THE
POLITICS
OF
CYBERSPACE

A *NEW POLITICAL SCIENCE* READER

CHRIS TOULOUSE AND TIMOTHY W. LUKE, editors

ROUTLEDGE
New York and London

Published in 1998 by
Routledge
29 West 35th Street
New York, NY 10001

Published in Great Britain in 1998 by
Routledge
11 New Fetter Lane
London EC4P 4EE

Library of Congress Cataloging-in-Publication Data

The politics of cyberspace : a new political science reader /
    edited by Chris Toulouse and Timothy W. Luke.
        p.   cm.
Includes bibliographical references.
ISBN 0–415–92167–8 (pbk.)
    1. Political participation—United States—Computer network resources. 2. United States—Politics and government—Computer network resources. 3. Internet (Computer network).
4. World Wide Web (Information retrieval system). I. Toulouse, Chris. II. Luke, Timothy W.
    JK1764.P67   1998
    025.06'3230420973—dc21   98–23865
                                                                        CIP

10 9 8 7 6 5 4 3 2 1

Contents

Introduction

Chris Toulouse
Hofstra University

I. The Internet & the Millennium

It says a lot about the character of our times, and the uneasy prosperity of the mid-1990s, that there is so little millennial sentiment in the developed world. Perhaps it is the postmodern fragmentation of consumer consciousness or the rationalization of culture (Ritzer's *McDonaldization)* that inhibits people from investing much faith in the possibility of wholesale social and political change. Visions of a better future no longer fire the imagination and inspire large-scale social movements; they have been reduced to just another lifestyle option, something we wear and discard – like a Greenpeace T-shirt – according to personal taste. Perhaps it is popular cynicism about politics, born of frustration with political parties that cling desperately to the old ideologies of national politics, even as globalization erodes their options, and effective power over the economy leaches away to international financial markets. People don't believe in "Progress" any more, but they don't know what to believe in instead. These are times when the old order established during the "Long Boom" (1947-73) has clearly been superseded, but we have only a tentative vocabulary of ideas to analyze the new one that has arisen in its place.[1]

And yet, for contemporaries, there are at least two phenomena of the 1990s that seem to have obvious millennial import – in the sense that they hold out the possibility of decisively shaping the world of the 21st century. The first is the collapse of communism in Eastern Europe in 1989. The 1990s have seen free-market economies and liberal democracies struggling to grow in the rocky ground left by the disintegration of the Soviet empire. More importantly, the 1990s have also seen the rise of a thriving market economy in China, bringing with it the spectre of a new

1. George Ritzer *The McDonaldization of Society: An Investigation into the Changing Character of Contemporary Social Life* (Pine Forge Press, Thousand Oaks, CA. 1993). I have written on this theme elsewhere in Chris Toulouse (1995) "Political Economy After Reagan" in Glen Perusek & Kent Worcester (eds) *Trade Union Politics: American Unions and Economic Change 1960s-1990s* (Humanities Press, New Jersey) pp. 22-56.

totalitarian superpower – trying to contain discontent at home with imperial aggression abroad – to haunt the first decades of the next century.

The second millennial phenomenon of the 1990s – and the subject of this volume – is the explosive growth of the Internet. Even in societies accustomed to rapid technological change (from hi fi to DVD in one generation) the rapid development of the Internet has been bewildering. Of course, network computing has been around since the 1960s: formally, it grew through the efforts of the US Department of Defense to develop a command & control system that would survive a Soviet nuclear strike; informally, it grew through the efforts of defense scientists to exchange e-mail and set up newsgroups discussing science fiction. However, even in the late 1980s, the Internet remained the province of scientists and graduate students, with their e-mail, library catalogues and neighborhood bulletin boards. What has made all the difference to the Internet – what brought in the middle class public and made it into a potential "millennial phenomenon" – is the invention of HTML (by the British physicist Tim Berners-Lee at CERN in Switzerland in 1991) and the extraordinary wild-fire development of the World Wide Web.

Hyper Text Markup Language freed network computing from the confines of academia by generating an alternative to the ugly esoteric "know-the-code" command-line interfaces of UNIX and DOS. In conjunction with the rapid development of desktop CPUs by Intel and Motorola, HTML browsers like Netscape's Navigator have made it possible for ordinary middle class computer owners who obtain an Internet connection to point-and-click to display Web pages and to bounce from Web site to Web site to Web site around the globe. Sites now feature sound and the Web is beginning to revolutionize the distribution of images as it exerts its technological prowess over the magazine, in terms of speed of distribution, and the television set, in terms of picture quality. Even television has been unsettled by the new upstart medium, as more and more prized viewers with disposable income give up on the terminally low-brow "goggle box" and shop for entertainment online instead.

In the terms coined by Negroponte (that have done so much to define how these changes are understood by the likes of Clinton, Gore, Blair and Gates) the *world of atoms* – of the physical packaging of our culture – seems to be disappearing before our very eyes into a *world of bits* – sights and sounds that come streaming into our computers. All of a sudden, it seems as if the whole material basis of the economy and the distribution of culture is about to undergo a far-reaching restructuring. All of a sudden (and perhaps for a brief and fleeting moment), the late 1990s look like the late 1940s or even the late 1960s – all bets are off and everything seems possible.[2]

II. Disorientation & Design

And yet, at the same time, people are profoundly disoriented by the Internet and the World Wide Web. When "all that is solid melts into air" right beneath your feet, people scramble hard to find firm ground. Among those who have a hard time with computers, and who have yet to spend much time online, misconceptions run rampant. People think that once a Web page is posted, any one in the world can find it; they believe that a simple inquiry to a search engine will yield a treasure trove of knowledge; and they worry that the Web is eroding originality in a sea of infinite revisions. In reality, as experienced Web surfers know, the Web is about as well-organized as a bookstore after a hurricane: unless you publicize the address of your page, no one will ever find it; much of the time, search engines yield a treasure trove of outdated junk, and miss the large proportion of Web sites that are not registered and which their robots never find; and new and quite original forms of expression are emerging out of the sea of text and images on personal home pages.[3]

There is also considerable disquiet about the implications of the Internet for free-expression and public morality. In particular there is anxiety about the availability of pornography on the Web and its accessibility to minors. Public opinion may begin to shift as more people gain experience online, but right now (in late 1997) there have seldom been better examples of Durkheim's "anomie" – the state of normlessness – or of Stanley Cohen's "moral panic" – where society's "collective conscience" acts to reinforce the boundaries of conventional morality by enacting new laws and conducting exemplary prosecutions.[4]

---

2. Nicholas Negroponte (1995) *Being Digital* (Vintage, New York, 1995). See also William Mitchell *City of Bits: Space, Place, and the Infobahn* (MIT Press, Boston, 1995) at http://www-mitpress.mit.edu:80/City_of_Bits/index.html

3. Emile Durkheim *Suicide* (Free Press, New York, 1951) and Stanley Cohen (1972) *Folk Devils & Moral Panics* (MacGibbon & Kee, London).

4. The typology outlined here is elaborated in a working paper Chris Toulouse (1997) *Designing Cyberspace: Voluntarism, Commercialism, Academia and the Future of the World Wide Web* at http://www.urbsoc.org/design/

The Web is certainly different from existing media of communication. Its rise challenges the balance of power between the publishers of content and consumers. Television, radio, newspapers and magazines are all "push" media – they pump product at the public whether consumers want it or not; whereas the Web is a "pull" media – consumers can decide for themselves whether they want to call up what the publishers are offering. The Web is also a more plastic medium; it can be configured and reconfigured to convert text or pictures or sounds to bits and deliver them in multiple combinations to any one with access to a computer and the Internet.

In the late 1990s powerful social blocs are contesting the design of the Internet and the primary purposes to which it will be put – they are trying to answer public disquiet by articulating a vision of what the Web will become. At least three "designs" for the future can be discerned. First is the voluntarist model of Internet pioneers, of Howard Rheingold and John Perry Barlow, who hold out hope that the Internet can still be used to revive civic virtues. Second is the commercial model, of Bill Gates and *Wired* magazine, who see the Internet as the railway of the post-industrial era. Third, there is the incipient public service model, which holds out the promise that universities and museums might repay taxpayer support by utilizing their considerable resources to provide information services for free.

The Internet, we are so often told by sceptics, will go the way of cable television in the US; for all the hype it will inevitably be turned into a bazaar for selling our culture back to us and recycling surplus product from the past. Yet so far the Web is proving stubbornly difficult to commercialize. Many firms are being misled by analogies between the Web and the ways the public use existing media – the Web is like television or the Web is like magazines... However, these analogies are not always helpful because they divert attention from the point that the Web can be made into something else besides. Indeed, where businesses succeed online it's often because of interactive (perhaps "participative" would be a better word) elements that could only have emerged through the Web. For example, the advertising revenue model borrowed from magazine publishing is struggling because advertisers have realized that people go to the Web precisely because it's easier to avoid the commercials than it is on TV. Now, in the wake of the success of Amazon Books, the catalog shopping model is coming into its own. However, Amazon is not a typical catalog warehouse, they hold very little stock of their own and make their money by passing orders on to book distributors. Furthermore, one of the main attractions of their site – the book reviews sent in by readers and the authors' home pages – are only possible because of the Web.[5]

Television producers are finding that the Web is an invaluable medium for publicizing their shows, but fan newsgroups and fan Web sites are not like the old official fan magazines; the producers cannot shape the content, and some are finding that the culture of their show – the myth, plot lines, character development – is spinning out of their control. In response, some corporate giants like Paramount have tried to protect the franchise by clamping down on *Star Trek* fan sites, while others, like Warner Brothers are content to ride the surf and have encouraged fans to make sites about their science fiction flagship *Babylon 5*. In a similar vein, some firms in the Internet industry, like Microsoft, AOL, and *Wired* magazine, have promoted "push" technologies, which attempt to turn the Web back into television by pumping content out in "channels" embedded in browser software. At the same time, others, like Geocities, are trying to make the most of what the Web already is by offering free Web pages and then organizing users into communities of interest. The commercialization of the Web may be a foregone conclusion then, but the terms and conditions of that commercialization are not.[6]

III. Social Science and Cyberspace

Out of e-mail and the growth of the World Wide Web comes the emergence of a new transnational realm of civil society – cyberspace. This volume focuses on the politics of this new realm. We cannot hope to cover every important implication of the emergence of cyberspace, but our contributions do touch on many of the most important themes: inequalities of access, the potential of an electronic Athena, the use of the Web by mainstream political parties, the challenge to the US First Amendment, the possibility

5. For the latest on the possibilities of electronic commerce see *the Economist* magazine's most recent survey "In Search of the Perfect Market: A Survey of Electronic Commerce" May 10th, 1997 at http://www.economist.com/editorial/freeforall/14-9-97/index_survey.html

6. On fan sites see Noah Robischon "The Empires Strike Back; Things Get Sticky For Fan Sites on The World Wide Web" *Entertainment Weekly* January 24, 1997 at http://cgi.pathfinder.com/ew/970124/multimedia/webwars.html See also the article by McIntosh & Cates in this volume. On "push" technologies see the front page op-ed by the editors of *Wired* in issue 5.03 March 1997 "Push! Kiss your browser goodbye" at http://www.wired.com/wired/5.03/features/ff_push.html

that the Web may foster new understandings of gender, and the need for progressive intellectuals to embrace and utilize the Internet in their political struggles.

We believe that this volume will be one of the first about cyberspace to move beyond a focus on the kinds of community generated by typing text. Indeed, this may well be the first volume that focuses on the politics of the broader Internet; that takes in e-mail and usenet groups, but also offers analyses of the social and political implications of the rise of the World Wide Web. It is worth dwelling for a moment on why it has taken social scientists – in the face of the Web's public prominence – so long to report back from the new realm.

First, the Web is a very new and rapidly developing phenomenon and very few social scientists are adept in computers. For the vast majority, word processing, e-mail and a little dabbling in spreadsheets are the outer limits. It takes time, effort and not in the least money (for a high-end computer at home) to jump on the Internet bandwagon, and not much less time, effort and money to stay on it.

Second, the rapid development of the Web defies conventional research methodologies. The Web is in a constant state of flux; at this early formative stage its essence is unending experimentation. How do you generate a valid sample of sites if there is a constant turnover of pages? How is it possible to make inferences about how surfers use sites if the only certainty is that the vast majority of people don't really know what they're doing? How can you make a "pull" technology "fit" in with the history of "push" technologies when "pull" holds out the possibility of rewriting the balance of power between publishers and consumers? The overwhelming rationale of social science has been to sit back and study well-established phenomena (such as television or poverty or homelessness) and then tell policy makers where they went wrong. The overwhelming temptation with the Internet is to jump in to the struggle over defining what the Web is really for and to help forge new uses. Nevermind the transition (in the popular phrase of the moment) from "the sage on the stage to the guide on the side"; what the Web offers academics is the possibility of moving from critic after the fact to the activist who helps create them. This is an unsettling prospect even to those who embrace the challenge.

Third, the advent of the Web is obviously deeply unsettling for authorities in academia. Deans, tenure committees and academic publishers are terrified of losing their grip on processes of authentication they have spent whole careers rising to control. Superstition runs rampant. There is no reason whatsoever why "peer review" should not work better through the Internet than it does through the US mail, and yet the prevailing wisdom over the department coffee-maker is that junior faculty would be wise to wait until they have tenure before publishing anything in an online journal (nevermind uploading "working papers" and mailing out the address to colleagues as an alternative to printing them on paper and mailing them out via the US Mail). Perhaps the paramount reason it has taken social scientists so long to generate research about the Web is that those who choose to study it have had to be – in the words of Apple's "Einstein" television commercial – "the crazy ones."

IV. In this volume

When social scientists have gone to the Web they have gone with two obvious sources of theory to interpret what they are studying – Habermas's work on the concept of civil society, and the work of authors such as Jameson, Baudrillard and Foucault on the postmodern fragmentation of culture. The authors in this volume draw on both.

Habermas & Cyberspace: The Possibility of an Electronic Athena

The articles by John Streck, David Resnick, Juliet Roper and Wayne McIntosh & Cynthia Cates all address issues arising from the tantalizing possibility that the Web can serve to reinvigorate liberal democracy and generate an electronic Athena in the 21st century. They are not optimistic.

John Streck focuses on the politics of usenet groups and listserv discussions and argues strongly that they cannot bear the weight of expectations loaded onto them. He points out that although many normal social cues are absent in text-based groups, users still bring a social history with them to the keyboard, and that this social history is often obvious in their interests and their writings. In his view text-based groups are caught in a bind: to conduct any kind of useful discussion at all existing members have to impose a social order that often marginalises and even stigmatizes new users; and yet without the imposition of such hierarchy groups often degenerate into free-for-alls in which discussion spins around and around in circles and flame wars break out. Streck worries that this bind will always restrict the potential of the Internet.

The articles by David Resnick and Juliet Roper look at the use mainstream political parties are making of the Web. David Resnick draws on the experience of the United States, while Roper discusses the use of sites by parties in New Zealand. Resnick makes a useful distinction between *politics within the Net* (which concerns the internal operation of the Internet), *politics which impacts the Net* (which concerns government attempts to regulate cyberspace), and *political uses of the net* (which concerns the use of Web sites to affect politics offline). He advances "the normalization thesis" – the argument that politics offline has flooded into cyberspace and shaped new uses in its image. Like Streck, Resnick argues that offline inequalities are being replicated in cyberspace, and he points to the growing division between the professional presenters who make Web sites and passive Web surfers sitting in front of their computer monitors. Juliet Roper's article proceeds along similar lines. Based on the New Zealand experience, her major worry is that political professionals will bring offline campaigning techniques to the Web, and that party sites will quickly degenerate into slick marketing tools which will be of no more help in raising the level of public discourse than the dismal negative advertising of American election campaigns.

Legal scholars Wayne McIntosh & Cynthia Cates examine the ramifications of the growth of the Internet for the most important single regulatory device affecting its future development – the First Amendment to the US Constitution. They begin by examining the principal arguments that are regularly made in support of the First Amendment. They then examine the process by which the First Amendment has been extended to cover new communications technologies in the past. McIntosh & Cates focus on the Court's habit of ruling by analogy with existing media, and are especially concerned about the power of corporations to take advantage of the plastic and undefined form of the Internet, and have property rights in cyberspace redefined to support their commercial interests.

Postmodernism & Cyberspace: Beyond the Fragmentation of Culture

The articles by Tim Luke, Anna Sampaio & Janni Aragon, and Doug Kellner all emerge from a progressive reading of postmodernism. All three abhor the negative and nihilistic ramifications of the postmodern fragmentation of culture – the notion (expounded by Baudrillard in particular) that the proliferation of media over the last generation has created a vast range of sources of identity, and that individuals are being carried away on a sea of signifiers, lost and directionless, utterly at the mercy of the entertainment corporations with the power to define meaning and authenticate identity. Our authors agree with the thesis about fragmentation, but they have a very different take on its consequences and the possibilities arising.

Tim Luke focuses on the politics of digital inequality and the emerging political economy of cyberspace. He dissects the ideology of gurus like Negroponte and Gates and takes them to task for overlooking the importance of inequalities of access. He discusses two types of inequality of access: whether groups have access at all and the hierarchy of access among those who do. Luke forsees a reconfiguring of social relations through cyberspace that will permit those in control to exercise a far more flexible type of dispersed authority than was possible through the top-down hierarchy of government or corporation.

Anna Sampaio & Janni Aragon examine the possibility that cyberspace has opened up a space for experimentation with language which may yet transform the way we understand gender. They draw on the writings of such authors as Baudrillard and Marc Poster to articulate the possibility in theoretical terms. They are not unaware of the practical limitations to the reconstruction of identities (of the kind John Streck discusses) but nevertheless they are optimistic that Web sites can provide a space for identity work of a kind that hasn't been seen before.

Doug Kellner's article extends into cyberspace his argument that progressive intellectuals must articulate a media politics and become adept in such media as local radio and public access television. Kellner makes a distinction between functional intellectuals, who do the work of the State, and critical-oppositional intellectuals, who expose injustice. Supporting his case with a broad range of concrete examples Kellner argues that oppositional intellectuals must now embrace the Internet or concede its exploitation to right-wing and reactionary forces.

V. Beyond the Millennium

Having begun on a millennial note it seems appropriate to conclude with a look into the future. Out in cyberspace, these are still very early days indeed, way back before the turn of the century, a time when people were first beginning to argue about the meaning of the Internet and grapple with its possibilities. In a sense this volume is like a book from the late 1890s about the way the automobile might shape the 20th century. On the whole, our authors are not optimistic about the way the Internet will shape the 21st century. In our own time, the forces of rationalization, the fragmentation of culture and the power of corporations to shape the law and regulate the Internet to their own ends, just seem too overwhelming for the possibilities of cyberspace to amount to much more than the occasional act of resistance and expression of discontent. In conclusion I want to try and tug the debate back the other way a little by framing some of the issues whose resolution will determine whether the Internet amounts to something more.

What becomes of cyberspace will turn on the resolution of at least three intensely political issues (although only the third is commonly recognized as having political import): the usability of the Internet; the extent to which the Internet is used for purposes other than entertainment; and the outcome of the upcoming conflict over intellectual property.

The Next 5 Years: The Usability of the Internet

If only the ubiquitous TV commercials for multimedia computers displayed anything close to the truth: in reality Internet access is still fiddly to configure, Internet connections still work unreliably, and Internet browsers still crash computers with mind-numbing regularity. There is much debate about how expensive the Internet is and whether you should count the initial computer purchase ($2-3000) or just the cost of Internet access ($20 a month); but what is really expensive about the Internet is not the cost in money but the cost in TIME.

Some of the cost in time arises from the fact that there are in the 1990s not one but two Internets – the high-speed one at work, shooting in over corporate or campus LANs, and the low-speed one at home, trundling in over a 28.8 modem. Commercial visions of what the Internet will become are premised on bringing the former to the latter – and indeed, many corporate web sites (replete with animated twirlies and Java applets) look (when they finally download) as if they have been designed in the belief that the transition is already complete. The transition is supposed to come about through the cable company upgrading to fibre optic cable and installing cable modems, and bringing about the much vaunted convergence between the Internet and television.

There are two problems with this transition. The first is well-known: the television set makes a lousy computer monitor – the US standard of 425 lines displays images poorly and is hopeless at displaying text. The answer is often said to be digital television. However, digital sets are likely to be expensive at first, and in order to recoup the cost of their investment cable companies will probably charge a premium ($50 a month?) for cable access to the Internet. Thus, it is not unlikely that high-speed home access will take some time to move out of the wealthy suburbs and elite urban enclaves. This is significant not only for the often commented upon informational inequalities it will generate, but also for the kinds of participative uses that will be developed through low-speed access in the interim (of which more in a moment).

The second problem with the transition is also well-known, but less well-recognized because too few ordinary users are familiar with the alternative. To put it bluntly, Windows still isn't very good. It may be better than it was, but it still falls short by comparison to the resourcefulness and ease-of-use of the Mac OS. The disorientation ordinary users experience with computers and the Internet (so often expressed in the existential lament "Er, what am I looking at?") is likely to be exacerbated rather than alleviated by Microsoft's plans to integrate Internet Explorer into Windows 98 because the move threatens to delete the most secure anchor users have in figuring out where they are – the sense of where their own machine ends and the Internet begins. If Microsoft didn't have legions of technicians dependent on keeping Windows running for their living, and if it didn't suit managers only too well to keep workers feeling stupid about the tools they use, PCs might be a lot easier to create with. In the end, the short term future of cyberspace may depend less on developments in the cable industry than on the success of Apple's Rhapsody OS in establishing an alternative to Windows NT.[7]

7. For a trenchant defence of Microsoft see Randall Stross *The Microsoft Way: The Real Story of How the Company Outsmarts its Competition* (Addison-Wesley, New York, 1996). On the Mac vs. PC debate Douglas Rushkoff "Confessions of a Macintosh deserter" in the *Guardian Online* April 23rd 1997 (search at http://go2.guardian.co.uk/) versus David Pogue "The Desktop Critic: The press says Apple's Dead? Two can play at that game. Why Windows is Doomed" in *MacWorld* June 1997 at http://www.macworld.com/pages/june97/Column.3700.html

The Next 10 Years: The Internet as an Information Appliance

The Internet can be used like television or the telephone as an entertainment device. Go to any campus computer lab and watch: the first thing students do when they go to the Internet is to try and turn it back into something familiar – they write e-mail to friends across the country (because it's cheaper than calling them up) or they surf the Web looking for pictures of celebrities (bouncing from site to site to site as if they were using a TV remote). However, this is not the only use to which it can be put, and it is in college that students must be trained to use the Internet as an information appliance.

The Internet is particularly important to social scientists. To use a science fiction metaphor, the Web is like a portal out onto the wider society. It can be used by students to visit organizations and retrieve documents that would previously have been available only in library document collections or in a matter of weeks via the US mail. If used properly, the Internet offers a range and immediacy that supersedes all existing media. As I like to tell my classes: the Internet is not like TV – you use it, it doesn't use you.[8]

This can be a challenging undertaking. Computer science students may know a lot more than the average professor, but the average undergraduate does not. University administrations may like to boast about their computer labs, but Computing Centers are accustomed to providing facilities for pre-professional technicians, not for the legions of ordinary students who are now flooding the labs looking for their e-mail accounts. There is a natural institutional reluctance to share the toys. Nevertheless, regular students can be taught how to find their way around Web sites and make judgments about their quality, to search the Web systematically (as opposed to haphazardly), and to use a course disk to store bookmarks and to save the text of web pages and develop a catalog of images.

The tricky bit comes when they go to write up their papers. Suddenly it is no longer clear quite what a paper is. On the Web, a paper may have an introduction, an argument and a conclusion, but the capacity to make hyperlinks means that a page has no necessary length. More importantly, a full range of colors and the capacity to include (properly referenced) images are now available to embellish the argument. Decisions that used to be

8. This section draws on another working paper, Chris Toulouse (1997) *Teaching with Course Home Pages* at http://www.urbsoc.org/teaching/CHP.html

left to pre-press are now in the province of ordinary users. *We are all designers now.*

These issues have profound import beyond academia because it is in college that future managers will get their first exposure to the differences between print, which is essentially fixed, and the Web, which is essentially fluid. The differences go beyond color and images; they go right to the heart of what text is for. In print, text is fixed on paper once it is printed and its potential audience is restricted to those who can obtain a copy of the original. On the Web however, text is endlessly revisable, and its potential audience is all those who are given the page's Web address. This is not for one minute to suggest that the Web will do away with the need for print publications; more likely the two will come to have a symbiotic relationship. Nevertheless, the availability of the Web, and its use as a tool for research and a means of distributing text and images cannot fail to have a powerful impact on printed text and on the way organizations are administered.

The Next 30 Years: The New Social Relations of Cultural Production in Cyberspace

The Web will also have a powerful impact on publishers and it may be that this is where its revolutionary significance lies. Those who package culture in the material form and distribute it to market are in for a very difficult period of adjustment. I want to argue here that the tensions generated in the social relations of production by the development of the new means of production are unlikely to be resolved through the courts, and they may not be resolved by everyone's favorite alternative solution – encryption – either.[9]

They are unlikely to be resolved through the courts because cyberspace makes a hall of mirrors out of conventional understandings of what constitutes private and public property. In everyday practice on the Web there is a vast difference between the following situations:

---

9. For an orientation to these issues see John Perry Barlow "Everything you know about intellectual property is wrong" in *Wired* 2.03 March 1994 at http://wwww.wired.com/wired/toc.html See also Peter Ludlow (ed) *High Noon on the Electronic Frontier: Conceptual Issues in Cyberspace* (MIT, Boston, MA. 1996) at http://semlab2.sbs.sunysb.edu/Users/pludlow/highnoon.html

One: posting a page and giving out its address to a circle of friends – in which case, the page can only be found by them and remains, in effect, private.

Two: publicizing a page to an occupational group – in which case, the page becomes semi-public, although how public depends on how large and geographically extensive the group is.

Three: listing a posted page with a search engine – in which case any one looking up the topic could, in theory, find it, and the page becomes fully public.

In the first instance the Web acts like a substitute for the US mail, in the second for the organizational newsletter, and in the third for the Yellow Pages. Now of course existing publishers will argue that all three instances are the same as selling a magazine through a newsstand; but presumably, eventually, the Courts will take note of the fact that in everyday practice out in cyberspace that is not how it works and this is not what these acts mean.

Already everyday practice on the Web is making a nonsense out of the understanding of copyright extended from the print world. By the law as it stands webmasters are supposed to ask for permission before reproducing any copyrighted images on their sites. In reality this is often impossible because a significant proportion of images on the Web are copied from elsewhere any way and no one knows (or cares) where they originally came from, and the practice is so ubiquitous that many webmasters won't take a request for copyright permission seriously. The most obvious analogies are with someone calling up a radio station and asking for permission to tape the music and play it at a party, or calling up a television station and asking for permission to tape a show and play it to their friends. The netiquette is to abide by any restrictions webmasters explicitly display on the use of their images and text. In practice most webmasters would probably settle for an acknowledgement of the source and a link to their site.

The social relations of production in cyberspace are not likely to be contained by encryption either. This is not because encryption won't be useful for securing transactions and distributing digitized goods – it will indispensable for that purpose, and encryption will be the backbone of the economy in cyberspace. However, encryption may not prevent an increasing proportion of cultural production taking a non-commodified or non-profit form. The public service design for the cyberspace – in which universities and museums provide information as a public service – will inevitably grow in the first years of the next century (if only because pressure on government spending will force them to explore new avenues for generating public support). In addition, the Web holds out the intriguing possibility that as the 21st century progresses more and more of our culture will be made by people for purposes of self-expression rather than for people by professional producers. As loopy as this sounds, it is already happening. Personal home pages are often derided as self-publicizing and indulgent, but as any experienced web surfer knows specialized sites made by inspired amateurs out of a love of their topic consistently outshine professionally-produced sites precisely because professional designers are only working for money and have no personal connection and deep abiding interest in what they are making a site about. [Individuals' sites also load far faster because they are made outside a LAN by people with 28.8 modems.][10]

One of the best examples of this trend is goth sites. Goths are a white youth cult like punks or grunge but they are not so tightly bound around a musical style as the others. They are highly visible in public because they nearly always appear in black and incorporate fetishistic elements into their dress. Goths draw on an eclectic mix of sources – including vampires, horror movies, comic books, romantic poetry, Victoriana, gothic churches, Halloween, and Arthurian mythology – and express themselves through an extraordinary variety of cultural practices – including music, dress, dance, jewelry, painting, make-up and body art, poetry, short stories and increasingly Web sites. There are "Goth Scenes" in New York, Toronto, San Francisco, Los Angeles, London, Northern England and Australia and the scenes are slowly but surely merging through the Web into a worldwide phenomenon. Goth sites feature some of the most visually effusive and exquisite imagery on the Web. Goths have fashioned themselves out of hole-in-the-wall boutiques, rundown dance

10. On personal versus professional sites compare for e.g. David Powell's *Sites of London* at http://ourworld.compuserve.com/homepages/David_J_Powell/ lonsite.htm with either *Metroscope London* at http://metroscope.com/lon.html or *Yahoo London* at http://www.yahoo.co.uk/Regional/Countries/United _Kingdom/England/Cities_and_Towns/London/. Or, similarly, Clay Irving's *New York Reference* at http://www.panix.com/~clay/nyc/with either *Metroscope New York* at http://metroscope.com/newyork.html or *Yahoo New York* at http://ny.yahoo.com/

clubs and Internet accounts, with very few major bands and no more than a cursory nod from the fashion industry. Of course kids have long made culture for themselves; in the future it just won't be as easy to commercialize it and sell it back to them because the Web will give them the means to distribute it among themselves.[11]

The Web will also make it possible for those who make cultural content to bypass physical marketplaces and the publishers who control them and to sell to the public directly. In principle over the medium term, and in reality over the long term, the awful ugly truth is that musicians don't need record companies any more, writers don't need publishers, artists don't need galleries, and so on and so on. This is not to imply that digital distribution won't be professionalized or that record companies, publishers and galleries will cease to exist. Many publishers will adapt and Web design firms are already big business. However over time it seems entirely possible that musicians, writers and artists will form co-operatives to publicize their Web sites and maintain them. It may take a long time to break their grip on existing markets, but there will be no going back to the days when the profit margins of publishers, and their definitions of what the customer wanted, controlled what the market has offered.

Too often the theme of commentaries on cyberspace echoes either AT&T's "You will..." commercial (for the resolutely optimistic) or Darth Vadar's march from *Star Wars* (for the relentlessly pessimistic). In concluding this introduction to the politics of cyberspace, it is worth recalling that way back before the turn of the century, you could also hear, faintly but distinctly in the distance, the strains of the Sorcerer's Apprentice. Wherever we are going on this journey we have embarked upon, it may just be that we have never seen the likes of it before.

---

11. For a sampling of the postmodern Gothic arts start with the index to the notorious but highly instructive *Goth Babe of the Week* at http://www.gothic.net/~cossack/gothbabe.html

John M. Streck
University of Iowa

Pulling the Plug on Electronic Town Meetings: Participatory Democracy and the Reality of the Usenet

Abstract: Drawing on the interactions commonly found on Usenet newsgroups and E-mail listservs, this paper challenges the conventional wisdom that computer mediated communication is potentially, if not necessarily, democratic and participatory. Specifically, the argument here is that essential and unavoidable characteristics of human interaction and communication place severe limits on the levels of diversity and equality which are experienced on the Internet. Most significantly, it is argued that interaction between individuals necessarily produces a history which in turn becomes the basis for social hierarchy. Finally, the point is made that whatever democratic potentials exist in cyberspace, the translation of those potentials into non-virtual worlds is problematic at best.

Call it Cyberspace, the Information Superhighway, the Matrix, the Net, or Virtual Reality. Think of it as a "consensual hallucination," a "New York City of the mind," or "that place you are in when you are talking on the telephone."[1] See it foreshadowed in the computer networks of the Internet, the cable television decoder (paying particular attention to the Home Shopping Network and the pay-per-view channels), and voice messaging services; see it championed in the novels of the cyberpunks, most newspapers, many magazines, and in the ubiquitous "You Will" commercials of AT&T.[2] The Information Age is coming home. The question is: Should we be bolting the doors or throwing them open? Do we question the corporate-sponsored visions of relationships made perfect through telecommunications and the Third Wave prophets who claim that information technologies "could make for warmer, more bonded families and closer, more

---

1. William Gibson (1984) *Neuromancer* (New York: Ace Books), p. 5. Clifford Stoll (1995) *Silicon Snake Oil: Second Thoughts on the Information Highway* (New York: Doubleday) p. 8. John Perry Barlow quoted in Phillip Elmer-DeWitt "Welcome to Cyberspace" *Time* Spring 1995 p. 8.

2. Currently, both *Time* and *Newsweek* include regular columns concerning the internet and cyberspace, and both have on multiple occassions devoted a full issue to the analysis and promotion of the new information technologies.

finely grained community life" or do we cash in our ten hours of free connection time from America Online without a second thought?[3] To date, the latter approach has largely won out. Like lemmings rushing to the sea (and with the media spurring them on), each month some 100,000 people are going on-line;[4] and given the rate of growth and the level of hype, it is doubtful many are giving serious thought to what awaits in the virtual world. If, however, we are unwilling to "assume all technology 'guilty until proven innocent'" as some have suggested, we must nevertheless realize that the promises of spiritual and/or social transcendence in cyberspace rest on a set of untenable assumptions concerning the nature of technology, experience, communication and culture.[5] Once those assumptions have been identified, moreover, the promise of salvation becomes a hollow one indeed. "You Will" becomes at best "You Might"; if you do it won't be nearly so rewarding as AT&T would have you believe.

Of Scientists, Cyberpunks and Politicians:
A Brief History of Cyberspace

How do government officials and military officers communicate and maintain control in the aftermath of global thermonuclear war? As the Cold War raged the RAND Corporation wrestled with this question and made their answer public in 1964: a computer network that "would use existing trunk lines, have no central authority, and would be designed from the beginning to operate as if it were already in tatters!" Based on a packet-switching technology developed by Paul Baran (whereby messages to be transmitted are fragmented into small, separately addressed pieces, "packets," which move independently through the computer network and are reassembled at the destination point), the proposed network would have no central hubs and, in the event of nuclear attack or other misfortune, could route the packets around any damaged nodes. Should, say, Denver suddenly cease to exist, the packets would simply go around whatever hole had

---

3. Alvin Toffler (1980) *The Third Wave* (New York: William Morrow and Company) p. 388. It is telling to compare America Online's offer of free connection time with the public service announcement from the Partnership for a Drug-free America which portrays a child being instructed in the ways of drug-dealing, told to first give the pills away for nothing and then to demand payment from those who come back for more. If nothing else, the comparison offers a striking metaphor for the experience of cyberspace.

4. Stoll (1995) p. 8.

5. Jerry Mander (1991) *In the Absence of the Sacred: The Failure of Technology and the Survival of the Indian Nations* (San Francisco: Sierra Club Books) p. 49.

been left in its place. Adopted by the Pentagon's Advanced Research Projects Agency (ARPA), RAND's concept became reality in December 1969 when four computers were linked together to form ARPANET.[6]

Expansion of the fledgling network was rapid. Provided it understood the packet-switching protocols, any computer could be connected to ARPANET, and with the development of TCP (Transmission Control Protocol) and IP (Internet Protocol) in the mid-seventies it became possible to link independent networks together using ARPANET as a backbone. ARPANET was evolving into the ARPA-Internet, and by 1981 linked together 213 separate host computers. By 1993, there were some 1,313,000 host computers linked to the network now called the Internet.[7] At the same time, while previously wary of inter-network connections, the commercial services such as America Online, Prodigy and CompuServe began scrambling to offer Internet access to their subscribers.[8] Currently then it is this network of networked computers that forms the foundation for the concept of cyberspace. Resting on that foundation, however, is a structure of metaphors and visions which articulate distinct and disparate meanings both for the network specifically and cyberspace more generally.[9]

While the Pentagon and the National Science Foundation were creating the computer networks that would come to be known as the Internet, science fiction writers were articulating a vision of a networked future. The vision was called "cyberpunk," and, if, like many genres, it was marked by ambiguous borders,

6. Michael R. Ogden (1994) "Politics in a Parallel Universe: Is There a Future for Cyberdemocracy?" *Futures* 26 p. 716.

7. Edward A. Cavazos and Gavino Morin (1994) *Cyberspace and the Law: Your Rights and Duties in the On-line World* (Cambridge: The MIT Press) p. 10. Two key moments in the development of the Internet came in 1983, when the U.S. military broke from the ARPANET backbone and established MILNET for its operational use, and in 1986 when the National Science Foundation's Office of Advanced Scientific Computing brought NSFNET on-line. With its newer, faster computers and faster, higher capacity lines, moreover, NSFNET eventually replaced ARPANET completely (Ogden p. 717).

8. June 1991 saw the volume of commercial traffic on the Internet surpass that of the academic systems which had traditionally accounted for the bulk of the communications (Ogden 719).

9. There are technologies not explicity connected to the Internet which are nevertheless generally included under the rubric of cyberspace (e.g., virtual reality). However, one finds that such technologies are frequently tied to projections of interactivity and decentralization (see, for example, Jaron Lanier and Frank Biocca (1992) "An Insider's View of the Future of Virtual Reality" *Journal of Communication,* 42 Autumn 1992 pp. 150-172), and it seems reasonable to argue that such projections imply a connection between these technologies and the Internet (or at least computer networking).

it nevertheless maintained a clear center: William Gibson's "Sprawl series": *Neuromancer* (1984), *Count Zero* (1986) and *Mona Lisa Overdrive* (1988).[10] Resonating with those who had found the 1980s leaving them at the crossroads of "the high tech, and the modern pop underground," Gibson's dystopian vision of anti-heroes augmented with surgical implants battling corporate consortiums in the data streams of cyberspace gave these "kids, freaks, [and] obsessive technophiles. . . a future they couldn't wait to build, couldn't wait to live in, couldn't wait to sell."[11] Not surprisingly, however, building it and living it quickly took a back seat to selling it. Cyberpunk was stripped of its literary mantle and developed into a marketing strategy "used to sell everything from comics to board games to specialty magazines for keyboard players."[12] More significantly, as subculture became market segment, control of the cyberpunk vision shifted from science fiction writers to advertising agencies and politicians; stories of jaded burnouts living in a technological dystopia gave way to thirty second vignettes celebrating life made perfect through telecommunications.

"Have you ever sent someone a fax from the beach?" asks the reassuringly masculine voice of Tom Selleck. "Studied abroad without leaving home? Looked in on your kids from a phone booth? You will – and the company that's going to bring it to you is AT&T."[13] If, moreover, they do not share the same motivations, AT&T's image of the future has come to be echoed by America's politicians. Vice-President Al Gore, for example, in a speech hawking the Clinton Administration's National Information Infrastructure (NII) to the Academy of Television Arts and Science, claimed "today's technology has made possible a global community united by instantaneous information and analysis," and further argued "our new ways of communicating will entertain as well as inform. . . . [T]hey will educate, promote

10. See Larry McCaffery (ed) (1991) *Storming the Reality Studio: A Casebook of Cyberpunk and Postmodern Science Fiction* (Durham: Duke University Press). George Slusser and Tom Shippey (eds) (1992) *Fiction 2000: Cyberpunk and the Future of Narrative* (Athens: University of Georgia Press).

11. Bruce Sterling (1986) "Preface" in *Mirrorshades: The Cyberpunk Anthology* Bruce Sterling (ed) (New York: Arbor House), p. ix; Peter von Brandenburg, producer, and Marianne Trench, director, *Cyberpunk*, Intercom Productions, Mystic Fire Video, 1990.

12. Lewis Shiner (1992) "Inside the Movement: Past, Present, and Future" in George Slusser and Tom Shippey (eds) *Fiction 2000: Cyberpunk and the Future of Narrative* (Athens: University of Georgia Press), p. 17.

13. A select group of the "You Will" spots is available on the World Wide Web at http://www.att.com/

democracy, and save lives."[14] More optimistic still, the Clinton Administration has claimed the particular combination of government bureaucracy and telecommunications technology found in the NII "can transform the lives of the American people – ameliorating the constraints of geography, disability, and economic status – giving all Americans a fair opportunity to go as far as their talents and ambitions will take them."[15]

The Democrats, moreover, are not the only ones manifesting such technological optimism. Republicans, too, are repositioning technologies found in the cyberpunk novels – computers, molecular medicine, breakthroughs in material technology, micro-miniaturization and virtual reality, among others – as the building blocks of a Utopian future. Thus, with futurist Alvin Toffler figuratively and/or literally at his side, House Speaker Newt Gingrich claims that through "the tremendous opportunities being created by the information technologies. . . America can be connected to the best learning, the best health care and the best work opportunities in the world."[16] It's a far cry from the world of *Neuromancer*.

While the most obvious impact of the corporate-political takeover of the public discourse concerning cyberspace has been the shift from a remarkably negative vision to a singularly positive one, a far more significant change concerns the relationship between technology and society. Although commonly portrayed as "purveyors of bizarre hard-edged, high-tech stuff," for the cyberpunk authors technology was in fact peripheral.[17] Theirs was admittedly a high-tech world, but it was not *principally* a high-tech world. Class conflict, corporate rule and the breakdown of the concept of human were as crucial to cyberpunk as neural disruptors and surgical implants; technology served not so much to define a future world but to explore our own. The result was the realization "that technology alone is not enough. Our problems are also sociological, spiritual, even moral."[18] This, however, is a conclusion explicitly denied by the future of Al Gore, Newt Gingrich and AT&T. In the corporate-political vision our problems are not social, spiritual or moral, but emphatically technological.

14. Albert Gore, "Speech to Academy of Television Arts and Sciences" 11 January, 1994 at http://sunsite.unc.edu/white-house/white-house.html

15. "The National Information Infrastructure: Agenda for Action" White House document, 1994 at http://enh.nist.gov/nii.dir/niiagenda.asc

16. Newt Gingrich, "Address to the Nation" 7 April, 1995 at http://house.gov/

17. Gardner Dozois, "Science Fiction in the Eighties" *Washington Post* 30 December, 1984, Book World, p. 9.

18. Shiner, p. 24.

Racism, sexism and class distinctions are not challenges to people, but to electrical engineers; justice, equality and love emerge not from a particular set of attitudes and behaviors, they flow from fiber optic phone lines. Thus, while the cyberpunks in effect turned technological questions into social issues, the politicians and advertisers have turned social issues into technological questions. The technological answer, moreover, is wide-area computer networking, code name: cyberspace.

The Meaning(s) of Technology

In 1962, Marshall McLuhan argued that "technological environments are not merely passive containers of people but are active processes that reshape people and other technologies alike."[19] Generally remembered in the more aphoristic (some would say cliché) formulation "the medium is the message," in certain circles at least McLuhan's idea has been accepted as a truism. Moreover, from Umberto Eco's assertion that "the Macintosh is Catholic and. . . DOS is Protestant" to Benedict Anderson's analysis of the roots of nationalism, one can now find McLuhan's ghost haunting a wide range of discourses.[20] Still, this is not to say that there is complete agreement on the meaning or implications of technology's "non-neutrality." Thus, Jerry Mander claims "every technology has *inherent and identifiable* social, political, and environmental consequences"; Neil Postman that "embedded in every tool lies an ideological bias," and Steve Steinberg that "the technology of the Net not only reflects, but fully embodies, the politics of the Net". And while all three reflect McLuhan, it can be argued that each presupposes a different relationship between device and design: design inherent to device, emerging *sua sponte*; design embedded in device, assigned by some outside force; and device embodying design, absorbing

19. Marshall McLuhan (1962) *The Gutenberg Galaxy: The Making of Typographic Man* (Toronto: University of Toronto Press).

20. Umberto Eco (1995) "The Software Schism" *Harper's* January 1995 33; Benedict Anderson (1983) *Imagined Communities* (London: Verso). While perhaps unique in his use of the Catholic/Protestant metaphor, Eco is not the only one to have noted important differences in the relationships between users and computers across distinct computer interfaces. The work of Sherry Turkle is perhaps most notable in dissecting the connection between individual ways of thinking and the computer interfaces individuals use. See, for example: Sherry Turkle (1984) *The Second Self: Computers and the Human Spirit* (New York: Simon & Schuster) and Sherry Turkle & Seymour Papert (1990) "Epistemological Pluralism: Styles and Voices within the Computer Culture" *Signs: Journal of Women in Culture and Society* 16, 1 pp. 128-157.

outside values or culture.[21]

Beyond these more nuanced questions, however, there is a more fundamental problem: McLuhan's idea assumes technology can be approached only as technology. Whether in the particular or in the general, the inherent meanings of technology which McLuhan and his followers have argued for are rooted in the material properties of a given technology. Printing press, steam engine, television, computer, and so forth – all conceived of in terms of their particular material properties, such properties imparting a particular set of meanings onto the individuals and culture in which they appear. Technology as material device, however, is not the only frame available, and in shifting to another frame – the frame of the consumer commodity – technology can be stripped of its inherent meanings.

In an analysis of contemporary advertising, Sut Jhally makes the McLuhanesque claim that "inherently, goods are communicators of social relations." Unlike McLuhan, however, Jhally qualifies this statement, limiting it to non-industrial societies. "The world of goods in industrial society," claims Jhally, "offers no meaning, its meanings having been 'emptied' out of them" by capitalist modes of production and consumption. Thus stripped of their inherent meanings, these commodified goods are assigned meaning through advertising. "Production empties. Advertising fills." Since the 1960s, moreover, Jhally argues that advertising has been used to suggest commodities offer "magical access to a previously closed world of group activities." "In modern industrial society," Jhally claims, "the link with nature has been shattered. . . . Our defining relationship is with technology . . . cloaked in magical and supernatural modes of representation."[22]

This, moreover, has probably never been more true than in the case of cyberspace, for cyberspace, with its inextricable ties to unfamiliar technologies, is all the more open to such magical meanings. Thus, the AT&T monopolized advertising found in the Spring 1995, "Welcome to Cyberspace" issue of *Time*, for example, presents a series of four one-page and twelve two-page advertisements woven together into a narrative based on classic stories and fables (eg. *Pinocchio, The Wizard of Oz, The Tortoise and the Hare*, etc). "Once upon a time," the campaign begins,

21. Mander, p. 49, emphasis original; Neil Postman (1992) *Technopoly: The Surrender of Culture to Technology* (New York: Alfred A. Knopf), p. 13; Steve G. Steinberg (1995) "Addressing the Future of the Net" *Wired* May 1995 p. 141.
22. Sut Jhally (1989) "Advertising as Religion: The Dialectic of Technology and Magic" in *Cultural Politics in Contemporary America* Ian Angus and Sut Jhally (eds) (New York: Routledge) pp. 217-229.

a new and unusual form of technology appeared. It promised to make all fantasies become reality. Some called it the Information Superhighway. Others called it Cyberspace. It had lots of names.

At first people didn't know what to make of it. And many were even confused by it. But there was a Wizard who understood this new technology was not as it appeared. He knew it was here to help people communicate in ways they never dreamed possible. So he got together with technology and created magical new products and services that everyone could use. Life in the kingdom became much easier. And much more enchanting.[23]

Through the magic of advertising AT&T is transformed into the wizard who controls the magic of cyberspace which can "make all fantasies become reality."

Arguably, then, these notions of the emptied commodity and magical modes of representation explain the corporate-political shift to a device-driven concept of cyberspace, for by defining cyberspace specifically in terms of its wiring – "a seamless web of communications networks, computers, databases, and consumer electronics" – the corporate-political vision drives a wedge between the technologies of cyberspace and the surrounding human/cultural environment, effectively shifting cyberspace out of the McLuhanesque frame of technology as technology and into the frame of consumer commodities.[24] This opens cyberspace to Jhally's magical and supernatural representations.

Paradoxical though it may seem, with a device-driven conception of cyberspace the device slips away leaving an empty vessel to be filled with whatever meanings those who control the discourse might choose to assign it. Thus, through a sort of conceptual sleight-of-hand, cyberspace, ostensibly defined in terms of wide-area computer networking, becomes "the land of knowledge" and "a flowering remnant of the '60s, when hippie communalism and libertarian politics formed the root of the modern cyberrevolution" – even, for a substantially smaller group,

---

23. *Time* Spring 1995 Special Issue "Welcome to Cyberspace."

24. "The National Information Infrastructure: Agenda for Action" White House document, 1994 at http://enh.nist.gov/nii.dir/niiagenda.asc

"an enormous, leaking landfill of vicarious crap."[25] Cyberspace becomes a matter of competing metaphors, the metaphors with significant consequences. A "cultural Brigadoon," cyberspace represents "a whopping stealth victory for the counter-culture"; "interactive pay TV," it is just another eddy in the revenue streams of the telecommunications industries.[26] Whoever controls the metaphors, controls cyberspace.

The Experience of Cyberspace

Undoubtedly, the preceding argument places great faith in the power of words, for to suggest that those who control the metaphors of cyberspace thereby control cyberspace one must necessarily accept that changes in the way we describe a thing can change the nature of that thing. There are those, however, who argue for this very idea. According to Heinze von Foerster, for example, "our experiences and ideas are not expressed *through* language . . . [but] rather, we have accepted language as *controlling* our ideas and experiences."[27] Experience, or at least our understanding of it, follows language, it does not precede it. Thus, changes in the way we describe an experience will transform it into something new. In this context, then, the significance of Philip Elmer-DeWitt's claim that "cyberspace. . . is an experience, not a wiring system" becomes self-evident.[28] Just as cyberspace defined in terms of technology is opened to metaphor through the nature of commodities, cyberspace as experience is similarly opened through the relationship between language and experience. In the connection between language and experience lie the roots of the transformation that, to borrow from an episode of Tom Tomorrow's strip, *This Modern World*, changes "sitting on your butt staring at a computer screen" into "cruising down the information highway in high gear . . . riding the waves of the digital ocean . . . exploring the uncharted regions of cyberspace!"[29] But while played for laughs in Tomorrow's strip there is reason to worry about this transformation.

25. Elmer-DeWitt "Welcome to Cyberspace" p. 6; Stewart Brand "We Owe it All to the Hippies" *Time* Spring 1995 p. 54; Robert Hughes "Take this Revolution..." *Time* Spring 1995 p. 77.
26. Brand p. 54; Frank Rich "Bit by Bit: The Internet Turns on Newt" *New York Times* 5 March, 1995 Sec. 4, p. 15; Franklin Saige "Mega Buys" *Utne Reader* March/April 1995, 66.
27. Heinz von Foerster (1980) "Epistemology of Communication" in Kathleen Woodward (ed)*The Myths of Information: Technology and Postindustrial Society* (Madison: Coda Press) p. 18, emphasis original.
28. Elmer-DeWitt "Welcome to Cyberspace" p. 8.
29. Tom Tomorrow [Dan Perkins] (1994)*Tune in Tomorrow* (New York: St. Martin's Press) p. 103.

Cyberspace is already an extremely heterogeneous grouping: it includes large commercial providers such as America Online, CompuServe and Prodigy; independent bulletin board systems run by hobbyists and small organizations; privately held in-house computer systems; and large public networks. The apparent "nature" of cyberspace, moreover, will be largely dependent upon one's point of entry. The experience of a user logged into the icon-based environment of America Online, for example, will likely be quite different than that of a user logged into one of the Unix-based systems still found on most university campuses. Similarly, the experience in cyberspace is also influenced, in some instances quite profoundly, by the tools available. The differences between, say, Fetch, Anarchie, and the standard anonymous FTP (File Transfer Protocol); Lynx, Mosaic, and Netscape; or T1 line, a 28.8 kbps modem, and a 300 bps modem are in many ways analogous to the difference between riding down the Pacific Coast Highway in a Mercedes Benz 500SL and driving the same stretch of road in a Yugo. True, both will likely bring you safely to your destination, but in the latter case you may wish you'd never left home. (In the case of the computer, moreover, last year's Mercedes Benz can quickly become this year's Yugo.[30]) Finally, then, the experience of cyberspace will also depend on the activities people seek to perform while there, and within the confines of cyberspace one can find people exchanging E-mail, surfing the World Wide Web and authoring home pages, reading and posting to Usenet newsgroups, downloading GIFs and software, MUDing, and shopping (among many other forms of work, play and commerce). However, despite heterogeneous environments, heterogeneous tools, and heterogeneous activities, cyberspace has largely been reduced to the single, homogenous experience of "cruising the information highway."

Perhaps not surprisingly, in reducing the heterogeneity of cyberspace to a single archetype, the tendency has been to choose the best possible example to characterize the concept as a whole. Hence, the WELL. Run by the *Whole Earth Review* out of Sausalito, California, the Whole Earth 'Lectronic Link (WELL) is a computer network comprising (as of 1991) 3,800 subscribers which Gareth

---

30. This is particularly true in the case of the World Wide Web. As home page designers have added more and more bells and whistles to their sites as a means to cut through the clutter, the basic requirements placed on the user's system have become more and more demanding. Today, the text-based systems described by Sandfort and Frissell as the solution to problem of access would be next to useless. See Sandy Sandfort and Duncan Frissell"Net Access for Next to Nothing" *Wired* May 1995, p. 141.

Branwyn characterizes as "a rich and rather bohemian constellation
of writers, artists, scientists, and other obsessively curious people."
These people, Branwyn claims, "treat the WELL like a second
home and spend lots of time 'hanging out' there, wending their
way through dense conversations with themes like 'The Works
of James Joyce' and 'The Evolution of Consciousness.'"[31] Simply
put, the WELL is a computer-based instance of Jürgen Habermas's
bourgeois public sphere, in which the educated and affluent come
together outside both home and state for critical discussion of
art, literature and politics. The WELL, therefore, is at once
significantly empowering – it seems anyone who wants to argue
seriously for the communal value of cyberspace cites their
experience in the WELL as a testament to that position – and
significantly limited.[32] As positive as the experience may be, one
cannot generalize from the WELL, with its 3,800 obsessively
curious people (largely drawn from the well-educated middle
class of the San Francisco Bay Area) to America Online, the Usenet,
or one of the many other elements of cyberspace. Demographics
notwithstanding, the mere difference in scale (on the order of
thousands to hundreds of thousands if not millions) is enough to
make such comparisons dubious at best. The comparisons,
however, have been routinely made – and, moreover, used to
sell cyberspace to people who have no way of recognizing the
deceit.[33] In the discourse of cyberspace, the passive becomes active,
the exceptional commonplace.

At this point, however, some back-pedaling is necessary,
for if the metaphors of cyberspace routinely minimize the diversity
of the experience, it must nevertheless be recognized that there is
one crucial factor common to most experiences of cyberspace:
cyberspace is text-based. Though the virtual reality (VR) evan-
gelists promise experiences in cyberspace wholly divorced from
the limitations of language, in its current formulation, cyberspace,
in its interactive forms, is largely reliant on language. Consider,

31. Gareth Branwyn "The Salon Virtual: Plugging in to a Transcontinental Creative
Community" *Utne Reader* March/April 1991, p. 86.

32. See, for example, John Perry Barlow "Is there a There in Cyberspace?" *Utne
Reader* March/April 1995 pp. 53-56.

33. While at this point the fascination with the WELL on the part of most people
writing on the Internet has largely been abandoned in favor of a new focus on the
more expansive World Wide Web, the WELL nevertheless remains important for
understanding our conceptions of computer mediated social interaction in much
the same way that understanding Greek democracy is important for understanding
American democracy. Thus, while the WELL may be unknown to many (if not
most) users of the Internet, it arguably remains the locus classicus for the application
of the ideals of participatory democracy to cyberspace.

for example, the notion of computer-mediated sexual encounters, "cybersex": While the popular media have taken to presenting computer-mediated sex as an idealized, multi-sensory experience taking place in dream worlds where anything is possible (see, for example, *The Lawnmower Man* and Fox Television's short-lived *VR.5*, in reality cybersex is "an odd brand of interactive and sexually explicit story telling" – "phone sex pecked out onto a keyboard."[34] In this extreme case, then, despite the dreams of the visionaries, cyberspace is not expanding our experience, but rather taking what is presumably one of the least lingual and most multi-sensory experiences and boiling it down into ASCII. Cybersex, moreover, is just one (extreme) example among many. From "ROTFL" to ";o)" – that is, from rolling on the floor laughing to winking – "much of what happens over the networks is a metaphor – we chat without speaking, smile without grinning, and hug without touching."[35] Cyberspace does not expand text into experience, it reduces experience to text.

Now clearly there are those who will take issue with the claim that cyberspace is fundamentally lingual in nature, particularly in the context of the World Wide Web and virtual reality technologies. Virtual reality, run the claims, "promises to be a multi-sensory merger of the telephone, the graphic workstation, and the television set," and the results of this merger will be "a rich environment to be traversed, manipulated, and experienced much in the fashion of an adventure game."[36] Within this environment, moreover, "knowledge structures become landscapes – perhaps fields of concepts, whose details can be harvested, winnowed, and stored."[37] Furthermore, in by far the most radical conception of virtual reality, Jaron Lanier argues that not only will VR give us the potential for new codes, but

> there's also the possibility of communicating without codes. . . . [In virtual reality] it's possible to do something that goes beyond sharing codes with people, because you can just make the stuff directly with them. . . . It's

34. Gareth Branwyn (1993) "Erotica for Cybernauts" *South Atlantic Quarterly* 92, p. 780; Gerard van der Leun "Twilight Zone of the Id" *Time* Spring 1995, p. 37.

35. Stoll (1995) p. 43.

36. Frank Biocca (1992) "Virtual Reality Technology: A Tutorial" *Journal of Communication* 42 Autumn 1992, p. 24; Patricia A. Carlson and George Gonzalez (1993) "When Books Become Environments: Virtual Reality and the Technology of Text" *Felix* 1, No. 3, p. 24. It is interesting to note the tendency to use the computer (game) as a metaphor for the computer (VR).

37. Carlson and Gonzalez (1993) p. 31.

that direct creation of reality; that's what I call post-symbolic communication.[38]

It's what I call utter nonsense. While virtual reality may one day merge computer, telephone and television and offer some degree of physical interaction with a computer-generated environment, the suggestion that this will move us away from language-based (much less symbolic) communication is absurd. Granted, there will be some reconfiguration in the manner in which language is used. Already we are seeing word processors change our relationship to words, and hypertext (eg. CD-ROMs and the World Wide Web) change our relationship to argument.[39] Moreover, as the telegraph was largely responsible for Ernest Hemingway, no doubt we will soon be presented with writers trained in cyberspace and using some of the conventions and grammatical oddities (eg. the "emoticon" or "smiley" 8-} :o) etc) employed there. Still, this cyberspace-inspired evolution of language usage hardly implies language will be abandoned anytime soon. The particular role of language in cyberspace may change as virtual reality is refined, but in so far as cyberspace is defined as fundamentally interactive, language, text, the ability to read and write, is and will remain crucial to the experience.

An Amazing Web of New People, Places and Ideas

"Cyberspace," writes James Beniger, ". . . is nothing if not public," and quoting Fisher, Margolis and Resnick he claims "the civic life of the virtual community may resemble the mutuality of a barn raising or a pot luck supper."[40] With similar enthusiasm, Philip Elmer-DeWitt gushes that cyberspace

> has unleashed a great rush of direct, person-to-person communications, organized not in the top-down, one-to-many structure of traditional media but in a many-to-many model that may – just may – be a vehicle for revolutionary change. In a world already too divided against itself – rich against poor, producer against consumer – cyberspace offers the nearest thing to a level playing field. . . .[41]

38. Lanier and Biocca (1992) p. 160.

39. David Gates, "Of Texts and Hypertexts" *Newsweek* 27 February 1995, pp. 71-73.

40. James R. Beniger "Cyberspace as Public Space: Toward the Commodification of Collective Representation" presented to *The Annenberg Scholars Program Conference on Public Space* Philadelphia, PA. 1-4 March 1995, p. 1, 4.

41. Elmer-DeWitt "Battle for the Soul of the Internet" *Time* 5 July, 1994, p. 64.

Cyberspace, we are told, is a place where "anybody can play and everybody is afforded the same level of respect," where those "who don't do well in spontaneous spoken interaction . . . [can make] valuable contributions," where "your chances of making friends are increased by several orders of magnitude over the old methods of finding a peer group," where "nobody has the power to kick anybody off," and where "people are judged by the content of what they say."[42] Described in these terms, cyberspace becomes a veritable hothouse of virtue: equality, inclusion, friendship, community, democracy – the list no doubt goes on. Again, social problems become technological problems, and all it takes to create the virtuous society is the right combination of copper and silicon. Approaching cyberspace as a lingual practice, however, it becomes clear this is more problematic than we are led to believe.

Consider diversity. According to Howard Fineman, "cyberspace may be everywhere in America, but it is not yet representative of it."[43] This is putting it mildly. Repeated surveys of the Internet have found it to be "dominated by the opinions of a highly-educated and well-paid young technocratic elite that is overwhelmingly male, white, and suburban-urban."[44] The citizens of cyberspace are "white males under 50 with plenty of computer terminal time, great typing skills, high math SATs, strongly held opinions on just about everything, and an excruciating face-to-face shyness, especially with the opposite sex."[45] The consequences of this are significant. If, for example, one accepts the argument that "access to the information highway may determine the basic ability to function in a democratic culture," then it would follow that large segments of our population are going to find themselves excluded if changes are not made.[46] Furthermore, it is little surprise that the patterns of allocation vis-à -vis this wealth of electronic information and participation correspond to traditional class breakdowns. As Suneel Ratan asks, "In an era in which success is increasingly identified with the ability to use computers and gain access to cyberspace, will the new technology only widen the gap between rich and poor, educated and uneducated, blacks,

42. Elmer-DeWitt "Welcome to Cyberspace," p. 9; Howard Rheingold "The Virtual Community," *Utne Reader* March/April 1995, p. 62; Wayne Gregori quoted in Mark Dery "Flame Wars" *South Atlantic Quarterly* 2 1993, p. 561.

43. Howard Fineman "The Brave New World of Cybertribes" *Newsweek* 27 February, 1995, p. 32.

44. Beniger (1995) "Cyberspace as Public Space" p. 4.

45. Barlow (1995) p. 55.

46. Suneel Ratan "A New Divide Between Haves and Have-nots?" *Time* Spring 1995, p. 25.

whites and Hispanics?"[47] And if the answer to Ratan's question has not yet emerged, at this point the demographics of cyberspace do not inspire much optimism.

However, there are those who are hopeful. In response to the fear that the new technologies will widen the established gap between rich and poor, Ratan claims that there is "considerable evidence" to support the belief of the telecommunications industries that "the forces of competition and the marketplace will drive the prices of equipment and online services downward and make both increasingly available to the less affluent."[48] Supporting this claim, Sandfort argues that "computers are like kids' toys: they aren't worn out, they're outgrown. . . . If you want to get online, all you need is any piece of hardware that can emulate a VT-100 terminal."[49] A doorway into cyberspace, they claim, can be had for as little as $35.[50] Diversity will come just as soon as people realize they want to be wired; when women, the poor, the uneducated, African-Americans, Hispanics, and other disenfranchised groups realize that they want to go online, cyberspace will blossom into multiculturalism. In response to such arguments, Kadi suggests that "what this whole delirious, interconnected, global community of a world needs is a little reality check."[51]

Hoping to "expose some of the realities lurking behind the regurgitated media rhetoric and the religious fanaticism of net junkies," Kadi argues that there are two reasons cyberspace will never possess a diverse population. The first is financial. Unlike Sandfort and Frissell who focus on the equipment costs, Kadi

47. Ratan p. 25.

48. Ratan p. 25-26.

49. Sandfort and Frissell p. 141.

50. I would challenge most of these assumptions. First, the general lack of downward compatibility in the computer industry suggests that computers are not exactly like children's clothing. Yes, that original Mac will still run, but it's not going to run software that's less than six or seven years old. Consequently, I think the problems associated with merging old and new technologies are being underestimated. Moreover, as noted earlier, there are many different experiences of being online; some of them simply aren't worth the effort. If, for example, reading E-mail, participating in one newsgroup and lurking on four others takes me at least an hour a day using a 9600 baud modem, what is that going to mean for someone using Sandfort and Frissell's $35 system with its 300 baud modem which runs 32 times slower? Admittedly, not everyone needs a PowerPC to go online, but I would argue that the financial barriers are far more substantial than these writers suggest. I dare say, moreover, that if Sandfort and Frissell were limited to one of those $35 systems for a few weeks, they would likely come to agree.

51. M. Kadi "Welcome to Cyberbia" *Utne Reader* March/April 1995, p. 57.

explores the connection costs. Believing that "as surely as the Department of Defense started this whole thing, AT&T or Ted Turner is going to end up running it," Kadi assembles an argument for $120 as a reasonable estimate of what a person can expect to spend each month to be connected to the Information Super-highway. To wit: The current average of $15 dollars a month for the service combined with the knowledge that "the average, one-step-above-neophyte user has at least two distinct . . . accounts" equals $30. Add to this the charge of $3 per hour of use times 30 hours a month – roughly equivalent to "the evening news plus a weekly *Seinfeld/Frasier* hour. . . . [and] less time than the average car-phone owner spends on the phone while commuting" – and the result is $120 a month.[52] So much for diversity.

Today, of course, Kadi's argument seems woefully out of touch with reality. As of July 1997, unlimited Internet access is available in Iowa City, Iowa, without an hourly fee, for roughly $20 a month – a far cry from Kadi's $120 estimate. One, however, must ask: In their distance from current conditions, are Kadi's arguments horrifyingly out-of-date or astutely prescient? While most would assume the former, there is reason to at least consider the possibility that the cost of Internet access may soon move closer to Kadi's figure. First, as students in Iowa were recently reminded, the Internet currently rests on a foundation of government subsidies. The future of such subsidies, however, is far from certain. So, for example, in April of 1997 the Iowa state legislature, pressured by local telephone companies, passed Senate File 519 which proposed ending government support for dial-in access at colleges and universities connected to the Iowa Communications Network.[53] And while a fairly small move toward the privatization of the Internet (and one ultimately vetoed by the governor), Senate File 519 may nevertheless emerge as a first step toward Kadi's vision of an Internet controlled by the telecommunications corporations. Indeed, the telephone comp-anies are right: the universities are engaging in a kind of unfair competition. And as more politicians become convinced that the "right" to free Internet access is not something guaranteed by the Constitution, more bills like Senate File 519 will be passed.

However, setting aside the questionable status of government subsidized access, there is a more basic consideration in the fact that providing Internet access remains a very young industry. As

---

52. Kadi p. 57-58.
53 See Kelley Chorley "Internet Bill Passes Senate" *The Daily Iowan* 16 April, 1997, p. 1Aff.

such it is characterized by numerous small players and competitive pricing. Pure competition, however, seldom lasts; and as numerous historians of radio have noted, an industry controlled by amateurs involved in pure competition can very quickly give way to oligopolies controlled by corporate giants.[54] Consequently, if Kadi's $120 today seems out of line, the $20 we pay today may one day seem little more than a fond memory.

Irrespective of the actual costs associated with going on-line, the possibility that the Internet will become a playground for the rich is something many have considered. But cyberspace as an outpost for the wealthy is not quite the image the politicians have in mind, and so in March 1995, for example, the Clinton Administration announced a program to break down the gap between rich and poor in cyberspace. While in part little more than political grandstanding – "We . . . want to change buying patterns and priorities of families" stated Commerce Secretary Ron Brown, apparently oblivious to the fact that if you don't have money for food and shelter a personal computer might be considered an odd priority – the proposal also included a plan to "establish. . . centers around the country that will give people access to computers and train them."[55] Perhaps then, Kadi is overly pessimistic in arguing that only those with $120 a month to spare will be able to go on line. Possibly, but Kadi also makes a stronger argument against the assumption of diversity, one that cannot be repaired with a government program.

Consider the Usenet. Currently it comprises more than 5,000 separate groups, each with its own distinct topic of conversation. Now, "Let's say you choose 10 folders. . . . Each folder contains an average of 50 posts. Five hundred posts, at, say, one paragraph each, and you're now looking at the equivalent of a 200-page book."[56] How many people have the time or inclination to wade through that much text each and every day? It is impossible for anyone to process all the information that is available on the Net and so choices must be made: Do you subscribe to alt.abuse.recovery or alt.abuse.offender.recovery? Alt.comics.batman or alt.comics.superman? Misc.invest.funds or misc.invest.stocks? Rec.music.classical or rec.music.country.western? Soc.feminism or soc.men? Soc.culture.argentina or

54. See Michele Hilmes (1990) *Hollywood and Broadcasting: From Radio to Cable* (Urbana: University of Illinois Press) and Daniel Czitron (1982) *Media and the American Mind: From Morse to McLuhan* (Chapel Hill: University of North Carolina Press).
55. Jeannine Aversa "Clinton Puts up New Plan Introducing Computer Age" *The Daily Iowan* 10 March, 1995, p. 5A.
56. Kadi p. 58.

soc.culture.yugoslavia? The list goes on (and on and on) but the point should be clear: Cyberspace, like the "real world,"

> is not a place where you will enter an "amazing web of new people, places, and ideas." One does not encounter people from "all walks of life" because there are too many people and too many folders. Diversity might be out there . . . but the simple fact is that the average person will not encounter it because with one brain, one job, one partner, one family, and one life, no one has the time![57]

Now, for some, this is a benefit. Howard Rheingold, for example, believes that because "in a virtual community we can go directly to the place where our favorite subjects are being discussed, then get acquainted with people who share our passions. . . . [our] chances of making friends are increased by several orders of magnitude over the old methods of finding a peer group."[58] However, if making friends is easier in cyberspace than the real word, meeting a diverse set of people is all the more difficult. Thus, despite claims that cyberspace is going to deliver us into a world of diversity, the simple fact is that limitations in our ability to process information will inevitably preclude that from happening.

In Cyberspace, Nobody Knows You're a Dog

If diversity is the fervent wish for cyberspace, egalitarianism is its sacred cow. In the real world we see clear power differentials based on differences of gender, race, ability, and appearance, yet in the realm of cyberspace these differences drop away. The particular circumstances of the fat, the thin, the tall, the short, the beautiful, the homely, the man, the woman, the gay, the straight, the Hispanic, the African-American, the Caucasian and so on are not revealed by the computer screen. Accordingly, Howard Rheingold claims "people whose physical handicaps make it difficult to form new friendships find that virtual communities treat them as they always wanted to be treated – as thinkers and transmitters of ideas and feeling beings, not carnal vessels with a certain appearance and way of walking and talking (or not walking

---

57. Kadi p. 59.
58. Rheingold p. 64.

and talking)."[59] Taking Rheingold's point one step further, some also argue that given this ability of those somehow marked by the material world – that is, everybody – to escape those markings in cyberspace, cyberspace must necessarily be egalitarian in nature. "Stripped of the external trappings of wealth, power, beauty and social status, people tend to be judged in the cyberspace of the Internet only by their ideas and their ability to get them across in terse, vigorous prose."[60] However, while on the surface this argument would appear to make sense, upon reflection one can begin to identify a number of significant flaws in the logic.

Like Elmer-DeWitt, Mark Dery argues that "on line, users can float free of biological and sociocultural determinants, at least to the degree that their idiosyncratic language usage does not mark them as white, black, college-educated, a high-school dropout, and so on." However, while Dery makes an important point in introducing the question of idiosyncratic language usage, he backs away from this complication and quotes Wayne Gregori, a computer consultant, who, like Elmer-DeWitt, claims "people are judged by the content of what they say."[61] Dery's reversal is unfortunate. Language in cyberspace is not nearly so generic as these arguments would suggest, and, for example, any given post on the Usenet or any given E-mail message will likely be riddled with clues to the sender's identity. When "Summer," who posts from an account associated with Seattle Pacific University, repeatedly refers to her favorite band as being "spifforama" it doesn't take much to begin to construct a rudimentary identity for her.

Moreover, there is at least anecdotal evidence suggesting that, well aware of the limitations of ASCII, many people intentionally amplify the idiosyncrasies of their language usage, replacing as best they can what the medium takes out. Thus, in a posting to one of the rec.music newsgroups, one user writes:

> Just came from the bookstore, and let me tell y'all somethin'. I picked up "Jesus Smoke" and "Tha Life of a Hoodlum". Y'all need to get this e-roc joint. 3NP produced this thing (which scared me at first). These boys deserve an album NOW. They also did a lot of rappin' on there. They got musical sense for real.

---

59. Rheingold p. 64.
60. Elmer-DeWitt "Welcome to Cyberspace" p. 9.
61. Dery p. 561.

Arguably, with the apostrophes replacing dropped vowels and final "g"s, the text here represents not so much an unfamiliarity with the rules of grammar and spelling, but rather a conscious attempt to manipulate those rules so as to create a particular cultural identity for the writer. What the medium takes out, the message attempts to put back in.

Of course, there are those who will challenge this argument, claiming, first, that cyberspace offers no irrefutable evidence that the peculiarities of one's language usage correspond to the reality of one's socioeconomic condition, and second, that it is quite common for users – particularly those on the MUDs and IRCs – to create personalities for themselves that have no connection to who they are in the material world (and given anonymous remailers and other tools it is possible to manipulate the data that is attached to any given message). This is, admittedly, quite true. Summer may well be a fifty-two-year-old male Native American and not the teenage female WASP her messages suggest, while the author of the post quoted above may well belong to the Daughters of the American Revolution; there is no way to tell. However, there are issues here that bear exploration. First, at a practical level, one might ask how many people have both the technical skills necessary to use these tools and the intellectual skills necessary to maintain the illusion of an alternate identity? Despite the media exposés, I would argue such individuals are few and far between.

Second, and more importantly, if cyberspace were the egalitarian environment it is claimed to be, beyond a sort of delight in the hoax, there would be little motivation for adopting an alternate identity. If men and women are equal in cyberspace, both judged on the content of what they say, then there is little reason for a man to pretend to be a woman and vice-versa. Thus, the very fact that there are those who choose to manipulate their identities in cyberspace, I would argue, refutes the notion that socio-economic indicators are meaningless in cyberspace.

Finally, the argument that without proof of identity there can be no prejudice fails to recognize that while we may not *know* a person belongs to this or that social category we can nevertheless respond to them as if they do. As a real world analogy, consider a woman passing as a man: It may be possible that this "man" is in fact a woman, but that does not preclude us from treating her as a man. Hence, whatever socio-economic categories you may belong to in the real world, in so far as your contributions in cyberspace position you in this or that group, you will be responded to as a member of that group.

Ultimately, there is a rather peculiar assumption underlying the claim that cyberspace is necessarily egalitarian in nature: the belief that material, socio-economic differences are the only distinctions that can translate into power differentials. Is it not possible that cyberspace has its own culture, and that differences in that culture could translate into social stratification as easily as differences in race or gender do in the real world? Not only is it possible, it is reality.

Consider, for example, the treatment newcomers generally receive upon entering cyberspace. "For all the talk of friendly, open systems, there's no warm welcome for novices" in cyberspace; "newbie" is emphatically not a term of endearment.[62] The difference between new users and old-timers, however, is not the only line of stratification in cyberspace. Steven Jones, for example, argues that "there are users and super-users. . . [and] E-mail addresses that have more status than others."[63] Jones might well have been thinking of America Online when he made that statement.

To understand America Online, and the hostility received by its users, it is necessary to look back to the early days of the Internet. Originally, the Internet was computer networking of the computer scientist, by the computer scientist, for the computer scientist. Not surprisingly, then, the Net spoke a computer scientist's language, Unix, a dense and archaic command-line language that is "a bear to set up . . . a nightmare to administer" and almost impossible to use.[64] Consequently, the Internet provides "a user interface designed by adolescents and constructed deliberately so as to make access as difficult as possible for the novice."[65] This brings us to America Online. Created explicitly (at least at first) for the Macintosh user, America Online utilizes an icon-based interface similar to Microsoft Windows. By definition then, America Online users fall on the wrong side in the religious war that is computer science. As if that weren't enough, moreover, when America Online first joined the Internet and gave Usenet access to its users, a flaw in the system caused any messages they posted to be repeated eight times. Thus, as America Online users proceed to make the usual newbie mistakes, these mistakes were amplified eight times over, and the users became "sitting

---

62. Stoll p. 60. In the hope of minimizing conflict, new users are generally encouraged to "lurk" for a few weeks before actively participating. Of course, how the new users are supposed to know to do this remains a mystery.

63. Quoted in Jill Smolowe, "Intimate Strangers" *Time* Spring 1995, p. 24.

64. Bill Cheswick quoted in Stoll (1995) p. 66. Another large selling point of Unix is that it's free.

65. Rachel Padman quoted in Stoll p. 66.

targets for locals already disposed to resent their presence on the Net."[66] Hence, if it's not the equivalent of a yellow star, in cyberspace an "@aol.com" tacked to the end of your login ID – the signature of the computer networking dilettante, perhaps? – can nevertheless be enough to draw hostility.

If newbies eventually evolve into experienced users and resentment against America Online users has begun to subside (though it's far from gone), there is nevertheless a more crucial form of discrimination in cyberspace, one that rests on the fundamental nature of human interaction. Responding to the claim that "people are judged by the content of what they say," I would like to argue that this is only true the first time. Consider: If in cyberspace one is judged only on the content of one's messages, then it would follow that whatever identity the individual possesses is based on those messages. This plural noun, moreover, is crucial. As in life, identity in cyberspace is cumulative; each contribution a person makes to the interactions of a given group will also contribute to that person's identity within the group, becoming part of a greater whole. Those individual contributions, moreover, come to be judged not individually but rather in the context of that whole. An inflammatory statement made from a user with a history of calm and rational discourse, for example, will be received much differently than that same statement coming from one with a reputation for hostility. In cyberspace, then, as is the case everywhere people interact, individuals build histories, they develop reputations. Reputation, moreover, as much as race, class and gender can become the basis for distinction. Thus, in the newsgroup rec.music.christian, for example, a select group of users have taken to reposting the messages of one Andy Whitman, pining for his hoped for return. We may mouth platitudes about individuals being evaluated solely on the basis of what they say, but it seems far more true to argue that people are judged on the basis of the history of their interactions. In cyberspace, as elsewhere, history leads to stratification. The only way cyberspace could ever be truly egalitarian would be if everyone were always a newcomer, and history weren't allowed to emerge.

Take Nothing With You, Bring Nothing Back

Can cyberspace offer us new opportunities for developing community and furthering democracy? Can cyberspace become a modern day public sphere for the "rational-critical debate of

---

66. Elmer-DeWitt "Battle for the Soul of the Internet," p. 54.

political matters. . . . [and] the self-articulation of civil society"?[67] For many, these are the crucial questions we must bring to the debate, and here again we find no shortage of believers. "Not only is the Internet public," argues James Beniger,

> it is also a public space. Against the Pentagon's efforts at hierarchical control, in the mid-1970s, the voices of the ARPA researchers who enjoyed public discussions of science fiction eventually prevailed. These first citizens of cyberspace were eventually allowed to make and enforce their own rules, bottom up, with relatively little centralized control. Two decades later, cyberspace continues to flourish in this way. . . .[68]

Similarly, Philip Elmer-DeWitt claims the Internet is "rabidly democratic," while Alvin Toffler expects the Information Society to be "more sane, sensible, and sustainable, more decent and more democratic than any we have ever known."[69] More concretely, Beniger reveals that "a 1993 survey of the EON Group, a Virginia public affairs firm, found that 81 percent of the potential cruisers of the information superhighway would use this interactive medium primarily to voice their opinions on social and political issues."[70]

Undoubtedly, there is a bit of intellectual sleight-of-hand at work here. In claims for the public and democratic nature of cyberspace, there seems to be the built-in implication that this nature can somehow be translated into the material world; that democracy in cyberspace means democracy in the world. The suggestion, however, is false. One might, for example, note that activity in cyberspace is bracketed apart from the rest of life. "Visiting and posting frequently in Internet newsgroups about exercise equipment are not the same as exercising," writes Tom Mandel, "[and] discussing lingerie via my online service's 'chat'

---

67. Jurgen Habermas (1989) *The Structural Transformation of the Public Sphere: An Inquiry into a Category of Bourgeois Society* translated by Thomas Buger (Cambridge: The MIT Press).

68. Beniger p. 1.

69. Elmer-DeWitt "Welcome to Cyberspace," p. 9; Toffler, p. 19.

70. Beniger p. 14. Given that the Usenet newsgroups with the most traffic are the ones found in the alt.sex hierarchy, unless the category of "social issues" is defined so broadly as to include most anything, this finding would seem to involve more than a few people telling the researchers what they expected the researchers wanted to hear.

utility . . . [is] not a good substitute for a Friday-night date."[71]
Contemplating the communal value of cyberspace, John Perry
Barlow, who, while finding some promise in the technology (he's
a WELL user), also finds a number of qualities conspicuously
missing. Philosophically, Barlow wonders if "the central question
of the virtual age is whether or not *prana* [the Hindu term for
breath or spirit] can somehow be made to fit through any
disembodied medium," but more pragmatically Barlow also
laments the loss of "body language, sex, death, tone of voice,
clothing, beauty (or homeliness), weather, violence, vegetation,
wildlife, pets, architecture, music, smells, sunlight, and that ol'
harvest moon. In short, most of the things that make my life real
to me."[72]

It seems, then, that the same power that allows us to rise
above our material conditions also necessarily separates us from
them. In a sense, cyberspace offers *too much* freedom; it's too
easy. Community depends on "an absence of alternatives and a
sense of genuine adversity, genuinely shared," but in cyberspace
there is no sense of adversity or constraint.[73] A command to the
computer, a click of the mouse, and you can go anywhere, leave
anywhere, join or abandon any group. Cyberspace offers complete
freedom. However, as Jean-Pierre Dupuy notes, "a world without
constraints, without order, a world in which everything would
be possible, would have no meaning."[74] Should we be surprised
to find the community and democracy of cyberspace strangely
empty?

Perhaps a result of the lack of materiality, perhaps the product
of design, there is another difficulty associated with democracy
in cyberspace: it lacks a defining structure of rules and sanctions
(thus becoming more anarchic than democratic). To again quote
Dupuy, "The first requirement of any communality of life is that
each person must be responsible for his own acts, including their
unforeseeable unwanted consequences."[75] In cyberspace, however,
there is no such responsibility as there is no one to demand it.
"Nobody has the power to kick anybody off for good," nor to

---

71. Tom Mandel "Confessions of a Cyberholic" *Time* Spring 1995, p. 57.

72. Barlow "Is there a There in Cyberspace?" p. 54.

73. Barlow "Is there a There in Cyberspace?" p. 55.

74. Jean-Pierre Dupuy (1980) "Myths of the Information Society" in Kathleen
Woodward (ed) *The Myths of Information: Technology and Postindustrial Society*
(Madison: Coda Press) p. 13.

75. Dupuy p. 16.

enforce any other sanction.[76] Thus, when lawyers Canter and Siegel wrote a program to automatically post an advertisement for their legal services on every Usenet newsgroup worldwide ("spamming" in the lingo of the Net) there was little anyone could do. Though enough hate mail was sent to their account to repeatedly crash the system, their "fax machine began spewing out page after page of blank paper. . . bogus magazine subscriptions began showing up on their doorstep," and eventually their service provider shut down their account, the two lawyers refused to give in. Insisting the ads had generated business, they got their account back (threatening to sue Internet Direct for cutting them off) and told the *New York Times* they would advertise on the Net again.[77]

Subsequently, the Usenet has begun to slip into a state of guerrilla warfare between the spammers who broadcast advertisements, surveys, and political harangues across the newsgroups and self-appointed vigilante censors who write programs ("cancelbots") designed to seek out such messages and cancel them before they appear.[78] And while each side draws wrath from some members of the Internet community – spammers from those who fear the declining signal-to-noise ratio, vigilantes from those who fear censorship – with "netiquette" the only reigning power there is no way to resolve the conflict. Without the possibility of sanction, users are free to act as they see fit.

If there is little consequence to the actions which take place in cyberspace within cyberspace, the impact is arguably even less in the material world. The battles which rage in cyberspace have little important in the world of the flesh, and issues like spamming, the Communications Decency Act of 1995 and the Clipper Chip, issues which generate megabytes of computer discussion and petition drives on the Net, are non-issues to those outside. As Clifford Stoll writes, "technologists [like everybody else] speak to their own concerns. The single overriding common interest among the network users is the medium itself."[79] CDA

76. Elmer-DeWitt "Battle for the Soul of the Internet" p. 53. In some case, service providers do have the ability to close the account of someone who flagrantly violates the norms of cyberspace. Thus, a university or business can police their users if they so desire. However, as David Wilson has argued, this has been an extremely rare occurrence. See David Wilson "Social Pressure Guides Behavior on Usenet's Bulletin Boards" *The Chronicle of Higher Education* 13 January, 1995, p. A19).

77. Elmer-DeWitt "Battle for the Soul of the Internet" p. 52.

78. David L. Wilson "Vigilantes Gain Quiet Approval on Networks" *The Chronicle of Higher Education* 13 January 1995, p. A17.

79. Stoll p. 47.

and the Clipper Chip aside, this focus on the medium further manifests itself (though less flamboyantly) in the continual practice of self-definition one routinely finds on listservs and the Usenet. Whatever their subject matter and whatever the nature of their membership, such groups spend an inordinate amount of time working to define who they are and where their boundaries lie. Thus, a recent post to the Comgrads listserv (now roughly five years old) offered "Things to Avoid" and "Things to Do" in facilitating civil interaction among the list's members. Included in the same post, moreover, was the identification of "the stages that all lists go through. . . . 1) initial enthusiasm; 2) evangelism; 3) growth; 4) community; 5) discomfort with diversity; 6a) stagnation, or 6b) maturity."[80] Quoted from a post to still another listserv (and seen elsewhere by this author as well), this identification and discussion of "the stages that all lists go through," is just one example of the continued obsession with the nature of the medium. (The obsession with netiquette one finds on the Usenet is another.) One has to wonder: If discussion in the salons of 18th century England and France concerned only the status of the salons as salons, would Habermas have called them public spheres?

Soap Boxes and Public Spheres

According to Jeffrey Abramson, "face-to-face deliberation should not be idealized as a cure-all for conflict."[81] Indeed not, but at the same time it seems worth exploring the nature of face-to-face deliberation for the purposes of evaluating communication and debate in cyberspace. In comparing cyberspace to the early townhalls, for example, Howard Fineman argues that

> In de Tocqueville's America, members of "voluntary associations met face to face" and talked of other things before the meeting was called to order. There was a sense of the whole community outside the hall. "In cyberspace you only 'meet' to talk about one specific thing," says Claremont McKenna's [Jack] Pitney.[82]

---

80. Norman Clark "Pulling Things Together" [post to Comgrads listserv] 12 May, 1997.

81. Jeffrey B. Abramson "Electronic Town Meetings: Proposals for Democracy's Future" presented to *The Annenberg Scholars Program Conference on Public Space*, Philadelphia, PA. 1-4 March 1995, p. 3.

82. Fineman p. 33.

The question we have to ask, then, is how crucial is this cross-topic talk? How important is it for people who have come together for the purposes of governing themselves to talk about the weather, their jobs, and all those things people talk about when they're standing around waiting for something to happen? What role does small talk serve? I do not have an answer, but I do have a suggestion: such talk, I would argue, serves to remind us that we are dealing with unique and complex individuals who cannot be reduced to the mere stance on an issue. Accepting this idea, however, puts a great burden on communication in cyberspace. If cyberspace transforms us from "carnal vessels with a certain appearance and way of walking and talking (or not walking and talking" into "thinkers and transmitters of ideas and feelings," it also restricts those ideas and feelings to a single domain.[83] Here you are a music fan, your opinions on abortion are not welcome; there you are Republican, your questions on car repair do not belong. Thus, without idealizing the face-to-face, it nevertheless seems worth wondering if the fragmented individuals of cyberspace could ever productively reason together on the issues of self-government.

Continuing this exploration of cyberspace vis-à -vis the face-to-face, consider Abramson's claims for the necessary conditions for deliberation. Abramson argues that for true democratic deliberation there must be the opportunities for 1) messages of substance to be exchanged at length, 2) reflection, and 3) interaction.[84] At first blush, cyberspace would seem to meet these criteria in spades: the threads on the Usenet, for example, often seem to go on forever; there is no point at which a person may no longer respond; and people may respond to, and interact with, whomever they desire. If, however, that is the normative condition, in practice things are much different. First, while threads may last forever, they are woefully circular; discussion reduces to the same people saying the same things in the same ways. Second, while substantive responses are possible, "just as television gives us sound bites, the online interview proves one-line answers" and messages on the Internet are woefully empty of substance.[85] Third, while there is no technical reason one must respond without reflection, as a practical matter "the Internet propagates a sense of urgency"; it offers instantaneous communication and so we

83. Rheingold p. 64.

84. Abramson p. 3.

85. Stoll p. 33.

feel obligated to communicate instantaneously.[86] Finally, then, there is the question of interactivity. "Anyone," claims Clifford Stoll, "can post messages on the Net. Practically everyone does. The resulting cacophony drowns out serious discussion."[87]

Cyberspace, in other words, on a day to day basis is about as interactive as a shouting match. Offering freedom from sanction and the power of anonymity and untraceability, cyberspace becomes not an environment for rational discussion, but a soapbox for extreme opinions which would not be entertained anywhere else. Unfortunately, it would seem a great many people have forgotten one basic rule of telecommunications: just because you've typed it into a computer and broadcast it to the world doesn't mean it's important. In the words of Benjamin Barber, democracy is "about defending your views in front of a group, not registering your biases from home or your car phone."[88]

So, given all this, why the faith in cyberspace as an empowering and democratic environment? I would like to suggest that for Americans at least this reflects a particular blindness concerning the requirements of democracy. Protected by the First Amendment, in America the freedom of speech has become the *sine qua non* of liberal democracy, and as a people we have, for the most part, done all we can to assure the right of the individual to speak her mind. More than any other, it is this goal that seems to motivate our discussions of cyberspace. "The Internet challenges our commitment to free speech," writes a local columnist, "precisely because it exposes us to its most extreme manifestations. This exposure has altered the terms of the free speech debate in cyberspace, leaving some Americans' fundamental commitment to free speech deeply shaken."[89] The implication I think is clear: keep fighting the good fight, don't let the censors come online. However, while an admirable sentiment, the time has come to complicate the situation. We must, I think, consider that as crucial as the freedom of speech is to our democratic ideals, the responsibility to *listen* may be far more significant.

This, of course, is not a new idea. Alexander Meiklejohn, for example, argues that

---

86. Stoll p. 167.

87. Stoll p. 32.

88. Quoted in Jonathan Alter "The Couch Potato Vote" *Newsweek* 27 February, 1995, p. 34.

89. Kim Painter "Understanding the Fight for a Free Cyberspace" *The Daily Iowan* 13 March, 1995 p. 6A.

> the First Amendment . . . . is not the guardian of unregulated talkativeness. It does not require that, on every occasion, every citizen shall take part in public debate. Nor can it even give assurance that everyone shall have the opportunity to do so . . . . What is essential is not that everyone shall speak, but that everything worth saying shall be said.[90]

And if Meiklejohn isn't willing to make the leap to hearing completely, Hannah Arendt is. Outlining her definition of the term "public," Arendt argues that pubic "means, first, that everything that appears in public can be seen and heard by everybody and has the widest possible publicity."[91] Reality, she argues, is something that comes from *being seen* and *being heard*, not from seeing or speaking. Nicholas Garnham, moreover, has more recently argued that "while the rights to free expression inherent in democratic theory have been continually stressed, what has been lost is any sense of the reciprocal duties." Crucial to democracy is "the duty to listen to the views of others and to alternative versions of events."[92]

What I want to argue, then, is that the crucial flaw of cyberspace is that it elevates the right to speak above all others, and all but eliminates the responsibility to listen. Writing on a somewhat different topic – universities, actually – Milan Kundera claimed that "culture is perishing in overproduction, in an avalanche of words, in the madness of quantity."[93] Nowhere is that more true than in cyberspace. "Our networks are awash in data," and everyone wants to add to the flood.[94] Is it too late to suggest that we perhaps need fewer tools allowing people to speak and more tools which will help them to listen?

Conclusion: New Media and Established Patterns

New technologies, we have been told, tend to create new human environments. Perhaps, but such environments are still necessarily human, and as such subject to human limitation. Thus, while in

90. Alexander Meiklejohn (1948) *Political Freedom* (New York: Harpers) p. 25.

91. Hannah Arendt (1958) *The Human Condition* (Chicago: The University of Chicago Press) p. 50.

92. Nicholas Garnham (1992) "The Media and the Public Sphere" in Craig Calhoun (ed) *Habermas and the Public Sphere*, (Cambridge: The MIT Press) p. 367-368.

93. Milan Kundera (1984)*The Unbearable Lightness of Being* (New York: Harper & Row).

94. Stoll (1995) p. 193.

the case of cyberspace it has been claimed that this new environment will be "more sane, sensible, and sustainable, more decent and more democratic than any we have ever known," the argument rests on false assumptions about the nature of human beings and human interactions.[95] As Kevin Kelly notes, cyberspace "is not a computer revolution, it's a communications revolution."[96] As such, it is limited by the nature of communication. Cyberspace will not produce non-symbolic (i.e., perfect) communication because there is no such thing. Cyberspace will not produce unlimited diversity, the human mind lacks the ability to process the information that would entail. Cyberspace will not produce equality, for history – that is, the simple passage of time – produces distinction. Similar problems, moreover, will thwart efforts to find in cyberspace community, democracy, justice, inclusion and the rest of the virtues routinely claimed to exist in cyberspace on a mass scale. So what will we find in cyberspace? A world much like our present one: a heterogeneous place of community, isolation, prejudice, love, hate, intelligence, stupidity, culture, commerce, respect, disregard and just about everything else that makes life at once worth living and almost more than we can stand.

---

95. Toffler (1980) p. 19.

96. John Perry Barlow, Sven Birkerts, Kevin Kelly and Mark Slouka "Forum: What Are We Doing On-Line?" *Harper's* August 1995, p. 39.

48

David Resnick
University of Cincinnati

Politics on the Internet:
The Normalization of Cyberspace

Abstract: The creation of the Internet gave rise to utopian fantasies of citizen empowerment and the revitalization of democracy as well as dystopian fears of technocratic domination. Neither of these possibilities seems likely. Cyberspace has been transformed from a virtual state of nature into a virtual pluralistic civil society with commercial activity, organized interest groups and parties, and an emerging legal regulatory structure. The early Net relied on text-based technology and limited access. It fostered a fluid relatively egalitarian politics relying on newsgroups, listservs and e-mail. The new Net created by the Web with its graphical interface and mass appeal, transformed Cyberspace into a mass medium which became attractive to the economic, social, and political forces that had previously ignored it. Politics in contemporary Cyberspace constitutes three distinct types: 1) *politics within the Net,* concerning the internal operation of the Net and involving those online 2) *politics which impacts the Net,* dealing with the policies and regulation of governments affecting Cyberspace and 3) *political uses of the Net,* concerning how Cyberspace is used to affect political life off line. Virtual reality has come to resemble the real world; ordinary everyday politics has captured Cyberspace.

Not long ago the Internet was heralded as a technology for creating new forms of community, empowering citizens, and challenging existing power structures. Rheingold, one of the leading popularizers of the idea said: "The political significance of CMC [Computer Mediated Communication] lies in its capacity to challenge the existing political hierarchy's monopoly on powerful communications media, and perhaps thus revitalize citizen-based democracy. . . The vision of a citizen-designed, citizen-controlled worldwide communications network is a version of technological utopianism that could be called the vision of 'the electronic agora.'" [1] There was also a darker contrary vision, an Orwellian dystopia of computers, electronic data bases and new media, a panopticon, in which governments employ powerful new information technologies to oppress, manipulate and dominate ordinary citizens.

---

1. Howard Rheingold (1993) *The Virtual Community: Homesteading on the Electronic Frontier* (Reading, MA: Addison-Wesley) p. 14.

Cyberspace has become wildly popular and undergone major technological transformations in recent years, but it has not had nearly the effects on society that either its proponents or its detractors predicted. Perhaps it is too early to fully assess the effects of the Internet, but so far, both the utopians and dystopians had it wrong. Cyberspace is neither a mass breeding ground for liberated virtual communitarians nor a launching pad for electronic storm troopers bent on stamping out free expression and dissent.

It is the thesis of this essay that what has occurred in recent years is the normalization of Cyberspace. Cyberspace has not become the locus of a new politics that spills out of the computer screen and revitalizes citizenship and democracy. If anything, ordinary politics in all its complexity and vitality has invaded and captured Cyberspace.

The fluid and unstructured politics of newsgroups and listservs was once the only significant politics that existed on the Net. Cyberspace sheltered an individualistic, free-flowing inchoate politics of discussion and polemic, of conversation and passion. It was relatively egalitarian and participatory and often bounded by the discussion group itself. While still important, this type of politics has been largely replaced by the organized politics of the Web structured by formal presentations which are the product of thought and deliberation, and open to all comers. While movement within a site appears to be totally free, there are only various degrees of structured freedom. Web sites are intended to present coherent positions, and to inform, influence and persuade those who log onto them. Though the majority of political sites are probably still created by individual volunteers, the most important, most visited sites are now sponsored, designed and paid for by organizations and professionals.

Popular press stories on politics and the Net almost always refer to the Web. While there may be a few passing references to newsgroups, those citizens who are interested in politics are guided to the flashy Web sites. The Web presents itself as the first and most exciting place for those new to Cyberspace. It creates a political experience unlike the amorphous dialogue of newsgroups and listservs. Web sites are designed to be graphic, attractive and informative. Politics on the Web are structured in a double sense, presenting a structured experience, and reflecting the organized structure of pluralistic political life in the real world. It is truly a creature of modern democratic politics.

On the day of the 1996 U.S. presidential election there was a tremendous increase in Net traffic. The traffic jams at the various web sites promising election news led some to claim that the Net was not yet ready for prime time.[2] While this phenomenon was a sign of the great number of people who see the Web as a ready source of information, such usage is not significantly different from using newspapers, or radio and television. The true potential for the Net changing the way we experience politics lies in other, less flashy but more manipulative uses of Web sites.

Many of those who are organized to influence electoral outcomes and to bring to bear the pressure of public opinion on public policy now feel that they must have their own Web site. While an organized group may occasionally respond to a posting on a newsgroup, these groups are not seen as the main vehicles for influencing a mass public. The public which is ripe for persuasion and manipulation, if it exists at all on the Net, is a free-floating agglomeration of Web surfers and searchers. The World Wide Web has transformed Cyberspace, creating new opportunities for the politically skilled and sophisticated. But for all the hype about a qualitatively new virtual world, Cyberspace is nevertheless coming to resemble our old familiar world of everyday economics and politics.[3]

The next section of this essay presents a theoretical perspective which illuminates the social-structural changes that have occurred in Cyberspace as it has developed from a simple text-based communication medium with limited access into a multimedia phenomenon with a mass audience. The postings of ordinary citizens have been supplemented by the sophisticated creations of professional content providers: individuals communicating with others have been joined by government agencies, political parties, interest groups, media conglomerates and commercial

2. "Internet Users Overwhelm Many Election Web Sites" *San Francisco Chronicles* November 6, 1996; "The numbers were there - if you could get through," *Nandonet* November 6, 1996.

3. W.B.H.J. van de Donk and P. W. Tops (1995) "Orwell or Athens?: Informatization and the Future of Democracy, A Review of the Literature" in *Orwell in Athens: A Perspective on Informatization and Democracy* (Amsterdam,: IOS Press) p. 13-32 contains a number of useful references on the relationship between new media and democratic theory. Orwell or Athens refers to the fact that the new technologies have evoked both negative and positive images. For optimistic assessments of the use of the Internet for enhancing democratic citizenship see Rheingold; Bill Mann (1995) *Politics on the Net* (Indianapolis, IN: Que Corporation); Edward Schwartz (1996) *Net Activism: How Citizens Use the Internet* (Sebastopol, CA: Songline Studios); Mark Bonchek, "Grassroots in Cyberspace: Using Computer Networks to Facilitate Political Participation," *Political Participation Project* at http://www.ai.mit.edu/projects/ppp/home.html

businesses of all sorts. The final section of the essay turns to the political implications of this transformation and discusses three types of politics spawned by this new mass media.

I. Politics on the Net: The Great Transformation and Beyond

Once the Net was like a Lockean state of nature. All individuals were free and equal. Each was a producer and a consumer, though some were more likely to consume than to produce. The dominant ethos was altruism, and there was a spirit of mutual aid. Though some were more skilled, there was no rigid division of labor. The land of Cyberspace seemed to stretch from virtual horizon to horizon, but was sparsely settled. There was hardly any real politics – certainly no concerted efforts to manipulate the opinions and actions of a mass public. Communities formed around common interests, and differences of opinion served to spur thought and discussion. People were more innocent. They led simple lives online, and life was fun, if not particularly profitable.

What happened? Locke attributes the transformation of the original state of nature to the invention of money, a medium of exchange which made it rational for men and women to work hard and use the surplus created by their labor. When it became profitable for people to invest more and more of their time in productive activities, the division of labor intensified, and the ways in which men and women interacted and organized themselves were radically transformed. With the invention of money came the need for laws and the creation of civil society and politics.[4] I suggest that something similar happened on the Internet. There is no question that the Net today looks much more like a pluralistic civil society than an individualistic state of nature. It has its own economy, complete with overly optimistic business forecasts; it has developed a complicated division of labor with its attendant inequalities; and it has heard the call for laws and regulation and the protection of private property. The Net has lost its political innocence.

Once activity on the Net came to be seen as a form of productive labor, the potential value of the time spent online greatly increased. Then new institutions, organizations, practices and politics appeared. The primitive exchange economy of altruistic producers and consumers was pushed to the periphery. The center became dominated by a relatively sophisticated political

4. John Locke *Two Treatises of Government* (Cambridge: Cambridge University Press, 1988) Second Treatise ch. 5 pp. 285-302.

economy which, in traditional fashion, can be divided into three sectors: the public, the nonprofit and the for-profit. Now the amateurs and hobbyists have been crowded out by the professionals and a mass audience of consumers, entertainment and information seekers and curious tourists. Some of the early stalwart settlers online dropped off in disgust. Those who remained online did not need their own Frederick Jackson Turner to tell them the frontier was fading fast.

When various professionals began to see time spent on the Internet as work rather than recreation,things changed forever. Now professionals are paid to construct Web pages, provide content for Web sites or log onto the Web in the course of their paid work. Though the boundary between technical support people and content and service providers is not sharp, this distinction should be adequate as a working concept. Political, economic, social and recreational life on the Net for the mass public is increasingly designed and guided by Web professionals.

This transformation of the Internet from a virtual state of nature to a virtual pluralistic civil society has been facilitated by technological innovation. What is now popularly known as the Net is dominated by the World Wide Web. The initial expansion of the Net from its early beginnings as a project of the Department of Defense occurred when those online started using it for communication; e-mail became the killer app and the functionality of the Net increased along with its popularity. The creation of the Web with its graphical interface and its hypertext site-based focus changed things forever. No longer was the Net a text-based system centered around dialogic communication and postings, an anarchic mélange of newsgroups and listservs and gopher sites. It had become a multimedia phenomenon of linked Web sites where search engines, advertisements, commerce and entertainment existed alongside the traditional text-based Net of old.

The invention and rapid spread of the World Wide Web has dramatically changed the feel of the Net for the overwhelming majority of users. Without the development of Web Browsers with their graphical user interfaces and point and click technology, Cyberspace would most likely have remained underpopulated. Despite all the hype about interactivity Web Browsers and Home Pages were also largely responsible for transforming the Net into a relatively passive medium, significantly more passive than the one envisioned by those who celebrate the Web as a spectacular breakthrough in interactivity. For web boosters it seems as if it could miraculously transform couch potatoes into actively engaged seekers after knowledge and new experiences. Surfing and using hypertext is still very like clicking a TV remote, albeit a remote freed from the tyranny of the fixed broadcast schedule and able to choose from an enormously expanded list of channels. The ability to actively respond to Web Sites by posting e-mail is only one step above being able to write fan letters to TV programs. Chat rooms and other opportunities to interact with like-minded individuals do exist, but they are not central features of the most popular politically relevant Web sites. To be sure, the Web can involve more participation on the part of the person online than other media, but it is not the kind of active participation that is required of someone engaged in conversation.

The Web site is typical of the new Net, just as the newsgroup or listserv is typical of the old text-based Net. Newsgroups are, by nature, interactive since they are conversations transplanted to a new medium. Conversation is not a finished product, but an ongoing process. Any bit of dialogue in the middle of a conversation is open at both ends; it responds to what has gone before and looks forward to a response. Whether it is conducted on the Net in real time or asynchronously, it still feels alive and spontaneous. Those who lurk, logging onto newsgroups without actually posting anything, are like those who stand around and listen to a conversation at a party, able to add to the conversation if they wish or move on to another conversation. Engaging in conversation requires no special training. Creating and maintaining a successful sophisticated Web site which attracts a significant number of hits, at least up until now, requires both dedication and technical skills.

If human conversation is the real world paradigm of a newsgroup, a presentation is the paradigm of a Web site. By a "presentation," I mean such things as a published book, a dramatic or musical performance, a TV program or advertisement, and the like. A presentation is based on a script, can be repeated without losing its essential qualities, and, what is most important, is intended for an audience. While there are brilliant conversationalists, conversation is essentially egalitarian. Presentations may use some of the same skills we use in conversation, but they also call on a host of other aptitudes and abilities. Unlike conversation, they value talents and demand expertise. They are inegalitarian.

Presentations encourage experiments in new media to convey meaning in more sophisticated and elaborate ways. They develop expertise in speech, the visual arts, dance and music. An audience is ordinarily not expected to participate in the presentation. They are there to be entertained, informed, inspired, awed, manipulated, energized and the like. The real class division in Cyberspace is between the Webmasters and the Surfers. Undoubtedly all producers of presentations are consumers of other presentations, but assuredly relatively few consumers are producers.

Web pages are Net-based presentations that are more suitable to a mass audience than are text-based conversations. It takes less effort to be an anonymous member of an audience, to go from presentation to presentation as the spirit moves you, than to actively engage in conversation, whether on the Internet or in the real world. Unlike being a member of an audience, participating in a conversation often requires discipline and effort. It is truly utopian to believe that the Internet by itself will radically transform politics in advanced industrial society, that it will make politics more like a conversation among equals than a series of elaborate presentations which attempt to elicit the support and approval of relatively passive consumers.

Political life on the Internet has moved away from fluid Cybercommunities in which civic life centers around free discussion and debate. It has entered an era of organized civil society and structured group pluralism with a relatively passive citizenry. A randomly selected on-line citizen is certainly more able, and as for now, probably more willing, to air personal and political opinions than his or her counterpart off line, but this is not sufficient to conclude that Cyberspace will transform the nature of citizenship in advanced industrial countries in the next century. As virtual reality comes to mirror the real world, Cyberspace simply becomes another arena for the ongoing struggle for wealth, power and political influence.

The Web today has a strong and growing commercial sector. Around $3 billion worth of commerce was conducted on the Internet during 1996, and it is predicted that this will rise to $100 billion by the year 2000.[5] Although the Federal government had always subsidized and owned significant parts of the Internet until recently, government remained virtually invisible to the average user. With the advent of the Web a formal public sector emerged. Now American governments at all levels increasingly use the Web to disseminate and gather information, deliver

---

5. "Unprecedented Growth in Global Usage of the Internet and the World Wide Web" *The Global Market Forecast for Internet Commerce,* International Data Corporation at http://www.idcresearch.com/HNR/cpr41c.htm

services, improve government operations and pursue the public interest as they see it, both nationally and internationally. As the Web increasingly becomes a venue for commerce, governments become increasingly interested in extending their regulatory supervision and taxing authority.

The Net has clearly met its promise of easy access to information for ordinary citizens, but it has not successfully challenged the power of established media conglomerates. In the early days of the Internet, people posted data for altruistic reasons, and no one thought much about its costs or reliability. Though now there are many more people able to provide information, the sheer quantity of information has led to problems with quality and selectivity. Good information is often costly to the provider and, increasingly, to the consumer who values accuracy and whose time is not a free good. How can providers be adequately compensated and true costs be reduced for the consumer? Commercial services which provide search engines and media conglomerates which run elaborate Web news sites have appeared on the Net to try and solve the latter problem. How providers will be compensated is still to be worked out. People are reluctant to pay for information that was once free, so advertisements have proliferated.

What we call news on the Internet has moved beyond the simple sharing of information among people online. Amateur news gatherers and presenters have been all but supplanted by the pros with their superior resources and technical expertise. While going online is hardly profitable now, big media corporations hope to turn a profit in the future. Alternative news sources are still flourishing, but they seem destined to either remain minor niche players, or if successful, be bought out by the majors.

II. Three Types of Internet Politics

Politics and the Internet comprises at least three political phenomena: politics within the Net, politics which impacts the Net, and political uses of the Net. Politics within the Net includes the political life of Cybercommunities and other Net activities which have little or no impact on life off the net. Politics which impacts the Net refers to the host of public policy issues raised by the fact that the Internet is both a new form of mass communication and a vehicle for commerce. Political uses of the Net include the activities of ordinary citizens, political activists, organized interests, political parties and governments to achieve political goals having little or nothing to do with the Internet per se.

II a. Politics within the Net

Politics within the Net, or intra-Net politics, has as its object the operation of the Net or some portion of it. It concerns arrangements which can be settled without reference to political or legal entities outside the Net community itself, and includes such things as establishing technical standards and behavioral norms, settling disputes internal to newsgroups and listservs, creating and structuring new virtual communities and the like. This type of Net politics conceives of Cyberspace as if it were a state of nature or, perhaps, a world consisting of one or more Sovereign countries whose inhabitants exercise authority over their own domain. Intra-net politics is based on a mixture of consensus, participation and, in the technical area, deference to civic-minded technical elites, although of late the civic-minded have been joined by commercial interests. The overall ethos is laissez faire and libertarian. Rule enforcement is through moral suasion, shunning and in extreme cases, excommunication (outlawing Web sites, blocking postings and so on).

Politics within the Net in the old days inspired utopian speculation. It was personal, egalitarian and voluntary in contrast to the corrupt politics of elites and organized interests, of money and power in the real world. This type of political life continues on the Web, but it has not turned out to be a model for politics in the real world, nor has it affected the consciousness of many of the millions of new users who have signed on in the last few years. If anything, the newcomers introduced a number of unpleasant attitudes and assumptions about politics which have upset the older generation of Internet users. In addition, with the advent of Internet commerce, as well as disputes about domain names, cybercrimes, terrorist sites, pornography and many other phenomena which attract the attention of organized advocacy groups and governments, the old types of Internet self-regulation have been challenged by external forces. The age of almost total laissez faire belongs to the past of the Net.

II b. Politics which Impact the Net

Politics which impacts the Net consists of actions and policies taken by political entities, usually but not always nation states. This type of Net politics is often seen as an unwarranted, if not illegitimate, intrusion by those who believe that the only legitimate Net politics is intra-Net politics. Since the Net has become an important and popular phenomenon off line, it has come under scrutiny by governments which assert jurisdiction over what happens online. Governments certainly do not accept any claim of extraterritoriality for Cyberspace. Governments cannot and will not acknowledge that Cyberspace is a free territory inhabited by free people acting beyond the writ of governments.

Those who log on to the Internet are citizens over whom states have ordinary legal authority. However, it is not perfectly obvious how we are to extend such legal concepts as property, libel, copyright, fair usage, community standards and free speech to Cyberspace. The unsettled state of the law has not stopped lawyers who see Cyberspace as a growth area from staking their own claims in the new territory. In major U.S. cities there are at least 53 law firms that claim expertise in the digital domain, and more than a score of U.S. Law Schools are now offering courses on aspects of law and the Internet.[6]

In the United States most of these legal issues probably will not be decided by new legislation, but by the old-fashioned case-by-case method of common-law adjudication. Although there is debate about how various legal concepts and principles are to be applied in Cyberspace, lawyers and judges will undoubtedly find satisfactory solutions – i.e., solutions satisfactory to lawyers and courts.[7] If this method of extending and adapting the law proves unsatisfactory in particular policy areas, politicians and regulators will step into the breach.

The impact of politics on the Net will only increase. The Communications Decency Act, though struck down by the Supreme Court in June of 1997 (*Reno vs. American Civil Liberties*

---

6. Courtney Macavinta "Law Schools Note Net Law Boom" CNET December 24, 1996. For a comprehensive treatment of the current state of the law in Cyberspace see Henry H. Perritt, Jr. (1996) *Law and the Information Superhighway* (New York, NY: John Wiley & Sons).

7. Peter Huber "The End of Law, and the Beginning" in "The Digital Revolution: Where Do We Go From Here?" *Forbes ASAP* December 2, 1996, p. 268. A good place to follow the evolving common law of the net through court opinions is in the CaseWatch section of *The Voters Telecommunications Watch* at http://www.vtw.org/

Union), still shows the sensitivity of politicians to public pressure and their attempt to respond to it.[8] Though, no doubt, a great triumph for free speech, it is only one victory in an ongoing war against attempts by governments to interfere with the free flow of information in Cyberspace. With the rise of commerce on the Net, politicians have become increasingly interested in the tax consequences.[9] As the Net becomes more a part of ordinary life, it will provide governments with excuses and opportunities to extend both their general regulatory and taxing authority. As Net activities become more varied and more public, they become subject to the intense scrutiny of political authorities. Much of the political discussion on the Net now concerns the possible impact of actions contemplated or taken by states which infringe on user freedom.[10]

Fears have centered around efforts by governments to censor visual and textural material on the Net which runs afoul of moral and cultural values. In addition to protecting children from pornography, a concern of all governments, authoritarian governments want to protect their citizens from dangerous social and political ideas. Singapore has a system of regulations which not only bans access to pornography for children but also for adults. It closes off access to Web sites and newsgroups providing information on homosexuality, defaming any race or religion, or containing what the government judges to be politically dangerous and subversive materials. China has blocked access to many Web sites, including those which discuss China's human rights record. German prosecutors have used threats of legal action to pressure online services to restrict access to Web sites providing neo-Nazi propaganda and information useful to terrorists. Recently, the French government sued an English language Web site in France affiliated with an American University because it offered services in English but not in French.[11] In July of 1996 the Group of Seven

8. Linda Greenhouse "High Court Voids Curb on 'Indecent' Internet Material" *The New York Times CyberTimes* June 27, 1997.

9. "Straight Talk: Internet, Tax and Interstate Commerce" *Information Technology Association of America*, at http://www.itaa.org/p7.htm; "Global Co-operation Needed to Avoid Multiple Taxation on the Internet" *Internet IT Informer* October 12, 1996.

10. At the forefront of this struggle to protect privacy and free expression on the Net is *The Electronic Frontier Foundation*. It boasts that it is now one of the 6 most-linked-to sites on the entire World Wide Web at http://www.eff.org/

11. Anne Swardson "French Groups Sue to Bar English-Only Internet Sites" Washington Post Foreign Service, December 24, 1996; Gail Russell Chaddock "English Web Sites In France Flamed by Language Police" *Christian Science Monitor International*, January 10, 1997. Though the lawsuit was thrown out of court on procedural grounds (Bruno Giussani, "French Court Dismisses Suit on Georgia Tech Site" *The New York Time CyberTimes*, June 10, 1997) at almost the same time a Quebec computer store owner got in similar trouble with Quebec's Office de la Langue Francaise for having an English only web site (Mike King "Quebec's Language Cops Slammed over Net Policy" *Calgary Herald Online* June 16, 1997).

industrialized countries, along with Russia, agreed to devise methods to prevent terrorists from using the Internet. In September the Association of Southeast Asian Nations agreed that the Internet should be regulated to protect "our cherished values, traditions and cultures" from the onslaught of Western values.[12]

The call to regulate has caused a furor among those devoted to privacy and freedom in Cyberspace. Many believe that attempts to control information on the Internet are likely to fail: the Net's ability to provide uncensored instantaneous information has proven invaluable in International trade, and the attempt to regulate it might prove more costly than it is worth. Attempts to block information also might prove useless because of the sheer size of Cyberspace and the ability of sophisticated users to circumvent limits on freedom of speech. Many Internet users put their faith in sophisticated encryption techniques to preserve privacy and block governments from snooping. Strong encryption would make it virtually impossible for the government to "wiretap" or "eavesdrop." (Interestingly, both words refer to earlier technologies, but you get the point.)

Policing Cyberspace clearly transcends national borders. The U.S. government as well as the Organization for Economic Cooperation and Development are exploring ways to establish guidelines for encryption. There have been calls for the United Nations to get involved in regulating Cyberspace to catch pornographers, neo-Nazis and terrorists. If fact, many in the legal community believe that a new area of international law will emerge as the Internet becomes subject to international treaties.[13]

The impact of the Net on society in general generates a host of political controversies. Issues of distributive justice are raised by the creation of this new and powerful good. Should everyone have a right to share in it? Should we subsidize its distribution? Many people fear that the new computer communication technology will further widen the gap between the rich and the poor. They worry that lack of either financial resources or technical skill will effectively deny the Internet to significant segments of the population. There are policy proposals which range from House Speaker Newt Gingrich's offhand comment that we might consider giving every poor person a laptop, to more serious

12. Alan Boyle "Government Take on the Net" MSNBC November 11, 1996.

13. Alan Boyle "Internet Issues on the International Stage" MSNBC, November 11, 1996. For an analysis of the problems of trying to adapt concepts grounded on territorial sovereignty to Cyberspace, a territory without traditional geographical boundaries, see David R. Johnson and David G. Post, "Law and Borders - The Rise of Law in Cyberspace" at http://www.cli.org/X0025_LBFIN.html

proposals. In the latest State of the Union address, President Clinton repeated his call for connecting every classroom and library to the Internet by the year 2000. He linked the Internet to education goals: "Every 8-year-old must be able to read; every 12-year-old must be able to log on to the Internet; every 18-year-old must be able to go to college, and every adult American must be able to keep on learning." [14]

It is hard to predict the outcome of the national and international struggle, between the civil libertarians and the regulators. Besides the clash of cultural values and issues of free speech and privacy, we will see the politics of distributive justice. As the Internet becomes enmeshed in the fabric of everyday life, demand will grow for universal access within nations and equitable access across nations. The pressure to spread the benefits of the *Rechtsstaat*, if not ultimately the welfare state, to Cyberspace will increase. The regulation of Cyberspace is part of the process of normalization – of transforming a marginal frontier into a populous settled territory of advanced industrial society. For some people this transformation marks the loss of freedom, but settling the frontier means establishing law and order; it means building fences and rounding up outlaws, making Cyberspace a nice place to raise a family and conduct a business. It also means lawyers, tax collectors and government officials, but that is the price of "progress."

III c. Political Uses of the Net

Political uses of the Net refers to employing the Net to influence political activities off line. Political parties and candidates design Web sites to affect the political behavior of those who visit the sites. Special interests, pressure groups and nonpartisan public interest groups have found the Net a cheap and fast way to communicate with their members and to inform and plead their causes to the general Web population. Political sites often urge visitors to get involved in the political process by taking actions such as e-mailing their representatives in Congress. There is a free wheeling political life on the Net, but it is mostly an extension of political life off the Net.

The types of political activities conducted on the Internet such as campaigning, lobbying, policy advocacy and organizing existed before the Net and would exist without it. The Net and especially the Web certainly will have an influence on off line

14. "State of the Union Address" *The New York Times*, February 5, 1997, A14.

political life, although the nature of this influence is unclear. Speculation about the impact of the Net often takes a metaphor, Cyberspace, and reifies it, as if Cyberspace actually exists in a parallel universe. Our mundane existence is presumably transformed when we enter this free space. Long ago Marx observed the false freedom which results from positing ourselves as free, all-powerful sovereign citizens in our public capacity, while actually living out limited and alienated lives in civil society.[15] Is the abstract freedom of Cyberspace really liberating or is it deeply illusory? The more we experience life online the more it looks like life off line.

The new pluralistic politics of the Web will not necessarily entail a politics of elite domination. There are countervailing tendencies. Optimists believe that voting via the Net would provide great benefits for our modern democratic society. The problem of the depressingly low turnout of the American electorate could be solved. If voters could log on at home, the voting process would be immune from the vagaries of weather, take hardly any time at all, be a boon to the sick and disabled and so on. Voting turnout could be increased thus reinvigorating our democracy. A recent American survey found that 51 percent favored voting via the Internet as long as there were proper safeguards in place; 28 percent were strongly in favor, but 48 percent were opposed.[16]

Voting via the Net could increase not only the amount but also the quality of participation. Before voting a citizen could visit both partisan and nonpartisan Web sites for information about the issues and candidates. In the last American National election a surprising number of people used the Net to follow the campaign and gather political information. A survey on American Internet usage, according to Andrew Kohut of the Pew Research Center in Washington, found that 12 percent of the voting age population said that they followed the campaign through their computers, and a great many more sought news about local elections. Observers have noted that while national newspapers and television do a fair job covering presidential and congressional races, local papers and local television carry much less political news than a decade ago. Web sites dedicated

15. Karl Marx "On the Jewish Question" *The Marx-Engels Reader* Robert C. Tucker (ed) (New York: W.W. Norton, 1978), 26-52.

16. "Majority of Americans Favor Voting by Internet" Proxcom Press Release at http://www.proxicom.com/press

to local politics may be filling this gap in coverage.[17]

The 1996 American national election was the first for which there was significant campaigning on the Web.[18] Nonpartisan public interest groups constructed sites to educate voters about candidates and issues. Major media corporations set up political news sites which attracted great attention and loyal followers. These sites provided a wealth of information about candidates, policies and positions for citizens who were genuinely interested in becoming well-informed voters, and detailed election news for political junkies who follow campaigns the way others follow sports.[19]

There were official and unofficial party and candidate sites, including the Democratic and the Republican parties and several minor parties. Although the minor parties had a jump in utilizing the Internet before the growth of the Web, particularly through Usenet newsgroups and listserv e-mail lists, during the campaign, major party sites greatly outnumbered those of the minor parties. The Web accelerated the growth of Internet use, bringing millions of new users online. It put a premium on sophisticated Web sites which are easy to access, visually attractive and fun to use. Constructing, maintaining and updating such sites requires much more time and money than running a newsgroup or a mailing list.[20] Newsgroups and mailing lists can count on active subscribers to create content and continually update it. Those responsible for Web sites have to rely on their own resources to keep the sites fresh and appealing for both first timers and repeat visitors.

---

17. Eleanor Randolph "Heard on the Beat" *Los Angeles Times* December 16, 1996; for the entire survey and detailed results see the web site of *The Pew Research Center for The People and The Press* at http://www.people-press.org/tec96que.htm

18. Michael Margolis, David Resnick, and Chin-chang Tu "Campaigning on the Internet: Parties and Candidates on the World Wide Web in the 1996 Primary Season" *Annual Meeting of the Midwest Political Science Association*, April 1996. Forthcoming in a revised version in *The Harvard International Journal of Press/Politics*; Michael Margolis "Electioneering in Cyberspace: Parties, Candidates, and Interest Groups and the 1996 Presidential Race on the Internet" *Annual Meeting of the American Political Science Association*, September 1996.

19. Michael Saunders "Internet Hums with Political Inquiries" *The Boston Globe*, September 6, 1996, A25; David Armstrong, "Digital Democracy: The Internet is crawling with ideas at election time" *San Francisco Examiner*, November 4, 1996, B 1. For those interested in following campaigns around the world, not just in the United States, Klipsan Press provides *Election Notes_* an excellent wide-ranging daily summary of electoral news at http://www.klipsan.com/elecnews.html

20. Michael Miley "Good interactive sites take time, hard work" *MacWeek* April 1, 1996, 32-34; Jeff Ubois "Ten essential steps for maintaining a Web site" *MacWeek* April 1, 1996, 28-30.

If we ask which political parties and candidates are likely to provide sophisticated Web sites, the answer is clear: those who command the resources to hire the talent to produce them. A study of campaigning on the Internet during the 1996 American national election confirmed this hypothesis. A comparison of the Web sites of the Democratic and Republican parties and their candidates with those of minor parties and candidates showed that the major parties dominated. They not only had more sites, but the sites were more technically sophisticated and attractive and contained more information, graphics and links to other sites. They were also updated more often. While most minor parties and candidates relied heavily on amateur talent (the leading exception was Ross Perot), the major parties hired professionals.[21]

Campaigning on the Internet is still in its infancy. Party and candidate Web sites will undoubtedly become more elaborate and sophisticated as more multi-media tools are employed in their creation, but it is not yet clear that the returns are there to justify the monies invested. If sales are the bottom line for businesses on the Web, so votes are for politicians. Campaigners have hoped that the Web would not only win votes, but also help perform other functions important to campaigning such as fund raising and mobilizing volunteers.

To evaluate the effectiveness of the Web as a means for campaigning, at least from the point of view of those who put parties and candidates online, contact persons and Webmasters at the national, state and local level were reached by e-mail or telephone after the campaign. No one claimed that their Web site affected the election outcome, changed public opinion, raised substantial sums of money or turned out numerous activists.[22] A Web journalist who covered the campaign online reached the same conclusion: "What effect did the Web have on the conduct of the presidential campaign? Answer: non, nada, zip, zilch."[23] The fact that American politicians had so little to show for their efforts on the Web in the last election does not mean that they will abandon Cyberspace. No doubt, they will simply try harder next time.

The last campaign did show that major American political parties and candidates now feel they must have a presence on

---

21. Margolis, Resnick and Tu.

22. Margolis.

23. John Heileman, "Netizen Columnist Bids Farewell to the Year of the Net" at http//www.wired.com/news/story/729.html?/news/96/49/1/politics_section-1c.html

the Web. The Web encourages what I have called "presentations," and these are suited to mass audiences and traditional top-down electoral politics. Entering such a site is like entering a little campaign headquarters with literature tables, candidates' pictures and solicitations for funds and volunteers. The more sophisticated sites have graphics that move around a little, but they are certainly not up to the standards of broadcast television. Yet the Internet does have a distinct advantage over the broadcast media since it enables a citizen to stop the show and concentrate on an interesting aspect of the presentation, and if desired, to download and preserve it for future consideration, or mark the site for a return visit. In this sense the Web is like traditional print media. No doubt, Web sites will get glitzier in the future, but, up to now, campaigns in Cyberspace have been dependent on tried-and-true real world campaign techniques. Campaigning on the Web might capture the attention of those who are unreachable by traditional campaign techniques, but, for now, a Web site often seems to exist merely to demonstrate that a candidate is aware of current trends and is committed to the latest technology.

On the other hand, the Internet might facilitate the particular style of democratic politics favored by activists, a style which, unlike that of traditional political parties, does not concentrate on voting and elections. One of the great advantages of the Web for political activists is that it enables them to access up-to-the-minute information on a huge variety of topics that are relevant to developing their own policy positions and political strategies. Policy relevant research developed by one group and put up on the Web can also be of great value to other groups which share their general political orientation.

Yet interestingly, Schwartz has recently argued that the political activist should not think only in terms of the Web because the older text-based area of the Internet will still have a crucial role to play in the politics of the future. He observed that "The public discussion of the Internet now revolves almost entirely around the World Wide Web . . . That's fine, but what activists – in fact, most people – want from the Internet is email." [24] The Internet can be used to build up discussion lists of activists who can develop political strategies and policy positions and to connect with those who, though devoted to different issues and policies, share similar general political orientations. Activists not affiliated with major political parties are always chronically short of resources, and listservs and e-mail can help raise money and organize political activity.

24. Schwartz p. 179.

If the Internet were to provide a significant boost to non-party political activism, the traditional American political parties, already in decline, might be further weakened. A form of hyperpluralism might emerge in issue areas where popular participation is facilitated by old Progressive participatory reforms. Many states have adopted the initiative which permits citizens by petition to put an issue on the ballot for public approval or rejection, thus bypassing the standard legislative procedure. In those states the Web could be a focus for continuous campaigns. The Net reduces transaction costs. The high cost of petition drives serves as a barrier to many interest groups that would like to circumvent the ordinary process of representative democracy and go directly to the voters. If it were legal to sign petitions on the Net, the actual dollar costs of putting new initiatives on the ballot would decrease significantly. If this practice became common-place, representative institutions would be significantly undermined.

It is far more likely that political activists will use the Net to locate and disseminate information, to contact and organize political sympathizers and to lobby government officials and political representatives. For all their commitment to radical change, the presence of activists on the Net is part of the process of political normalization. Along with the political parties and interest groups, they represent a familiar element of democratic pluralism.

Organized interest groups are another type of player in democratic politics. They also advocate familiar types of political participation. They urge visitors to learn more about the group and its policy concerns, to contact public officials, to contribute to the cause, to support candidates sympathetic to the group, to vote and the like.[25] They offer Web presentations of their positions, some more glitzy than others, but it is hard to see how their presence in Cyberspace will add anything to ordinary interest group politics. Traditional political parties and interest groups will probably not increase their power and influence by going online. They construct Web sites now because it is expected of them, and perhaps because they need to in order to prevent being outflanked by newer groups. For most, it is simply part of the struggle to remain competitive in all areas of mass appeal. As part of their constituency moves into Cyberspace, organized groups migrate with them.

---

25. Margolis p. 8.

Traditionally, mass media serve a mass public, while specialized media serve select audiences. The Web is a hybrid, both a specialized medium and a mass medium. There is room for groups and causes which appeal to narrow constituencies. A presence on the Web could greatly increase the exposure of a narrow interest group both to its own potential constituency and to the public at large. Small relatively obscure interest groups probably have more to gain by going online than mainstream well-established groups which are skilled in using traditional mass media. Because of the hypertext linkages which permeate the Web, even a very specialized interest can be categorized in more general terms and become linked to more popular sites. In any case, no matter how obscure or outré the cause, if it has a Home Page it can probably be located by employing a search engine (though this is often not as simple as it is made out to be).

Though groups sponsoring such Web sites may not approach the number of hits in a year that the National Democratic Party site receives in a day, any exposure is important to them. Obscure groups and causes typically lack the money and membership to do off line what they can do online. Because it is relatively inexpensive for them to operate online, they can spread their message, recruit new members, raise funds, lobby politicians, mount petition drives and the like. Many of these familiar political strategies and activities would have been impossible even to attempt without the Web. Currently, the effects of such political activity are hardly visible in the real world; nevertheless, such activity does have some potential. Any significant political movement in the near future arising in the industrial world probably will not only have a strong presence on the Internet, but that presence will be one factor among many explaining its rise to prominence. Yet communication technology is no magic bullet. For the most part, marginal movements will remain marginal.

Just as activists, interest groups and parties use the Net for their purposes, governments are discovering that the Net is a way to achieve their own political objectives. Just as activists wish to know what the government is doing, so the government wants to know what activists are doing. An assessment of the strategic impact of the Internet written by Charles Swett, an assistant for Strategic Assessment for the U.S. Department of Defense (DoD), claims that "The Internet is a potentially lucrative source of intelligence useful to the DoD. This intelligence can include . . . Information about the plans and operations of politically active groups." It can even be used for counterintelligence. He cites as an example a message posted to a left-wing newsgroup which repeated for their benefit an AP article about an army training exercise directed at the St. Moritz Hotel in Miami Beach. He adds a cautionary note that if it became known that the DoD was monitoring the Internet for intelligence or counterintelligence purposes, then people would start leaving false messages, and "our analysis function would need to account for this." [26]

The world of spies and counterspies, intelligence and counter-intelligence has already invaded the Internet and more lies ahead. Swett suggests that as more foreign officials, military officers, business people and journalists get e-mail addresses, the Internet could be used as a medium for Psychological Operations (Psyops) campaigns. The Net could rapidly convey the official government perspective on a host of issues to a wide and influential audience. It could also be used in unconventional warfare to communicate with sympathetic groups abroad who might undertake missions which would otherwise be performed by U.S. special forces. [27]

Swett also foresees the use of the Internet as a tool of statecraft. Citing the use of dueling Web sites by Ecuador and Peru to lambast each other in a dispute over the Ecuadorian border, he sees a future in which nation states use the Internet for their diplomatic and propaganda efforts. To date, most official foreign government Web sites have been limited to routine public affairs information, heavy on statistics and descriptions of businesses, culture, industries and population. It is commonplace on the Web to see policy advocacy by political dissenters and activists of every persuasion. When countries become embroiled in disputes in the future, Web sites will be created to advocate government policies and positions. [28]

Conclusion

Cyberspace will undoubtedly facilitate the spread of democracy across the world. For the next round of coups, seizing the radio and TV station will not be as crucial as it has been in the past.

26. Charles Swett "Strategic Assessment: The Internet" Office of the Assistant Secretary of Defense for Special Operations and Low-Intensity Conflict, 22-3. The views expressed in this document are those of the author and do not necessarily represent the policies or positions of the DoD.

27. Swett p. 24.

28. Swett p. 21.

The origin and design of the Internet as a defense department project will make it virtually impossible to shut down. Along with other new media such as satellite TV, cell phones and faxes, the Internet will make it much more difficult for repressive political regimes to withhold vital information from their citizens.

The Internet also will continue to harbor a great variety of opinion and controversy. It can serve as a school for a truly democratic politics since it is not limited to official establishment sources. The Web is a wonderful vehicle for those who are already interested in politics. The ordinary citizen can acquire a plethora of data and gain access to the public face of the democratic political process. It has functioned well as a tool for citizen awareness campaigns, though so far, these have mostly concerned politics which impact the Net. It can mobilize activists and facilitate political organizing, campaigning and lobbying.

While some still hope Cyberspace can bring radical political change, that hope must be tempered by the facts. Both official government information and independent information have their limits. No matter how copious and detailed, government-provided materials will not make modern governments transparent to their citizens. The unofficial sources of information on the Internet are only as reliable as the providers themselves. Furthermore, things are not always what they seem; manipulation, deception and disinformation occur in Cyberspace. Even if we do manage to select what we need and sort the good from the bad, good information by itself does not make good citizens. Information is no substitute for education and motivation.

Cyberspace has undergone a great transformation. While those working on the cutting edge might still see the Internet as a wide-open frontier, it has taken on the characteristics of a settled territory. The utopian vision of a worldwide agora which would revitalize democracy has to confront the harsh reality of lawsuits and regulations, of commerce and entertainment, of political parties, organized interest groups and political activists, and most importantly, of masses of bored and indifferent citizens. Although revitalization is still possible, it is much more difficult than we once imagined.

Juliet Roper
University of Waikato

New Zealand Political Parties Online: the World Wide Web as a tool for democratization or for political marketing?

Abstract: Media centered political communication theory and research is looking increasingly at the use and potential of new technologies such as cable television, televised "town hall" meetings, telematics, such as Minitel in France, and various "talk" media, especially radio and television. This paper looks at the emergence of World Wide Web sites for political parties contesting general elections in a range of countries, with a particular focus on those sites established in New Zealand in 1996. The sites are discussed both as potential contributors to the formation of a new public sphere in the Habermasian sense, and also in the light of their removal from that role by public relations practitioners and advertisers as the sites are moved more towards an entertainment format targeted at political consumers in a private domestic sphere.

Introduction

From a political economy perspective, mass media theory has for many years looked at the encroachment and subsequent domination of the arena of public communication by free market politics. The focus has largely been on the traditional media of newspapers and television. Today, however, it is to the new technologies of public communication that media theory must turn. The Internet, or, more specifically, the World Wide Web, is being used increasingly as a medium for public information and debate. As such it provides scope for the development of a new public sphere. However, the Web is already being affected by the same forces of political economy which have changed the basis of traditional media production and distribution.

Much has already been written about the potential of new technologies for the development of new public spheres, building on the Habermasian ideal of the early seventeenth and late eighteenth century bourgeois public sphere in which private interests and social barriers were put aside in favor of open discussion of matters of public concern. Nicholas Garnham[1] has

---

1. N. Garnham (1990) *Capitalism and Communication* (London: Sage Publications).

used the notion of the public sphere to argue for the maintenance of public service broadcasting. He makes his argument on the basis of public service broadcasting as "an embodiment of the principles of the public sphere,"[2] divorced from control by either forces of economy or of the State. Garnham's arguments for public service broadcasting need now to be expanded to new media forms.

In this paper I explore the notion of World Wide Web sites being used by political parties to such an extent that a plurality of interests may provide the range of perspectives required to form a basis of informed public debate, particularly during the pre-election campaign period. The notion is rejected, however, if the information provided by these web sites takes on an entertainment form which is increasingly targeted to individuals in a private domestic sphere. It is suggested that an ideologically independent vehicle for public service communication via the Internet is needed. This vehicle may be community free nets in which case, following Garnham's rationale for the maintenance of public service broadcasting, it can be argued that they should be publicly funded in order to protect their independence and integrity.

The Public Sphere

The principles upon which Habermas' public sphere was based were "general accessibility, especially to information, the elimination of privilege, and the search for general norms and their rational legitimation."[3] Of course, the viability of such principles has been repeatedly called into question, but they can still serve as a set of ideals against which democratic participation in political matters can be measured. Legitimation of general norms is brought about through free participation in discussions which move towards consensus of public opinion. Participation is facilitated through the communicative functions of the public sphere: dissemination of information and provision of a forum for debate.[4] Participation cannot occur when citizens become passive consumers of information, divorced from interaction with either other citizens or the disseminators of the information, as is the case with the current linear models of mass communi-

2. Garnham (1992) p.109.
3. Garnham (1990) p.108.
4. Garnham (1990) p.111.

cation.[5]

For large societies, Habermas stressed, open communication can only be achieved through the agency of the mass media, including newspapers and magazines, radio and television.[6] To these, I would add computers and, indeed, Morris and Ogan have argued convincingly for inclusion of the Internet as a mass medium.[7] Other new technologies have also expanded the list beyond traditional television and radio with the development of cable television, televised town hall meetings, telematics, such as Minitel in France, and various "talk" media, including those which have resulted from the convergence of television and computer technologies. However, the contribution of these alternative media to a public sphere is again dependent upon their use in an interactive manner, allowing for participation in discussion rather than simply serving as alternative means of information dissemination.

Public Access television in the United States has been set up through the introduction of cable television and has allowed the production and broadcast of alternative programs free from the constraints of political economy and diplomacy. With minimal resources of equipment, money and technical knowledge, in some cities anyone who wishes can produce a program and have it broadcast through cable television.[8] Computer networks such as PeaceNet and HandsNet have enabled discussion and dissemination of information at a grass roots level. PeaceNet and similar networks exist in order to facilitate a sharing of resources, hosting conferences in which members can provide such items as news releases and alternative news services. Members can also discuss openly and laterally a wide range of issues.[9] Used in such ways these alternative media do, to a limited extent, fulfil the criteria

5. J.W. Carey (1987). "The Press and Public Discourse" *Center Magazine* March/April; K. Hacker (1996) "Missing links in the evolution of electronic democratization" *Media, Culture & Society* 18 pp. 213-232.

6. J. Habermas (1979)"The Public Sphere" (FRG, 1964) in A. Mattelart & S. Siegelaub (eds) *Communication & Class Struggle* Vol. 1, pp. 198 - 201 (New York: International General).

7. M. Morris & C. Ogan (1996) "The Internet as Mass Medium" *Journal of Communication* 46 (1) Winter pp. 39-50.

8. D. Kellner (1992) "Public-Access Television and the Struggle for Democracy" in J. Wasko & V. Mosco (eds)*Democratic Communities in the Information Age* (Toronto and Norwood: Garamond Press and Ablex Publishing Corp).

9. J. Downing (1989) "Computers for Political Change: PeaceNet and Public Data Access" *Journal of Communication* (Summer) pp. 154-161; H. Sachs (1995) "Computer networks and the formation of public opinion: an ethnographic study" *Media, Culture & Society* 17 p. 81-99; L. Friedland (1996)"Electronic democracy and the new citizenship" *Media, Culture & Society* 18 pp. 185-212.

of enabling general accessibility of information and the elimination
of privilege, especially if we accept Kellner's (1995) argument
that, at least in the United States, most individuals will soon
have access to computers both through schools and as standard
household items.[10] They also provide a forum for debate, allowing
for interactive participation by interested citizens and in this way
can certainly contribute to the formation of public opinion.

While it may be accepted that a political public sphere is
dependent upon interactive discussion and availability of
information, there are different ways in which the word "public"
can be interpreted. It is clear that "the political public sphere
constitutes a space – a discursive, institutional, topographical
space."[11] But what is "public"? Does the word refer to the nature
of the space – its openness or publicity – or does it refer to the
occupants of the space? In Habermas' public sphere, before it
was transformed, the participants in discussions of political
concern were members of the late seventeenth and early eighteenth
century male bourgeoisie. Aufderheide, writing of public television and its potential role in the formation and maintenance of
a public sphere, defines "public" as a social concept ..[which]
needs social spaces in which to exist, to learn about the public
interest, to debate it and to act."[12]

Such a general interpretation of "public," however, does not
allow for the multiple strata which exist within societies, either
in the seventeenth century or today. There is no uniform broadly
based "public" which makes up the sum of politically interested
people within a given society. Nor is a space truly public if access
to it is limited to specific groups of people. One frequent criticism
of the Habermasian public sphere is its inattention to the existence
of groups other than the male bourgeoisie or to the exclusion of
these other groups from the political public sphere. Nancy Fraser
has taken up this issue of multiple publics, challenging the
Habermasian notion that one overarching public is not only
possible but preferable to stratified societies made up of multiple
publics.[13] She points out that within a society stratified by divisions
of class, gender or race full parity of participation in a single

10. D. Kellner (1995) "Intellectuals and new technologies" *Media, Culture & Society*
17 pp. 427-448.

11. P. Dahlgren (1995) *Television and the Public Sphere* (London, Thousand Oaks:
Sage Publications) p. 9.

12. P. Aufderheide (1991) "Public Television and the Public Sphere" *Critical Studies
in Mass Communication* 8 pp. 168-183, p.169.

13. N. Fraser (1994) "Rethinking the Public Sphere: A Contribution to the Critique
of Actually Existing Democracy" in C. Calhoun (ed) *Habermas and the Public Sphere*
(London: MIT Press) pp. 109 -142.

public sphere is impossible. It is better to allow for a range of views from a number of competing publics. Even in societies with an absence of such divisions, Fraser argues, cultural differences must give rise to a plurality of publics and multiple public spheres.

When the term "public" is given the perspective of the spaces of debate rather than the participants of the debate (e.g. Calabrese & Borchert) the question resides in the accessibility of the space to all comers without interference of the state nor of commercialization. Habermas laid the blame for the demise or "transformation" of the late seventeenth and early eighteenth century public sphere at the feet of monopoly capitalism as it caused the public sphere to become "more an arena for advertising than a setting for rational-critical debate."[14] The public sphere thus became depoliticised while its members adopted a mass consumption mentality. Similarly, while the Internet is held up as a potentially democratic space, available to diverse groups and individuals, so is it feared this potential will be diminished by the drive for increased commercialization of cyberspace.[15]

Calabrese & Borchert have suggested that the rapid encroachment of capitalism on to the economy of the Internet will result in two separate but interdependent models of electronic network activity, based on dictates of political economy: the civic and the consumer models. In the civic model an elite class of technological and professional members will emerge. They will form a new class of intelligentsia who, although still important members of a consumer public, will demand input in debates of public policy making. Because of their concern with political discussions and policy formation, coupled with resources of knowledge and income, they will access relevant information and, in many ways, will function in a manner similar to the eighteenth century bourgeoisie.

The consumer model, on the other hand, will be targeted towards those of lower socio-economic status and will center on the sale of goods, services and political ideas and representatives. In this model the bulk of the flow of information will be broad and downward.[16] In line with the prediction, use of the Internet is already increasingly following a consumer model with a

14. C. Calhoun (1994) "Introdution: Habermas and the Public Sphere" in C. Calhoun (ed)*Habermas and the Public Sphere* p. 26.

15. A. Calabrese & M. Borchert (1996) "Prospects for electronic democracy in the United States: rethinking communication and social policy" *Media, Culture & Society* 18 pp. 249-268.

16. Calabrese & Borchert (1996) pp. 251-53.

growing proportion of activity geared towards entertainment and the sale of goods and services. These include Internet related merchandise such as software and consulting but there is also an increasing use of the Internet for online advertising and direct selling.[17]

Capitalism has brought with it a continued development of the techniques and practices of marketing, political marketing and public relations. Part of the success of these disciplines is attributable to their development of more precise definitions of the word "public." In the world of marketing and public relations, the existence of a general public is not considered. Instead, communication is targeted specifically to various "publics." Each public affects or is affected by an organization or individual in different ways and has, therefore, different vested interests in the behavior of that organization.[18] Communication to each public is tailored by public relations practitioners and marketers in order to appeal specifically to those vested interests. In this case, Aufderheide's comment that consumers are not a public becomes invalid[19] as consumers become a public of paramount importance, be they buyers of goods and services or of political ideologies which are bought with a vote. This does not mean that groups of publics do not overlap. Each member of a public is likely to have a range of vested interests; at once a consumer of specific goods and, for example, a retired pensioner reliant on government superannuation.

Elections, Public Relations and New Technologies

One of the institutions within which public opinion is formed is that of the media of public communication. Another is that of elections.[20] 1996 was a year for general elections in several Western democracies, such as the USA, Australia and New Zealand while in Britain campaigning was underway for an election to be held in 1997. Consistent with a trend which has developed since 1988, the use of new technologies in the context of election campaigns

17. R. McChesney (1996) "The Internet and U.S. Communication Policy-Making in Historical and Critical Perspective" *Journal of Communication* 46 (1) Winter pp. 98-124.

18. J. Grunig & F. Repper (1992) "Strategic Management, Publics, and Issues" in J. Grunig (ed) *Excellence in Public Relations and Communication Management* (Hillsdale, NJ: Lawrence Erlbaum Associates) pp. 117-158.

19. P. Aufderheide (1991) "Public Television and the Public Sphere" *Critical Studies in Mass Communication* 8 pp. 168-183.

20. Garnham (1990) p.108.

has increased enormously. New technologies provide the means for increasingly sophisticated marketing to target specific publics, and the domain of political campaigning is certainly no exception.[21] Ever more sophisticated demographic computer software has resulted in databases which allow increasing precision in the targeting of direct mail; the development of cable and satellite technology has allowed, at least in the USA, broadcasts of candidates on media other than the traditional television channels; and a convergence of telecom, computer, television and radio technologies has resulted in televised talk shows and debates with immediate voter evaluation of candidates' comments and responses. It is argued that the use of new technologies, from early effective use of television to recent use of computer bulletin boards is related to successful election campaigns.[22] Senator Edward Kennedy's staff claim that his winning the 1994 US Senate election was due to his being the first US Senator to have a World Wide Web page.[23]

While the debate about the commercialization of the Internet continues, use of the Internet as a political marketing tool has emerged. In both the 1988 and the 1992 US elections a "Presidential Campaign Hotline" offered, upon payment of a monthly subscription fee, a computer service to candidates and news media. In October 1994 the US White House established an Internet site, an addition to the existing White House-citizen e-mail system.[24] However, the broader application of the World Wide Web to set up freely accessible (notwithstanding the question of access to computers and Internet software) web sites by political parties for campaign purposes does not appear to have featured prior to the run up to general elections of 1996.

---

21. P. Maarek (1995) *Political Marketing and Communication* (London: John Libbey and Co. Ltd); B. Newman (1994) *The Marketing of the President: Political Marketing as Campaign Strategy* (London and Thousand Oaks, Ca: Sage Publications, Inc).

22. D. Kellner (1995) "Intellectuals and new technologies" *Media, Culture & Society* 17 pp. 427-448, p.438.

23. B. Mann (1995) *Politics on the Net* (Indianapolis: Que Corp) p. 47.

24. K. Hacker (1996) "Missing links in the evolution of electronic democratization" *Media, Culture & Society* 18 pp. 213-232.

The New Zealand Case

The New Zealand election of 1996 was particularly notable not for the beginning of the use of the World Wide Web by political parties but for its being the country's first under a system of proportional representation (a Mixed Member Proportional system, or MMP). This system was voted in by referendum in 1993 after almost ten years of economic upheaval as each of the two main political parties in turn propelled the country rapidly towards neo-liberalism.[25] Through the referendum the majority of the voting public had expressed its disillusionment with elected representatives who no longer appeared to represent the wishes and interests of their constituencies but who, instead, continued to sell public assets and to retract the welfare state to the point of severe hardship for many. It follows that the referendum result was also a protest at the lack of involvement by citizens, through their representatives or directly, in the process of policy making. A similar discontent has been registered in the USA.[26]

It is worth noting at this point that in New Zealand, as in Britain and Australia, elections are contested by political parties with less of a focus on individual candidates than is the case of US elections. Because of the new electoral system, the New Zealand election was contested by 22 political parties, an unprecedented number. Because of the subsequent failure of the majority of parties to gain seats in Parliament, it is unlikely that such diverse representation will again be sought. In order to gain any Parliamentary seats, a party had to either cross a threshold of 5% of the total votes or win one electoral seat. In either case, the party would then be apportioned the percentage of available seats equal to the percentage of the overall vote it won. With so many new political parties attempting to establish themselves as both different and viable, political marketing practices gained new importance. Resources permitting, these political parties used what they could of new technologies as aids to election campaigning. The campaign manager of the incumbent, National Party, for example, claimed that their computers and demographic

25. J. Kelsey (1994) "Aotearoa/New Zealand: The anatomy of a state in crisis"in A. Sharp (ed) *Leap Into The Dark* pp. 178-205 (Auckland: Auckland University Press); J. Roper & S. Leitch (1995) "The Electoral Reform Campaigns in New Zealand: a political communication case study" *Australian Journal of Communication* 22 (1) pp. 123-135.

26. J. Lemert, W. Elliot, W.Rosenberg, & J. Bernstein (1996) *The Politics of Disenchantment* (Cresskill, NJ: Hampton Press, Inc).

software were second to none.[27]As a member of the International
Democrat Union, an association of center-right political parties
worldwide, the party was privy to advancements made by its
affiliates such as the Republicans in the USA and the Conservatives
of Britain. However, not all of the other parties could afford
access to databases and extensive market research. What many
of them did manage was to set up a web site on the Internet, the
content and implications of which I will discuss below.

    Despite the urgency of accurate and effective political
marketing practices, the reasons given for the parties' setting up
web sites were surprisingly simple. When campaign managers
were asked for reasons the general responses were: "We have to
be seen to be keeping up with technology" and "the site cost so
little to set up." Neither of these reasons betrays any consideration
of empowering the voter to make a rational decision informed
by access to a diverse range of opinions. Nor do they indicate
that the sites form part of any political marketing plan. Indeed,
the campaign manager of one of the major parties commented
that the direct mailing of letters is a practice which is virtually
obsolete for that party as their main demographic group of
supporters does not read.[28] It is unlikely that a group of people
who are unwilling to or cannot read will seek access to information
provided by a party political site on the Internet. It is more likely,
at this stage, that the sites were established because the political
parties believed that they could not, especially given the relatively
low monetary cost, afford the risk that another party might gain
an advantage, as yet undefined, through the Internet. Such a fear
would bear out the potential effectiveness of the advertisement
cited by McChesney which promoted the Internet as a business
"secret weapon against the other guys."[29]

    What constitutes a party political web site? Some of the
New Zealand sites were set up by political party members with
technological enthusiasm and skills[30] while others were set up by
companies which specialize in Internet sites. In either case a lack
of knowledge of the potential of the medium has resulted in the
content and format of the sites resembling those of more traditional
media, with little or no attempt at appealing to any one of a
variety of publics. Although the medium is as controlled as that
of any advertisement, standard political advertisements produced

27. Interview, March 1996.
28. Interview, April 1996.
29. McChesney (1996) p.105.
30. Interview, December 1996.

by public practitioners and advertisers are carefully targeted, usually on an issue basis. Web sites, like advertisements, are paid for by the political parties and are used for the promotion of a party's policies; the dissemination of that party's interpretation of events; and occasionally for the denunciation of opposing party policies (e.g. the National Party[31]). The format of each of the party political web sites, both from New Zealand and elsewhere, is similar and basic. Essentially, most sites provide access to copies of press releases put out by the party and by candidates; speeches made by candidates and policy statements of the party's stance on key issues. Many provide a link to an e-mail address to which comments and questions can be directed. The New Zealand Labour Party[32] during the 1996 election campaign claimed to select key issues from e-mail messages received and to address those issues weekly. In fact the "key" issues remained consistent with the party's campaign agenda, suggesting that they were chosen with the party's needs in view rather than those of any public. Some party web sites (eg the National Party) provide links to other parties and to related international sites. Certainly, during the election campaign period, none of the New Zealand party political web sites allowed for open, direct interaction with or between users. New Zealand First[33] did open their site with a link to a bulletin board but the link was soon removed, probably because of the negative comments which were being posted. Political parties, especially when facing an election, are likely to believe that they cannot afford the risk of opening themselves up to such negativity, either from voters or from political opponents.

Party Political Web Sites and the Public Sphere

Although e-mail links are a common feature of party political web sites, unless e-mail messages are given a personal reply and questions are answered or assertions directly addressed, then such e-mail facilities cannot be said to be interactive[34] and, therefore, cannot be claimed to be contributing to a public sphere. Providing personalized feedback is clearly problematic when the volume of incoming mail is great. There are, however, other features of the party political sites which are worth examining

31. The National Party at http://www.national.org.nz

32. The New Zealand Labour Party at http://www.labour.org.nz

33. New Zealand First at http://www.nzfirst.org.nz

34. K. Hacker (1996) "Missing links in the evolution of electronic democratization" *Media, Culture & Society* 18 pp. 213-232.

features of the party political sites which are worth examining
for their potential in increasing the range of opinions available to
the voter for consideration. The foremost of these is shared with
other forms of alternate media – direct access to a voting public
which bypasses traditional media filters.[35] Many of the sites
provide links to speeches made by candidates and to news releases.
Traditionally, the voting public has to rely on journalists of the
mass media and their editors to sift through such material, the
processes of which are well documented.[36] The consumers of the
edited product receive a narrative constructed out of concessions
to forces of political economy.[37] The product is crafted to suit a
target audience or public, the purchasers of the particular
newspaper or the viewers of the television channel. As such,
mass media products are arguably far removed from the variety
of perspectives required for the rational formation of public
opinion.

There is no disputing that news releases and political
speeches are just as carefully crafted as the news stories of the
mass media. Nor are they any less ideologically biased – almost
certainly more so. They are usually written by a public relations
practitioner trained in the art of "spin doctoring". That is, the
writers know how to write a "news" story from the perspective
which best serves their organization's or client's needs. They also
understand the institutional practices of the media and use this
understanding to provide "news" in a format and at a time most
useful to the target media. Their success in having the story
published depends upon a range of factors, including "news-
worthiness," such as the pre-eminence of the subject of the story.[38]

The posting of news releases through the Internet presents
an opportunity for public relations practitioners to by-pass
traditional media restrictions and to present their clients'
perspectives. Is this further demonstration of a public sphere
being transformed through the agency of public relations
practitioners? In some ways it is, yet it can be argued that if the
whole range of political parties uploads their news releases to

35. J. Lemert, W. Elliot, W. Rosenberg, & J. Bernstein (1996) *The Politics of
Disenchantment* (Cresskill, NJ: Hampton Press, Inc).

36. G. Tuchman (1978) *Making News: A Study in the Construction of Reality* (New
York: Free Press).

37. J. Keane (1991) *The Media and Democracy* (Cambridge, MA: Polity Press).

38. H. Gans (1979) *Deciding What's News: A Study of CBS Evening News, NBC
Nightly News, Newsweek, and Time* (New York: Pantheon Books); R. Tiffen
(1989)*News and power* (Sydney: Allen and Unwin); S. Leitch (1990) *News Talk*
(Palmerston North: Dunmore Press Ltd).

the Internet, those people who are interested are able to freely assess the range of viewpoints for themselves. Garnham stresses the need to recognize the communicative functions of the public sphere: dissemination of information and provision of a forum for debate.[39] In line with this he argued for greater access by public groups to direct dissemination of information, if necessary by the use of journalists to function as knowledge brokers.[40] This is essentially a public relations function which many journalists, because of their knowledge of the news industry, have "crossed the line" to adopt.

Within party political web sites are commonly found hypertextual links not only to news releases and speeches but also to other political parties, nationally and globally; and in some cases to selected on-line newspapers, television news pages, the US White House and organizations such as the World Bank and OECD (e.g. the New Zealand National Party site). The provision of these links begins to parallel the vertical layering of information put forward as a model for multimedia journalism which enables a merging of the functions of information dissemination and provision of a forum for public debate discussed above. Friedland's description is in the context of public journalism, put together by teams of "citizen-editors" and is thus removed from the advocacy of party political agendas.[41] However, as proposed above, the existence of multiple party political web sites, linked together hypertextually, could be said to approach the range of information required to provide the means of rational debate.

The "transformation" of the party political web site

Despite the absence of well-developed motives for the establishment of party political web sites there is no doubt that the use of these sites will continue to be a practice – one which will become increasingly sophisticated as the technology develops further, as more people gain access to computers and the Internet, and as the developers consider more fully the marketing potential of the medium. As argued above, with the addition of a forum for open debate, the plurality of views available through party

39. N. Garnham (1990) *Capitalism and Communication.* (London: Sage Publications) p. 111.

40. Garnham (1990). Also L.Friedland (1996) "Electronic democracy and the new citizenship" *Media, Culture & Society* 18 pp. 185-212.

41. Friedland (1996) p.202

political web sites could provide a new public sphere and so act as a tool for democratization. However, it is more likely that this public sphere will, in turn, be "transformed" in the same way as the Habermasian one. By building on Calabrese and Borchert's vision of civic and consumer models of the Internet discussed above, I will map out below the direction which I believe the format and use of party political web sites will take once they are "transformed" by public relations practitioners and advertisers.

To date surprisingly little thought or attention has been given to how the Internet can be used for political marketing aimed at target groups of voters or publics. This may well be because it has not yet been truly integrated into the campaign strategy, overseen by the same professionals who direct political marketing through traditional media. Garnham in his appeal for the continuation of public service broadcasting described the division of public communication into a two-tier market, one for the "information-rich" and one for the "information-poor" with the latter characterized by "homogenized entertainment services on a mass scale"[42] delivered to individuals in a privatized domestic sphere. Paralleling the civic and consumer models proposed by Calabrese and Borchert, this principle will be increasingly applied to new electronic communication. Used uni-directionally, the Internet, like television, addresses the individual privately rather than providing a forum for discussion. Such is the case with party political web sites whose added feature of e-mail merely creates an illusion of participation. Without the true function of interactive debate, a proposal of Garnham's can be equally applied to party political web sites: "[i]nteractive capacity may indeed be useful for financial and commercial transactions, but claims that it allows the consumer in some way to talk back or the voter to be more fully involved in political decision-making are highly misleading."[43]

Press releases and transcripts of speeches to voters can be of little interest to those who do not read. How can the information be otherwise delivered? The format of party political web sites has so far failed to use the full range of available technology. There is, typically, more of visual interest to be found in graphics offered by traditional media. Apart from interest derived from the novelty of their existence, the sites so far do little to encourage examination of their contents. The trend in both political advertising and traditional media coverage of political campaign-

42. Garnham (1990) p. 362.
43. Garnham (1990) p. 126.

ing has been towards ever shorter "sound bites"[44] and an increasing factor of entertainment, particularly in the case of television. This is likely to also be the case for party political web sites. Instead of a written news release or commentary, the "story" will be relayed as a short video narrative which will portray the desired version of events with the relevant ideological interpretation. Ideology will also be encapsulated in on-line video games – good versus evil with "good" winning by following the policies of the sponsor political party. Prizes will be offered to "winners" of the games. Prizes will also be offered as an incentive to log on to a particular site. Web sites, and what they have to offer, will be advertised through the purchase of links on more popular web sites, in the form of banner advertisements already common in commercial web sites.

Similar techniques have already been used in traditional media: The New Zealand party, Act, has offered attractive prizes for those who respond to data collecting questionnaires and has repeatedly used a narrative format to present scenarios in newspaper articles which condemn the status quo in favor of its own neo-liberal ideology.[45] The scenario described above is not far away. The technology is available and is already in use in some commercial web sites with the producers including the necessary software to make it available to receivers. For example, the Levis site[46] contains two full length commercials as QuickTime movies. The adaptation of the technology for advocacy advertising by political parties will signal the end of the already limited contribution made by those parties to the use of the Internet as a public sphere. Instead, political marketers would be able to use entertainment to more effectively target their voting publics and appeal directly to their perceived interests. The target voting publics would fit within the consumer model of the Internet and would be reached in a private domestic sphere without the information nor the facility to join in debate on public policy making. Traditional media, subject to editorial processes, would continue to be the primary source of political information.

Although one of the main existing reasons for setting up a party political web site may be the low cost of doing so, the maintenance of an entertainment format – with the incorporation

44. C.A. Steele & K.C. Barnhurst (1996) *The Journalism of Opinion: Network News Coverage of U.S. Presidential Campaigns, 1968-1988.*

45. J. Roper (1996) "New Right as Left? A critical analysis of the discourse of a political campaign at a site of hegemonic struggle" *Sites* 33 pp. 33-44.

46. http://www.levi.com/menu/

of video links created for the site, prizes and interactive games – will be expensive. In the absence of appropriate legislation, limits to the use of the Internet will be drawn only by the purchasing power of the political party in question. Even now advertising through the Internet is a grey area for electoral law in New Zealand. Campaign spending is strictly limited but in 1996 only some political parties declared the cost of their web sites. All campaign billboards are to be removed before election day when all political advertising is banned; the party web sites remained in place. Their introduction has moved more quickly than the legislators. It is unlikely that anything can be done to stop advocacy advertising through the Internet developing in the ways described. As the use of the Internet continues to increase, community networks such as PeaceNet appear to be the most likely vehicle for the dissemination of information and provision of a forum for debate in the tradition of a public sphere. As such they must be encouraged to continue to operate in order to provide access to a diverse range of data and opinions. Indeed, their use must be expanded internationally to provide material relevant to the diverse voting publics worldwide. The ongoing and increasing cost of personnel for the maintenance and updating of these sites is high and reliance on volunteers is, arguably, unrealistic in the long term. Community networks must be able to maintain their integrity by not selling banner advertisements to sites of advocacy advertising such as those of political parties. These requirements allow for an extension of Garnham's appeal for public service broadcasting to the funding of community networks as a public service. Public funding would be required to allow such networks to remain independent and to avoid being encroached upon by capitalism in the same way as public service broadcasting. Although individuals may well choose to seek entertainment and/or consumer-ism over information, others have expressed a desire for access to information and for new ways of participation in the processes of public policy making.[47] The satisfaction of such desires could be found via the Internet but only if the development of a consumer model at the expense of a civic model is resisted.

---

47. K. Hacker (1996) "Missing links in the evolution of electronic democratization" *Media, Culture & Society* 18 pp. 213-232.

84

Wayne V. McIntosh and Cynthia L. Cates
University of Maryland, College Park and Towson University

Hard Travelin': Free Speech in the Age of the Information Super Highway[1]

Abstract: The last twenty-five years have seen a massive restructuring of our basic market infrastructure. Some say that we have entered the "information age," and there is a real temptation to view what is happening primarily in technological terms. Technological development is important in its own right as a broad social phenomenon. It also has consequences within specific venues. In this article we explore one such venue – the courts. As the superhighway continues to develop, the courts will face a range of difficult First Amendment issues – judges are destined to do some hard travelin'. Until now, various forms of communications have appeared separately and in a series. This has allowed the courts to address issues according to technological differences as they have arisen, rather than taking a comprehensive view, yielding an array of internal contradictions that will need to be reconciled. Signals from the courts suggest that the drift of First Amendment reconciliation favors corporate interests.

Every time you get more technology and more access to people, they are creative with it. . . I think the computer will democratize communications, if we make sure that there is public access to it and it's not controlled just by a handful of powerful corporations.
Bill Moyers, *Larry King Live*, June 29, 1995.

Recently bought up by a number of commercial companies such as Sprint and MCI, the Internet is no longer funded by the government; there aren't any public parks or libraries in cyberspace – it has all been sold.
Edmund Lee, "Access Denied: Has The Carnegie Mellon Administration Started a New Age of Book Burning?" *The Village Voice* Aug 15, 1995, Education Supp't; Pg. 14.

---

1. We would like to thank Brad Canon and the anonymous *NPS* reviewers for their insight and constructive comments.

Communications technology is changing far faster than anyone can possibly keep up with. Print media seem to be in decline (perhaps destined to someday go the way of the phonograph record), telecommunications services are rapidly expanding while the various sectors of the media market are converging. Conventional definitions that helped to distinguish one medium from another are vanishing, as are traditional delineations between speaker and audience. Moreover, virtual space bears little resemblance to physical space, eviscerating conventional distinctions between public and private, and creating significant questions in some heretofore fairly clearly under-stood threshold areas, such as geographic location and jurisdiction. For the courts, this means ongoing challenges to existing First Amendment analysis.

In the face of the current revolution in telecommunications, the existing First Amendment theories from which free speech principles obtain are on a collision course. Individual autonomy arguments suffer in a world where tangible materials are digitized and easily transmitted through virtual space in absolute defiance of our traditional conceptualizations. Madisonian principles of governance could be rendered obsolete by expanded availability of communications technology, and the open marketplace theory is threatened by communications convergence.

Moreover, computerized transmission does not fit neatly into any traditional category of communication. As a rule, courts address new media by analogizing to existing technologies. And, as a rule, they have been reluctant to extend analytical models and the Constitutional principles derived from them into unfamiliar terrain. For example, when the U.S. Supreme Court first encountered electronic surveillance (*Olmstead v. U.S.*, 277 U.S. 438) in 1928 the Court found that because there was no physical intrusion nor anything tangible seized, a telephone wiretap did not implicate the Fourth Amendment. Four decades later (*Katz v. U.S.*, 389 U.S. 347, 351 (1967)) the Court reversed itself, finding that "the Fourth Amendment protects people not places." And, in *Mutual Film Corp. v. Industrial Comm'n*, 236 U.S. 230, 244 (1915) the Court stated that motion pictures "[are] not to be regarded . . . as part of the press of the country." Some thirty years later, the Justices saw things differently, finding that "moving pictures . . . are included in the press whose freedom is guaranteed by the First Amendment" (*U.S. v. Paramount Pictures, Inc.*, 334 U.S. 131, 166 (1948)). In other words, the courts generally have not adapted quickly to new communications technologies.

This article represents an attempt to flesh out some of the challenges to the First Amendment that are likely to arise in the short term as we begin the hard travelin' on the information superhighway. The first section discusses the major sets of principles that have been developed through the years to justify free speech and press. Part II assesses some of the technological challenges to rule by analogy, and this is followed by a discussion of the technological threshold problems associated with location, space and jurisdiction.

I. A PARAMOUNT RIGHT:
JUSTIFICATIONS FOR THE FIRST FREEDOM

Among the liberties protected by the Bill of Rights, freedom of speech holds a very obvious position of reverence. Not only is it, along with religious freedom, literally the first among several, but its attendant admonishing of Congress to "make no law . . . abridging," bespeaks a certain superiority. Notwithstanding the obvious, however, the fact that the Amendment has seldom been taken verbatim – despite its unambiguous importance, other interests, both social and individual, have frequently collided head-on with the "first freedom" – has forced courts, scholars, as well as monied interests and their lawyers, to struggle endlessly with the nuances of a seemingly straightforward phrase. Not the least of these subtleties is the nagging question of how to justify open expression within a civic culture. Why allow relatively unfettered speech (a potential source of chaos) within the structured polity? Because "Madison said so," has never, on its own, been held a sufficient rationale, and so liberal theorists wrangle with, and constitutional litigants pursue, a variety of explanations for the preferred place of speech.

In general these rationalizations can be categorized among three main arguments. The first grounds free speech in the deep-rooted, fundamental libertarian ideal of *individual autonomy and dignity;* the second, in *the search for ideological truth;* and the third,

in *the sovereign authority of a democratic people* over their government. In the following pages we briefly set forth each of these
models.

a. Free Speech and the Autonomous Individual

> The First Amendment serves . . . the needs of . . . the
> human spirit– a spirit that demands self-expression.
> *Procunier v. Martinez*, 416 U.S. 396, 497 (1974).

To speak freely is thus, arguably a basic human need. Call it
fundamental to "the . . . spirit,"[2] to "individual self-realization,"[3]
to private "autonomy,"[4] to personal "fulfillment,"[5] to "human
dignity,"[6] the ability to speak one's piece is transcendent among
those elements that make a person a person. This notion that free
speech is rooted in individual autonomy is the most broadly
libertarian of the justifications for open expression – after all, the
human being herself is at stake here. As such, the onus on the
state is particularly harsh, for "when the state suppresses . . . [a]
person's expression of . . . ideas, the state is insulting that person
and affronting his dignity."[7] Moreover, "recognition of the self-
realization value leads to the view that all forms of expression
are equally valuable for constitutional purposes," such that
regulatory schemes based on constitutionally preferred classes of
speech are inherently flawed and that the restriction of any speech
be done only in "extreme cases."[8]

　　Thus, only a few categories of expression, no matter how
they are communicated, have been declared outside the ambit of

2. Justice Thurgood Marshall writing for a unanimous Court in *Stanley v. Georgia*,
394 U.S. 557 (1969).

3. Martin H. Redish, "The Value of Free Speech," 130 *U. Penn. L.R.*, 591, 514
(1982).

4. Charles Fried, "Exchange: Speech in the Welfare State: The New First
Amendment Jurisprudence: A Threat to Liberty,"59 *U.Chi.L.Rev.*, 225, 233 (1992).

5. Thomas I. Emerson, *The System of Freedom of Expression* (NY: Vintage Books,
1970), at 6.

6. Rodney A. Smolla, *Free Speech in an Open Society* (NY: Knopf, 1992), at 9.

7. Frederick Schauer, *Free Speech: A Philosophical Enquiry* (New York: Cambridge
University Press, 1982), at 62.

8. Redish, *op. cit.*, at 595.

First Amendment protection based entirely upon the nature of their content – libel and slander, obscenity, and child pornography.[9] Even so, so strong is the autonomy principle that, despite its decisions to allow government restrictions on obscene speech, the Supreme Court sustained an individual's constitutional right to possess obscene material in *Stanley v. Georgia*, 394 U.S. 557 (1969) by refusing to uphold a conviction based on mere possession. Writing for a unanimous court, Justice Marshall eloquently invoked the autonomy model:

> It is now well established that the Constitution protects the right to receive information and ideas . . . . [Stanley] is asserting the right to read or observe what he pleases– the right to satisfy his intellectual and emotional needs in the privacy of his own home. He is asserting the right to be free from state inquiry into the contents of his library. . . . If the First Amendment means anything, it means that a State has no business telling a man, sitting alone in his own house, what books he may read or what films he may watch. Our whole constitutional heritage rebels at the thought of giving government the power to control men's minds.

Thus, while the State is obliged to protect the welfare of the larger community and can restrict sales and distribution of specified materials from any location within its jurisdiction, it must respect an individual's privacy and can neither restrict mere possession nor "control men's minds" (with the exception of child pornography).

The First Amendment autonomy principle also has given birth to several auxiliary rights. The right not to speak, for example, has been found to protect individuals from forced allegiance to an orthodox point of view.[10] The dignity rights of adults must be

9. Lawrence H. Tribe, *American Constitutional Law*, at 930 (Mineola, NY: The Foundation Press, 1988, 2d ed.).

10. See, e.g., *West Virginia Board of Education v. Barnette*, 319 U.S. 624 (1943) (disallowing the coercion of school children to salute the U.S. flag). Justice Jackson, writing for the Court: "If there is any fixed star in our constitutional constellation, it is that no official, high or petty, can prescribe what shall be orthodox in politics, nationalism, religion, or other matters of opinion or force citizens to confess by

respected such that they must be allowed to exercise individual discretion regarding the right to receive information and cannot be restricted to a child's menu of choices. Purveyors of information must respect the privacy interests of their audiences, and a speaker must act in the public interest when addressing a "captive audience." Many of these issues came together in *Stanley*. More recently the Court addressed a set of questions surrounding a "dial-a-porn" 900 telephone sex service which again joined many of the autonomy issues *(Sable Communications, Inc. v. FCC, 492 U.S. 115 (1989))*.[11] We will likely see more of such cases as all of our current mass communications media converge toward the home computer. Indeed, some foresee the home computer as a full-featured interactive telecommunications device that will connect the user to the entire world, combining telephone, broadcast television and radio, cable television, newspapers and magazines, motion pictures, and all other information and entertainment sources.[12]

Finally, as Justice Marshall stated in his *Stanley* opinion for the Court, the autonomy model emphasizes personal privacy. In a computer-mediated world, the issue of individual privacy is reflected in at least two important phenomena: anonymity and encryption. As Lawrence Lessig notes, "anonymity. . . enables individuals to control what about themselves is known by those with whom they interact – control, for example, whether others know a user's name or association or, more generally, any feature of that individual. . . [E]ncryption [enables] users . . . to speak a language that only intended recipients can understand."[13] We are

word or act their faith therein. If there are any circumstances which permit an exception, they do not now occur to us."

11. Sable sought injunctive relief against a recently amended statute that banned all indecent and obscene interstate commercial telephone messages. The Court found that Sable's "dial-a-porn"audience, who must take affirmative steps to access the service, was different from a broadcast audience comprised of unsuspecting listeners. Hence, the state's interest in protecting children was not served by the language of the statute, the effect of which was to impose a children's standard upon adults.

12. See e.g., Note "The Message in the Medium: The First Amendment on the Information Superhighway,"107 *Harv.L.Rev.* 1062 (1994).

13. Lawrence Lessig, "The Path of Cyberlaw," 104 *Yale L.J.* 1743, at 1749 (1995).

often reminded of the "power of information" and the self-empowerment that access to online information sources brings to individuals. However, when using the communications capabilities of computer networks, most individuals do not realize that their identity can easily be determined,[14] the full record of their activities can be traced and logged,[15] and their messages and files can be opened and read, even if encrypted.[16] Some employers are doing just that, concerned that employees are wasting company time frivolously surfing the Web and/or using the corporate system for personal correspondence (e-mail technically belongs to the corporate owner, not the individual recipient). Moreover, internet marketers are intensely interested in profiling as much information as possible about their Web-site visitors so that they can tailor follow-up sales pitches to the perceived interests of potential customers.[17]

b. Free Speech in the Marketplace of Ideas

> . . . [T]he best test of truth is the power of the thought
> to get itself accepted in the competition of the market.
> *Abrams v. United States,* 250 U.S 616, 630
> (Holmes, J., dissenting).

So goes the "marketplace of ideas theory," a principle which analogizes thought to products and unencumbered expression to commercial competition in a free market. Under such conditions, the public will "purchase" the good concept, reject the bad, and demand the cultivation or combination of notions containing some

14. Often a great deal can be found out about an individual user (e.g., name, home address, birth date, and so on) if one knows the right commands.

15. Internet activities leave traces that can be reconstructed into a log, much like the pen registers associated with telephone use.

16. The U.S. government is concerned about encryption technology and the capability that it would give to criminals. Hence, steps are being taken to ensure that top secret government files can be securely locked but that all others can be decoded. Indeed, the "Clipper Chip" standard, proposed by the Clinton Administration, has created considerable controversy. See, e.g., A. Michael Froomkin, "The Metaphor Is the Key: Cryptography, the Clipper Chip and the Constitution,"143 *U.Pa.L.Rev.* 709 (1995).

17. The Federal Trade Commission held several days of hearings on Internet privacy issues in June 1997 at http://www.ftc.gov/bcp/privacy2/index.html

element of worth. The free market, then, ultimately yields practical, valuable ideas – in conceptual terminology, it yields truth.[18] According to Holmes, this simple metaphorical scenario embodies "the sweeping command" of the First Amendment.[19]

The notion can be traced to any number of intellectual forebearers, but probably none so influential and forceful as J.S. Mill who offered it as a potential counterpoise to the theory of free speech grounded in individual autonomy as an end:

> If all mankind minus one were of one opinion, and only one person were of the contrary opinion, mankind would be no more justified in silencing that one person, than he, if he had the power, would be justified in silencing mankind. Were an opinion a personal possession of no value except to the owner; if to be obstructed in the enjoyment of it were simply a private injury, it would make some difference whether the injury was inflicted only on a few persons or on many. But the peculiar evil of silencing the expression of an opinion is, that it is robbing the human race; posterity as well as the existing generation; those who dissent from the opinion, still more than those who hold it. If the opinion is right, they are deprived of the opportunity of exchanging error for truth; if wrong, they lose, what is almost as great a benefit, the clearer perception and livelier impression of truth, produced by its collision with error.[20]

---

18. Notwithstanding, of course, the fact that Holmes, himself believed that truth was "generally illusion"! Holmes, "Natural Law,"32 *Harv. L. Rev.* 40 (1918).

19. *Abrams v. United States,* 250 U.S. 616, at 630 (Holmes, dissenting).

20. J.S. Mill, "On Liberty," in *Utilitarianism, On Liberty, and Considerations on Representative Government,* ed. by H. B. Acton (London: Everyman's Library, 1972), at 85. The marketplace idea long predates even Mill, however. In an address to Parliament in 1644, John Milton argued that "[T]hough all the windes of doctrin were let loose to play upon earth, so Truth be in the field, we do injuriously by licensing and prohibiting to misdoubt her strength. Let her and Falshood grapple; who ever knew Truth put to the wors, in a free and open encounter." Milton, Areopagitica (London 1644), in *Complete Prose Works of John Milton* (E. Sirluck, ed., 1959), at 561.

According to Mill, then, an open speech marketplace performs three vital functions. First, it may be an essential counterweight to opinions which, though widely held and sanctioned, are in fact false. Second, if popular inclinations are indeed true, erroneous dissenting opinions will strengthen belief in the veracity of the received wisdom. And, third if conflicting visions each hold a piece of the truth, their free intermingling will result in a more legitimate opinion – a truer truth, if you will.[21] But, if, in the beginning, there was Mill, the fact that Mill begat Holmes has given the marketplace theory of speech a particular legitimacy in American jurisprudence. Indeed, Holmes' dissent to *Abrams* has inspired a virtual cottage industry in opinions employing marketplace rhetoric to rationalize First Amendment decisions.[22]

To those who abide by the marketplace model, the First Amendment presumes a system of speech markets controlled by the forces of supply and demand, without benefit of government restriction. Indeed, the state must remain neutral with regard to content and viewpoint. Regulation intended to maintain the speech market within certain boundaries is not only highly suspect, it is prohibited. Some observers regard *Tornillo* (*Miami Herald Publishing Co. v. Tornillo*, 418 U.S. 241 (1974)), where the Court struck down a Florida "right of reply" statute and upheld the right of newspaper owners to exercise full editorial control over what they publish, as the quintessential marketplace model

---

21. Id., at 85-123.

22. See, for example, *Board of Educ. v. Pico*, 457 U.S. 853, 866 (1982); *Widmar v. Vincent*, 454 U.S. 263, 267 n.5 (1981); *Citizens Against Rent Control v. City of Berkeley*, 454 U.S. 290, 295 (1981); *Consolidated Edison Co. v. Public Serv. Comm'n*, 447 U.S. 530, 537, 538 (1980); *FCC v. Pacifica Foundation*, 438 U.S. 726, 745-46 (1978); *Virginia State Bd. of Pharmacy v. Virginia Citizens Consumer Council*, 425 U.S. 748, 760 (1975); *Bigelow v. Virginia*, 421 U.S. 809, 826 (1975); *Miami Herald Publishing Co. v. Tornillo*, 418 U.S. 241, 248 (1974); *Red Lion Broadcasting Co. v. FCC*, 395 U.S. 367, 390 (1969); *Time, Inc. v. Hill*, 385 U.S. 374, 382 (1966). Cited in Stanley Ingber, "The Marketplace of Ideas: A Legitimizing Myth,"1984 *Duke L.J.* 1, at 3, n.2 (1984). And, for more recent use of the metaphor, see, *Rosenberger v. Rector and Visitors of the University of Virginia*, 15 S. Ct. 2510 (1995); *McIntyre v. Ohio Elections Commission*, 115 S. Ct. 1511 (1995); *U.S. v. National Treasury Employees Union*, 115 S. Ct. 1003 (1995); *Turner Broadcasting v. FCC*, 114 S. Ct. 2445 (1994); *Edenfield v. Fane*, 113 S. Ct. 1792 (1993); *R. A. V. v. St. Paul*, 505 U.S. 377 (1992); and *Simon and Schuster v. Members of the New York State Crime Victims Board*, 502 U.S. 105 (1991).

opinion.[23]

In 1976 the Court struck down limitations on expenditures on behalf of a presidential candidate, made independently by individuals and organizations alike, as an unconstitutional restriction on political speech.[24] Hence, in the *Buckley* Court's view, independent cash expenditures to promote a political candidate is the constitutional equivalent of speech. In addition, the Court stated that the government cannot limit the amount of money a political candidate may personally spend to promote her own campaign (424 U.S. 1, at 54). And recent elections have seen a number of candidates spend lavishly to thrust themselves and their messages upon the electorate in a way that few could emulate– e.g., Ross Perot's third party quest for the presidency in 1992 and 1996, Michael Huffington's 1992 run for a California Senate seat, and Steve Forbes' foray into the 1996 Republican presidential primaries. Moreover, *Buckley* and its progeny make campaign finance reform a constitutionally suspect venture, even if Congress and the President can muster the wherewithal to do it, and despite the much publicized soft-money excesses of the 1996 election cycle.

Indeed, the *Buckley* Court accepted the proverb, "money talks," into the First Amendment universe.[25] Considered slightly differently, however, it is clear that the economic market is indelibly linked to the idea market. In many ways, speech, including political speech, has been transformed into just another

23. See, e.g., Cass R. Sunstein, "The First Amendment in Cyberspace," 104 *Yale L.J.* 1757, at 1760 (1995). He also notes that "[t]he FCC has at times come close to endorsing the market model, above all in its decision abandoning the fairness doctrine. (See *Syracuse Peace Council v. Television Station WTVH*, 2 F.C.C.R. 5043, 5055 (1987)). When the FCC did this, it referred to the operation of the forces of supply and demand, and suggested that those forces would produce an optimal mix of entertainment options"(Id.). Also see *Alliance for Community Media v. FCC*, 56 F.3d 105 (DC Cir. 1995) *(en banc)* (upholding editorial control rights to cable television owners and endorsing a marketplace First Amendment theory).

24. *Buckley v. Valeo*, 424 U.S. 1 (1976). And see *FEC v. NCPAC*, 470 U.S. 480 (1985).

25. Justice White put it thusly: " Proceeding from the maxim that 'money talks,' the Court finds that the expenditure limitations will seriously curtail political expression by candidates and interfere substantially with their chances for election." *Buckley v. Valeo*, 424 U.S. 1, at 262 (White, J., concurring in part and dissenting in part).

commodity market. Wealth and resources are directly correlated with the ability to distribute speech, to purchase time on radio or television for example, or advertising space in magazines and newspapers. In fact, the Perots and Huffingtons out there can buy the whole cable network, broadcast station, or newspaper (Forbes already owns his own magazine) if they choose to do so and use them to disseminate their ideas. This linkage between economic and idea markets, quite conceivably produces information distortion, as there is no necessary relationship between the soundness of an idea and the money used to promote it. As Ingber states it, "[r]estriction of entry to the economically advantaged quells voices today that might have been heard in the time of the town meeting and the pamphleteer."[26]

In the wake of the computer and cable revolutions, however, much has been made of the potential for democratizing communications – for opening up the marketplace of ideas to more and more voices, more and more ideas. Clearly, the twin specters of 500 channels and a limitless Internet would suggest heretofore undreamed of market potential for those with ideas to disseminate, from the single amateur scholar to the giant corporation.[27] Under such circumstances, the biggest problem would seem to be an embarrassment of riches – and certainly, much has already been made of the notion of information overload.

For Emord and others who prefer the marketplace First Amendment model, the biggest problem really rests with the specter of government interference. "Technology," he states, "is now carrying us into the greatest age of mass communication the world has ever known. The principal threat . . . is the same enemy of freedom that has always prevented civilized man from enjoying an unencumbered right to exchange information: the

26. Stanley Ingber, "The Marketplace of Ideas: A Legitimizing Myth,"1984 *Duke L.J.* 1, at 38 (1984).

27. As Jonathan Emord (*Freedom, Technology, and the First Amendment.* San Francisco, CA: Pacific Research Institute for Public Policy, 1991, at xiii-xiv) has projected, "In the twenty-first century, technology will afford the American public a profusion of new means to send and receive ideas and information. From the home, each person will command access to more information, opinion, and entertainment than ever before. For the first time, each person will be able to publish to hundreds or thousands of others in the United States and abroad at comparatively low costs."

government." Only a "self-governing media marketplace" can guarantee that "our freedom of speech and press [will] retain its meaning and protected status in the new media age."[28]

According to this view, government should restrict its role to providing a stable framework within which new communications technologies can thrive, deregulate the entire system, step back and watch as the telecommunications market-place empowers the consuming public. The only justification for a government regulatory role was the problem of scarcity, associated with the old days when people depended upon broadcast stations for entertainment and information.

Under prevailing precedent, supported by a long series of case law, significant broadcast regulation is allowed on the argument that, due to its finite physical limits, the electromagnetic spectrum is a scarce public resource. Because of the scarcity problem, a broadcaster is given exclusive rights to a frequency but must abide by regulations promulgated to ensure that it operates in the public interest. Justice Frankfurter first articulated the scarcity rationale in *National Broadcasting Co. v. U.S.*, 319 U.S. 190 (1943): "[radio broadcasting] facilities are limited; they are not available to all who may wish to use them; the radio spectrum simply is not large enough to accommodate everybody" (at 213). On the basis of this understanding, the Court thus upheld the FCC's authority to allocate broadcasting frequencies and to regulate and monitor the content of broadcasters' transmissions.

However, the scarcity argument, which has prevailed for more than 50 years, is now being seriously challenged. Not only has the number of broadcast stations dramatically proliferated, but the nation's households are rapidly being equipped to receive cable and satellite transmissions.[29] Moreover, with the convergence of all telecommunications media, probably in Internet cyberspace, scarcity will be replaced by infinity, and individuals will be able to customize their own preferred programming menu. We are al-

28. Emord, at xiii.
29. As of 1994, 60 percent of all homes were cable-connected. See *Turner Broadcasting System, Inc. v. FCC*, 114 S. Ct. 2445, at 2451 (1994). For a discussion of satellite communications see, e.g., John J. Gibbons, "Convergence in Communications Technology and the First Amendment," 25 *Seton Hall L. Rev.* 1375, at 1391ff (1995).

ready on the edge of such a world. The *Wall Street Journal*, for
example, provides an online service called the "Personal Journal,"
allowing subscribers to receive only individually customized
reports on selected topics without the bother of confronting
irrelevant information.[30][31] Others are following suit with "push"
information delivery systems like The PointCast Network,
NETdelivery, Netscape In-Box Direct, BackWeb (to name a few).
The much ballyhooed Web-site blocking software, such as
NetNanny, CyberSitter, SurfWatch (among many others) and the
television v-chip are additional steps in the same direction.

Sunstein suggests that, given the forces at work, an
unregulated idea marketplace will likely lead to "social balkanization in which most people's consumption choices simply
reinforce their own prejudices and platitudes, or even worse" (at
1763). Moreover, he argues,

> Quite outside of science fiction, it is foreseeable that
> free markets in communications will be a mixed
> blessing. They could create a kind of accelerating "race
> to the bottom," in which many or most people see
> low-quality programming involving trumped-up
> scandals or sensationalistic anecdotes calling for little
> in terms of quality or quantity of attention. It is easily
> imaginable that well-functioning markets in commun-
> ications will bring about a situation in which many of
> those interested in politics merely fortify their own
> unreflective judgments, and are exposed to little or
> nothing in the way of competing views. It is easily
> imaginable that the content of the most widely viewed
> programming will be affected by the desires of
> advertisers, in such a way as to produce shows that
> represent a bland, watered-down version of convent-
> ional morality, and that do not engage serious issues
> in a serious way for fear of offending some group in
> the audience.[31]

30. See Michael Putzel, "A Personal Journal from Dow Jones," *Boston Globe*, Feb.
6, 1995, at 19; *Morning Edition:* "'Personal Journal' Delivers News Based on
Need"(NPR radio broadcast, Mar. 11, 1995).
31. Sunstein, at 1763-64 (notes deleted).

It would be supremely ironic if the telecommunications revolution, which promises to make a nearly unimaginable array of information available to the individual at the click of a mouse, in reality produces a net reduction (perhaps a significant one) in informational, viewpoint, and communications diversity. Marketplace theorists would argue that, were this to happen, it would result from free individual choices. This is as it should be. Under our First Amendment, government is prohibited from making those decisions for us and must remain entirely neutral. Any intervention by the state should be facilitative to the market; if its actions are not content-neutral, they violate the constitution.

We already seem to be moving in the direction of social and political Balkanization. To move further could present some serious challenges to our governing system. And, this brings us to a discussion of the third First Amendment model.

c. Free Speech and Democratic Self-Governance

> [T]he right of freely examining public characters and measures, and of free communication among the people thereon . . . has ever been justly deemed the only effectual guardian of every other right . . . Let it be recollected . . . that the right of electing the members of the government constitutes more particularly the essence of a free and responsible government. The value and efficacy of this right depends on the knowledge of the comparative merits and demerits of the candidates for public trust, and on the equal freedom, consequently, of examining and discussing these merits and demerits of the candidates respectively.
>
> Virginia Resolutions of 1798, 4 Elliot's Debates, pp. 553-554, 575.[32]

An explanation for free speech grounded in the necessity for effective self-governance can point to the Father of the Constitution himself (with a nod to the constitutional paper trail, this is indeed the "because Madison said so" rationale). Thus, in the Virginia Resolutions cited above, Madison makes clear that free public

---

32. Cited in *New York Times v. Sullivan*, 376 U.S. 254, at 274-75 (1964).

discussion of policy and policymakers is the very essence of republican government. Speech is prized not as an end in itself nor as part of a broad emporium, the aim of which is to pit competing ideas one against the other, but rather as a specific crucial means to the end of popular sovereignty. The general and central object of the American political experiment, according to Madison, was a transfer of absolute power from the government to the people.[33] The particular rights and duties contained in the Constitution, then, including the First Amendment, function to preserve and enhance the sovereign authority of the people. We speak not merely to hear ourselves speak, but to engage in "those activities of thought and communication by which we 'govern'."[34]

Presumably, this self-governance function of the First Amendment is served in a variety of ways. Obviously, speech is the primary method of participation in democracy. Moreover, unfettered speech supposedly allows political truth to emerge; facilitates the accomplishment of the collective will; acts as a restraint on "tyranny, corruption and ineptitude;" and contributes to political stability by acting as a safety valve, allowing the legal venting of minority viewpoints.[35] In short, the Madisonian model of the First Amendment focuses on public deliberation. If Madison is interpreted correctly in this regard, then clearly his most articulate intellectual progeny has been the late Alexander Meiklejohn. Hence, Professor Meiklejohn argued that, "Political freedom . . . *is* self-government."[36]

---

33. Virginia Resolutions of 1798, 4 *Elliot's Debates*, at 569-70, 575. Cited in New York Times v. Sullivan, 376 U.S. 254, at 274. Of course, both Madison and Hamilton explicitly underscore this point numerous times throughout the Federalist Papers. For example, "the people are the only legitimate fountain of power"(Madison, *Federalist* 49); "all power should be derived from the people"(Madison, *Federalist* 37); and "[t]he fabric of the American empire ought to rest on the solid basis of THE CONSENT OF THE PEOPLE"(Hamilton, *Federalist* 22). *The Federalist Papers*, ed. by Roy P. Fairfield (New York: Doubleday, 2d ed., 1966).

34. Alexander Meiklejohn, "The First Amendment Is an Absolute,"1961 *Supreme Court Review* 245, at 255.

35. Smolla, op. cit., at 12-13.

36. Meiklejohn, op. cit., at 254.

Although the Supreme Court, unlike liberal philosophers, has never articulated a pure speech rationale theory,[37] it did produce at least one landmark decision which Dr. Meiklejohn viewed as "occasion for dancing in the streets."[38] In *New York Times v. Sullivan* (376 U.S. 254, 1964), the Court rejected its usual "tests" for determining the level of protection offered speech in favor of an examination of "history to discern the *central meaning* of the first amendment. . ."[39] And, that central "meaning was revealed in Madison's statement 'that the censorial power is in the people over the Government, and not in Government over the people.'"[40]

The model was reinforced soon afterward in *Red Lion*[41] (reaffirming the fairness doctrine), "with the Supreme Court's

37. Even while employing marketplace, self-governance, and, occasionally, autonomy rhetoric, the Court has tended to develop "tests,"rather than broadly philosophic arguments, for speech protection. Justice Brennan identifies four such tests: 1. Justice Black's minority view that speech is protected "absolutely;"2. Justice Holmes' "clear and present danger"analysis; 3. the divining of "redeeming social value,"an inquiry generally associated with obscenity caselaw; and 4. Justice Harlan's "balancing"of individual versus social interests. Brennan, "The Supreme Court and the Meiklejohn Interpretation of the First Amendment,"79 *Harvard Law Review* 1, at 4-10.

38. Harry Kalven, "The New York Times Case: A Note on 'The Central Meaning of the First Amendment,'"in 1964 *Supreme Court Review* 191, at 221. In addition, a variety of justices have, from time to time, argued the Madisonian case. For example, Justice Brandeis articulated it very well in his famous Whitney concurrence, stating in part:

> Those who won our independence by revolution were not cowards. They did not fear political change. They did not exalt order at the cost of liberty. To courageous self-reliant men, with confidence in the power of free and fearless reasoning applied through the processes of popular government, no danger flowing from speech can be deemed clear and present, unless the incidence of the evil apprehended is so imminent that it may befall before there is opportunity for full discussion. If there be time to expose through discussion the falsehood and fallacies, to avert the evil by the processes of education, the remedy to be applied is more speech, not enforced silence.

Whitney v. California, 274 U.S. 357, 375 (1927) (Brandeis, J., concurring).

39. Brennan, op. cit., at 15 (emphasis added).

40. Id., citing Madison at 4 *Annals of Congress* 934 (1794).

41. *Red Lion Broadcasting* Co. v. FCC, 395 U.S. 367 (1969).

suggestion that governmental efforts to encourage diverse views and attention to public issues are compatible with the free speech principle – even if they result in regulatory controls on the owners of speech sources."[42] As Sunstein sees it, the First Amendment's purpose is to promote democratic goals, and "[t]o the extent that the Madisonian view prizes education, democratic deliberation, and political equality, it is connected, as the marketplace conception is not, with the highest ideals of American constitutionalism."[43]And he issues the following challenge to lawmakers:

> In building law for an age of cyberspace, government officials – within the judiciary and elsewhere – should be particularly careful not to treat doctrinal categories as ends in themselves. Much less should they act as if the First Amendment is a purposeless abstraction unconnected to ascertainable social goals. Instead they should keep in mind that the free speech principle has a point, or a set of points. Among its points is the commitment to democratic self-government.[44]

Hence, it may well be necessary to intervene in the marketplace in order to ensure that general communication contains a wide diversity of viewpoints. This would necessarily entail content-based regulation – a direct contradiction of the marketplace of ideas rationale.[45] Hence, the Madisonian and Holmesean visions conflict.

While First Amendment scholarship wrangles endlessly over the one true rationale for the First Amendment, the search for philosophical purity has tended to end at the courthouse door.

---

42. Sunstein, at 1760.

43. Sunstein, at 1763.

44. Sunstein, at 1765.

45. On a number of occasions, the Court has indicated this necessity. See, e.g., *Associated Press v. U. S.*, 326 U.S. 1, 20 (1944) ("[T]he widest possible dissemination of information from diverse and antagonistic sources is essential to the welfare of the public. . . ."); *Turner Broadcasting Sys., Inc. v. FCC*, 114 S. Ct. 2445, 2470 (1994) ("[A]ssuring that the public has access to a multiplicity of information sources is a governmental purpose of the highest order, for it promotes values central to the First Amendment").

As the *New York Times*, *Abrams*, and *Procunier* opinions cited above demonstrate, the Court itself has been a great deal less than unadulterated in its approach to freedom of speech. Indeed, it has tended to place tests before hypotheses.

Yet, rationales do make a difference, and not just to those who sit in ivory towers. For example, the nation's advertising industry has argued strenuously for adoption of the autonomy model to justify elevation of commercial speech to a position of full First Amendment protection. "[F]rom the standpoint of an individual hearer," they posit, "it is often demonstrably more important to receive information about a product critical to health or happiness than to receive non-commercial information."[46] Hence, from the perspective of the business community, commercial advertisements offer information of critical importance to individual consumers, and advertisers should be free from government interference to present that information.[47] A great deal hangs in the balance (not to mention the fact that advertising is a multi-billion dollar industry). Similarly, cable operators have balked at Congress's attempt to require them to carry local broadcast stations as part of their basic service. Cable Corporations argue that "must carry" regulations constitute non-neutral, content-based interference in violation of First Amendment market principles. The government maintains that such rules are necessary to ensure the continued viability of broadcast stations and, hence, to ensure diversity of viewpoints and information.[48] The rationale employed in addressing these conflicts makes much difference, and the outcome often determines distribution of profits among corporations in competing market sectors.

Although only a small percentage of the American population communicates on computer networks, it very likely includes a "most" elite group – the very group, in fact, that tends to drive political discourse and economic consumption. The online popul-

---

46. *City of Cincinnati v. Discovery Network, Inc.* (113 S.Ct. 1505, 1993), Brief Amici Curiae of Association of National Advertisers, Inc.; American Association of Advertising Agencies; National Association of Manufacturers; Grocery Manufacturers of America, Inc.; and National Food Processors Association in support of respondents. (filed June 1, 1992).

47. Also see *Rubin v. Coors Brewing Company*, 115 S. Ct. 1585 (1995).

48. *Turner Broadcasting System v. FCC*, 1997 U.S. Lexis 2078 (1997).

ation is growing, and with escalating development and use, the information superhighway could conceivably supplant traditional media as the least expensive and most effective means of communicating to a large audience. Thus far, however, many First Amendment questions remain unanswered, and much depends upon how courts analogize from old media to the new.

II. RULE BY ANALOGY:
ROAD-KILL ON THE INFORMATION HIGHWAY

Telecommunications service currently comes in four broad forms – broadcast media, cable television, hard-wire telephone, and computer networks – but the dividing lines among them are collapsing in the wake of technological change. And, the Telecommunications Act of 1996 promises not only to hasten technological development but to blur distinctions among the various forms even further.[49]

The Courts have only begun to address some of these convergence issues, and already they are proving to be quite thorny. Justice Kennedy, writing for the *Turner* majority in 1994, began by noting:

49. However, as they currently exist, we can roughly differentiate them as follows: *Broadcast media* transmit non-interactive audio and video program signals on dedicated frequencies that can be accepted by any receiver within their respective broadcast range. *Cable television* transmits over coaxial cables within a specified service region. Again, the communication is non-interactive, and it is available only to those households able to pay the monthly fee. The typical franchise operates as a monopoly or near-monopoly and is required to carry local commercial and educational broadcast signals as part of their standard packages. *Telephone companies* transmit site to site, interactive audio communications over copper wires (carrying electronic impulses) and fiber-optic cables (carrying digitized signals with far-greater capacity than the older copper wire systems). Phone servers further break down into local and long distance carriers. However, telephone companies can send video programs over their lines, and cable companies have the capability to transmit telephone calls, and cordless telephones fall into the broadcast category, since messages are transmitted over the airwaves and can be received by anyone listening in on the appropriate frequency. Finally, *computer networks* provide a "host"informational system (all in a digital data form) that can be accessed by individuals who have a computer, modem and telephone. Computer networks already provide news and information services traditionally provided in hardcopy and allow transmission of interactive e-mail messages that approximate telephone conversations. Once connected, the individual can upload/download information to/from the host, send and receive e-mail messages from other users, and participate in on-line bulletin board conversations.

The role of cable television in the Nation's communications system has undergone dramatic change over the past 45 years. Given the pace of technological advancement and the increasing convergence between cable and other electronic media, the cable industry today stands at the center of an ongoing telecommunications revolution with still undefined potential to affect the way we communicate and develop our intellectual resources.[50]

This controversy required the Court to unravel at least four distinct sets of competing speech rights, those asserted in the name of cable programmers, cable operators, broadcasters, and a general audience.[51]

If cable has "undefined potential to affect the way we communicate" and has created a web of complexity, what of computer networks? With the convergence upon computer networks, all telecommunications activities will occur in a different dimension – cyberspace.[52] Although entirely dependent

---

50. *Turner v. FCC*, 114 S. Ct. 2445, at 2451 (1994).

51. The Court finally resolved the matter in favor of the government's "must carry"position. *Turner Broadcasting, Inc. v. FCC* 1997 U.S. Lexis 2078 (1997).

52. Science fiction author William Gibson is credited with coining the term in his novel *Neuromancer*. Cyberspace, as it is currently understood "is the conceptual 'location' of the electronic interactivity available using one's computer."(William S. Byassee, "Jurisdiction of Cyberspace: Applying Real World Precedent to the Virtual Community"30 *Wake Forest L. Rev.* 197, at 199, n5 (1995). It has also been characterized as the "words, human relationships, data, wealth, and power . . . by people using computer-mediated communications."(Howard Rheingold, *The Virtual Community: Homesteading the Electronic Frontier*, at 5 (1993)).
  The largest and most discussed region of cyberspace is the Internet. Originally created by the U.S. Department of Defense in the early 1970s as an experimental system to conduct military research, it was set up as system by which all manner of computer stations (there were no industry standards) could communicate with one another. Moreover, given the military influence the network was constructed without a central hub or governing unit, so that, in the event of a nuclear attack, a sector of the system could be wiped off the face of the earth without disabling the remaining portions. (For an excellent and thorough discussion see Ed Kroll, *The Whole Internet*, 2d ed. (Sebastopol, CA: O'Reilly & Associates, Inc., 1994)). The 1980s found the academic community beginning to go online to make use of the Internet's research and information base resources.

upon actions in real time in the concrete real world, cyberspace constitutes a "virtual reality."[53]

To comprehend cyberspace, itself, one must draw parallels to its analogs in the real world, and because of the diversity of activities that are possible, the comparisons are equally diverse. We may well have a case here where parallel lines do, in fact, cross. Because of the absence of a governing body, the lack of formal behavioral rules and regulations, and given its freeform quality and multi-faceted potentials, the Internet has given rise to a vast array of user communities, whose memberships are entirely voluntary, whose boundaries have no known contours, and whose activities are self-regulating based upon sets of informal rules of unknown origin. Some have characterized the "inhabitants" of such communities as early pioneers who are

Finally, the 1990s has seen nascent commercial exploitation, with the system being made available to the public. Indeed, web browsing software (such as that developed by Netscape) has rendered the Internet's WWW both far easier to use and capable of delivering full color graphics and sound to the end user. What has developed, especially over the past five years, is a mammoth collection of networks that connect computers from literally the world over and whose communications potential is infinite. It is also a system without a governing body and that has no central location. In the words of one technology policy analyst,

> The Internet is best thought of as a suite of digital communications – packet-switching protocols that, when adopted by many nonhomogeneous digital networks, create the equivalent of a virtual, interactive overlay network. The Internet is not a physical network. It has no owner, no control point, sells no services. Thus the Internet is better thought of not as a network, but as a remarkably powerful array of internetworking capabilities, through which great numbers of users can reach one another and a great array of sources of information around the world through the facilities of many networks.

Anne Wells Branscomb, "Anonymity, Autonomy, and Accountability: Challenges to the First Amendment in Cyberspaces," 104 *Yale L.J.* 1639, at 1640, n5 (1995) (quoting Lewis M. Branscomb, Professor of Science and Technology Policy).

53. See, e.g., Lawrence H. Tribe, "The Constitution in Cyberspace: Law and Liberty Beyond the Electronic Frontier,"*The Humanist*, Mar. 26, 1991, at 15. Computer-mediated activities likely to produce litigation in the near term (some already have) are difficult even to categorize, but can be tentatively differentiated by their distinct communications protocols, such as E-mail, Usenet, FTP, Telnet, and the World Wide Web (this list is admittedly not complete).

establishing colonies based upon absolute democracy in a new world (the "networld") that transcends traditional nation-states. As Anne Branscomb assesses it:

> These new experiments in democracy do not simply represent a futuristic vision. On the contrary, they pervade the electronic environment. Observers of online activity have recognized inclinations to preserve individual and group autonomy without governmental intrusion or authoritarian censorship. These inclinations are fully in accord with the motivations that brought the early pioneers to the new continent to preserve their religious independence, develop new frontiers, and exert self-determination in their systems of governance. Many of these new experiments have led to the development of user groups that look upon themselves as "virtual communities" entitled to deal with problems arising in the electronic environment as they find appropriate. Such virtual communities can be said to occupy separate and diverse cyberspaces, essentially carving out domains of their own over which they choose to exert jurisdiction.[54]

To many who still reside squarely in "hard space" or who only occasionally "surf," the unruliness of the Internet is not only inherently disquieting but also threatens social order. To governments it is seen as a potential encroachment upon political hegemony. To corporations it represents a marketing system of unknown dimensions that must be harnessed to prevent resource depletion (via copyright violations, outright piracy, and the like) and to ensure continued commercial exploitation. To cyber-libertarians any attempt to impose "real world" order on interactions in the Networld constitutes a threat to individual liberty and democracy, and it will block full development of the Internet's telecommunications potential.

In short, a constitutional battleground is beginning to take shape in which the courts will confront a dilemma. On the one

54. Branscomb, op cit., at 1640.

hand, the likely challenge they will face is to extend sometimes conflicting speech principles crafted from a somewhat orderly physical world to one that defies order by drawing a series of imperfect analogies. This is the common law tradition and represents a model with which judges feel most compatible. The alternative is to be creative, to address entirely new questions with a fresh First Amendment perspective.[55]

Extending First Amendment principles into cyberspace is complicated by the fact that the proper analogy can shift with a keystroke. To the extent that computer networks are used to distribute information such as news wires, electronic newsletters, and data bases, and to the extent that screens can be converted into hardcopy, they resemble traditional print media, or secondary distributors such as booksellers or libraries. Indeed, the *Washington Post, New York Times,* and a host of other newspapers now offer their text to subscribers in electronic form. Hundreds of "zines" are already online, with others being launched almost at their "editors'" whim; and many sites on the World Wide Web (WWW) offer full digitized versions of conventional library and museum materials, ranging from historical documents, classic novels and poetry, academic papers and journal articles, government and institutional documents and forms, to art collections and tours. Others are bulging with a range of files (e.g., games, data, operational, graphic, sound, and so on) available for viewing and/or downloading from any remote location, and additional such sites go online almost daily.

Because of the form they take and the manner in which information is transmitted and received, such computer communications could also be analogized to the traditional broadcast media. With the proper hardware-software combination (much like a television set or radio), one can view and/or download any material that is made available on the networks (much like tv and radio programming). Once material is downloaded (or self-generated), however, the receiver (or author), herself, can become a publisher/broadcaster by dispatching e-mail messages or posting downloadable files on her own web-site.

55. See, e.g., Lawrence Lessig, "The Path of Cyberlaw,"104 *Yale L.J.* 1743 (1995) (discussing such a dilemma with regard to issues of anonymity and privacy in cyberspace).

When e-mail is considered, the more appropriate model may be that of a common carrier, such as a telephone or telegraph operator; or a message could be analogized to traditional hard mail delivered door-to-door by the U.S. Postal Service. Public message areas resemble in varying degrees such things as the bulletin board at the local laundromat or the classified and personal sections of newspapers and magazines (privately operated and controlled), and a public library's or university's information kiosk, an open meeting of the county school board, streetcorner leafleting, or a gathering of likeminded souls to hear speakers on the Washington Monument grounds (public fora).

Moreover, individuals gain entry to the Networld either through a public agency (e.g., state universities, public libraries, government agencies) or a private internet service provider (there are hundreds of ISPs).[56] This creates a public/private question regarding any communications activities from the very point of departure. The First Amendment operates as a restriction on Congress, and through the Fourteenth, on the states, and it is clearly established that government may not prohibit speech on the basis of its content or viewpoint without a compelling interest. Private individuals or corporations, however, operate the majority of the nation's computer networks, and the First Amendment does not guarantee access to private property in order to engage in speech. Indeed, the owners of a speech outlet possess the right of editorial control over communications associated with their property,[57] unless it has been converted into a public forum.[58]

---

56. Access to computer networks is obtained through a range of possible routes, such as general online services (providing a fairly wide array of things like e-mail, interactive games, chat-rooms, Web access, and information packages from commercial vendors), basic access providers (e.g., e-mail and direct Internet connections), limited service providers (access to particular informational data bases, and related interactive chat-rooms), and electronic bulletin boards (e.g., chat-room discussions on specialized topics, game files for downloading or interactive play).

57. See e.g., *Miami Herald Publishing Co. v. Tornillo*, 418 U.S. 241 (1974) (recognizing a right of private censorship by newspaper editors).

58. The public forum doctrine was first announced in *Hague v. CIO* (307 U.S. 496 1939) and extended in *Marsh v. Alabama* (326 U.S. 501 1946). But the Court has recently shown renewed deference to the rights of property owners (see e.g., *International Society for Krishna Consciousness v. Lee*, 112 S.Ct. 2701 1992). The Court has attempted to draw a sharp line between violations of rights committed

To resolve the access issue in a computer network venue will require healing the breach between two significant sets of interests: the individual users' First Amendment right to disseminate and receive ideas, and the access providers' property interests. In traditional terms, some conflicts have been sorted out. Usually, editorial control rests with the party who originates communication, but there are differences associated with the various media technologies. For example, print media possess full editorial control. There is no scarcity of print outlets, and audience reception is based entirely upon individual choices among many alternatives. Because the airwaves are considered a public resource, broadcast media have partial control and are subject to government regulation. Audience reception is free, but choices are limited. The extent of editorial control of cable operators is in dispute; cable operators hold local monopolies but subscription requires an affirmative choice on the part of the audience. The general trend, however, seems to be to treat cable more like print than broadcast. Moreover, reconciliation of competing interests in each of the mass media is premised on non-interactive technologies, with a single information or program originator and a large, relatively passive audience.

Hard-wire telephonic communications are the only exception,[59] since the technology is interactive; however, any given transmission usually involves only two parties. The caller must respect the privacy interests of a receiver, who might not want the information (e.g., obscene phone calls, unsolicited sales pitches, and the like). On the other hand, calls coming in to a commodity exchange (e.g., a mail-order catalog outlet, phone sex service) represent autonomous choices (so long as filters are in place to screen out calls from juveniles; see e.g., *Sable*, 492 U.S. 115 (1989)).

by government and by private actors. In Jackson v. Metropolitan Edison Co., 419 U.S. 345 (1974), then Justice Rehnquist summarized the state action analysis: "The inquiry must be whether there is a sufficiently close nexus between the State and the challenged action of the ... entity so that the action of the latter may be fairly treated as that of the State itself"(at 351). The requirement is typically satisfied in one of two ways: The state authorizes or facilitates the action of a private entity, or the state delegates to a private entity a "[power] traditionally exclusively reserved to the State"(*Jackson*, at 352).

59. Transmission over cellular phones has been analogized to broadcast.

Like the telephone, computer networks allow for two or more speakers to exchange information interactively. However, unlike the telephone, the Networld allows individuals to communicate with an audience of unknown dimensions. Hence, information technology challenges a number of accepted First Amendment premises. Where all but telephonic communications were one-way, all are rendered interactive; transmissions of limited range and finite reach are transformed to undeterminable infinity; and an individual user can readily convert herself into a publisher, or the functional equivalent of a bookstore or library.

This occurs, for example, when an individual creates her own WWW homepage. Some newspapers (e.g., *Washington Post* and *New York Times*), radio broadcasters (e.g., *NPR*), and cable networks (e.g., *CNN*) have also established a presence on the WWW. Should a different First Amendment standard apply to different publishers? When the same information is provided in different technological forms?

The Internet is, like the airwaves, a public resource. But, unlike the airwaves, scarcity cannot be used to justify government regulation. Moreover, because choice of transmission content is exercised by the individual user rather than by a medium owner, the responsibility to transmit in the public interest is lost. Transmission falls into an area of singular private interest. Are "discussions" in cybernetic chat rooms and Usenet newsgroup messaging areas conducted in a public forum? Or, since the great bulk of these "locations" are provided by private operators, do they occur in a private domain?[60] The question can be answered in several ways with different implications.[61] For example, if an individual user posts a clearly libelous message for all visitors to read, the party suffering the defamation certainly has a cause of

---

60. See, e.g., Edward J. Naughton, "Is Cyberspace a Public Forum? Computer Bulletin Boards, Free Speech, and State Action,"81 *Geo.L.J.* 409 (1992).

61. The limited case law existing in this area offers conflicting guidance. In a $200 million libel suit against a computer bulletin board provider, *Stratton Oakmont, Inc. v. Prodigy Services Co*, 23 Media L.Rep. (BNA) 1794 (N.Y.Sup.Ct. 1995), the trial court rejected defendant Prodigy's claim that it could not be liable for alleged defamatory statements transmitted on its system because it served as a mere passive conduit for the communications of its users. However, in a libel case filed against another electronic bulletin board operator, a different court reasoned that CompuServe did not exercise editorial control over messages on its network. (*Cubby Inc. v. CompuServe Inc.*, 776 F. Supp. 135 (S.D.N.Y. 1991)).

action. But against whom? To hold all users (who think they are communicating anonymously or privately)[62] individually responsible for liability could well have a chilling effect on all cyberspace communications. On the other hand, to hold system operators liable would likely put all of the small ones out of business altogether.[63] In addition, a private system operator could claim to be analogous either to a print publisher or a book store owner, in which case different expectations apply.[64]

To confound the analysis further, conversion of Internet interactivity into a passive information retrieval system that would resemble a customized tv set is moving apace. Indeed, in the interest of expanding the community of users, corporate service providers are hard at work reducing the interactivity of the Web with push technology that promises to automatically retrieve specified information to the user's desktop. Apparently, according to market analyses, many people are intimidated by their perception of Internet complexity and would prefer to be able to use the medium passively, much as they do television.[65]

---

62. Indeed, one's private but libelous e-mail message could be posted by the intended receiver in a location accessible to all visitors.

63. Moreover, a small operator probably lacks the technological capability to monitor all messages and files on its system; whereas, a large-scale operator (e.g., America OnLine) does have this capacity. Such monitoring and the private censoring that it entails also presents some questions that will need to be worked through.

64. Branscomb (op cit., at 1651-52) notes some of the problems in drawing appropriate analogies:

> There is, however, a difficulty in applying existing legal metaphors to a Networld in which an information provider may logically seem to fall under the ambit of several legal regimes. On some channels offered by Prodigy, the information provider is acting in the normal manner of a publisher editing content; in others it is delivering e-mail and acting as a carrier legally forbidden to monitor content; in others it is offering a public forum for the discussion of public issues; and in still others it is acting as a distributor that would not be required to monitor content.

65. For a review of some of the push technology products, see David Lidsky, "News, sports, weather, and even more software come to your desktop," *PC Magazine* "Online Content: The Web Delivers," January 31, 1997 at http://www8.zdnet.com/pcmag/features/push/_open.htm

Property rights issues have moved to the forefront in our burgeoning information economy in another significant way. Since the introduction of the radio early in this century, followed more recently by broadcast television, cable television, computer networks, and multi-media communications mergers (combining newspapers, motion picture studios, book and magazine publishers, television and radio, telephone and computer networks under one roof), communication and information have been transformed into market commodities, owned and distributed by corporations. This is an extraordinarily significant development, allowing corporations to claim a property interest in information. In other words, speech is transformed into an intangible property asset. Copyright law is being wielded as a weapon by major market actors against individuals and small operators.[66] Viacom, for example, has been particularly aggressive in initiating copyright litigation against individual webmasters for placing downloadable image and sound files on homepages constructed for *Star Trek* devotees, and many other fan site operators have faced threatened legal actions from the likes of Sony, Paramount, and MSN.[67] Similar intimidation tactics are deployed against those who dare to register a coveted domain name.[68]

Because it is not clear whether such communications constitute a new medium or fall into one of the already established categories, the courts will soon face some difficult problems, particularly in the realm of obscenity. Indeed, a section of the Telecommunications Act of 1996 (known separately as the Communications Decency Act (CDA)) aimed at protecting children from objectionable matter on the Internet met with a legal challenge the day that President Clinton signed the bill into

66. See e.g., James Boyle, *Shamans, Software, and Spleens: Law and the Construction of the Information Society* (Cambridge, MA: Harvard University Press, 1996).

67. Noah Robischon, "The Empires Strike Back; Things Get Sticky For Fan Sites on The World Wide Web,"*Entertainment Weekly,* January 24, 1997, at 15; Brett Atwood, "Oasis In C'right Dispute With Fans' Web Sites Act Seeks Halt To Unauthorized Use Of Material On The Net," *Billboard,* May 24, 1997.

68. See e.g., *MTV Networks v. Curry,* 867 F. Supp. 202 (S.D.N.Y. 1994); James West Marcovitz, "ronald@mcdonalds.com - 'Owning a Bitchin" Corporate Trademark as an Internet Address - Infringement?"17 *Cardozo L. Rev.* 85 (1995).

law, February 8, 1996.[69] A special three-judge district court found the Act's language and scope to be unconstitutionally vague and overbroad (*ACLU v. Reno*, 929 F. Supp. 824 (E.D.PA 1996)). Upon review, the U.S. Supreme Court agreed with most of the lower court's opinion, unanimously finding the CDA's prohibitions against transmission of "indecent" and "patently offensive" materials over-broad, in violation of the First Amendment (*Reno v. ACLU*, Slip Opinion: 521 U.S., Decided June 26, 1997). Writing for the Court, Justice Stevens asserts: "We are persuaded that the CDA lacks the precision that the First Amendment requires when a statute regulates the content of speech. In order to deny minors access to potentially harmful speech, the CDA effectively suppresses a large amount of speech that adults have a constitutional right to receive and to address to one another. That burden on adult speech is unacceptable if less restrictive

69. *ACLU v. Reno*, 1996 U.S. Dist. LEXIS 1617 (E.D.PA, 1996) (issuing a temporary restraining order against enforcement of the Act's provisions). Judge Ronald L. Buckwalter (at *1-2) noted the challenged legislative language:

> Title V of the [Telecommunications] Act includes the provisions of the Communications Decency Act of 1996 (CDA), codified at 47 U.S.C. @223(a) to (h).
> Pertinent to the matter now before this court, @ 223(a)(1)(B) provides:
>   (a) Whoever—
>   (1) in interstate or foreign communications—(B) by means of a telecommunications device knowingly—(i) makes, creates, or solicits, and (ii) initiates the transmission of, any comment, request, suggestion, proposal, image, or other communication which is obscene or indecent, knowing that the recipient of the communication is under 18 years of age, regardless of whether the maker of such communication placed the call or initiated the communication;
>
> Section 223(d) provides:
>   (d) Whoever—
>   (1) in interstate or foreign communications knowingly—
> (A) uses an interactive computer service to send to a specific person or persons under 18 years of age, or
> (B) uses any interactive computer service to display in a manner available to a person under 18 years of age, any comment, request, suggestion, proposal, image, or other communication that, in context, depicts or describes, in terms patently offensive as measured by contemporary community standards, sexual or excretory activities or organs, regardless of whether the user of such service placed the call or initiated the communication; or
>   (2) knowingly permits any telecommunications facility under such person's control to be used for an activity prohibited by paragraph (1) with the intent that it be used for such activity, shall be fined under Title 18 United States Code, or imprisoned not more than two years, or both.

alternatives would be at least as effective in achieving the legitimate purpose that the statute was enacted to serve" (Slip, at 35).[70] Note that the Court places at least as much emphasis on citizens' "right to receive" information as it does on any speaker's right to disseminate, an important distinction to which we subsequently return.

A number of states have also gotten into the cyber-censorship act with statutes of their own, on the premise that the Tenth Amendment empowers the states to protect the psychological health and well-being of their respective children. Thus far, legislation in New York and Georgia have been struck down by federal courts, following a rationale similar to that issued by the *Reno* courts.[71] In addition, because Internet communications often (nearly always) cross state boundaries, sub-national regulatory effort also runs afoul of the interstate commerce clause, which brings us to a discussion of the locational problem.

III. VIRTUAL REALITY v. PHYSICAL REALITY

All of the Court's speech precedents are grounded upon accepted conceptions of geographic location and physical space. Indeed, until now all speech activity could be said to occur at a particular place, within a specifiable geographic region, on an identifiable electronic bandwidth, and so on. Moreover, given the nature of the physical world, space (as we have come to know it) is finite, which means that it can be either publicly or privately controlled, and it cannot be put to simultaneous use, so it must be shared. Much First Amendment jurisprudence hinges upon conceptions

---

70. Interestingly, Justice O'Connor, joined by Chief Justice Rehnquist, suggested that some sectors of the Internet be "zoned"for adults only, in the same fashion that cities use zoning ordinances to place some businesses off-limits to minors, by full implementation of gateway technology (Slip, O'Connor, J., concurring in part and dissenting in part). Also see Lawrence Lessig, "Reading the Constitution in Cyberspace,"45 *Emory L.J.* 869 (1996).

71. *ALA v. Pataki*, (S.D.NY 1997) at http://www.aclu.orgcourt/nycdadec.html); ACLU v. Miller, (N.D.GA 1997) at http://www.aclu.org/court/aclugavmiller. html. An additional challenge, filed in May, 1997, is currently pending in the Eastern District of Virginia (*Urofsky v. Allen*). For full discussion of these activities, as well as other regulatory actions at the state level, see ACLU, "The Threat of State Censorship Bills" at http://www.aclu.org/issues/cyber/censor/stbills.html (June 1997).

of the physicality of speech and the limitations that spring from it. Speech on computer networks falls into a completely different realm, posing problems for any analogies that one can draw.

An additional challenge presented by development of cybernetic communications is the question of court jurisdiction. All court jurisdictional boundaries are set by physical location. An event falls within a court's jurisdiction if it physically occurred within the boarders of that court's geographic reach. Telephonic messages often cross jurisdictional boundaries, but there are clear locations of transmission and reception, unambiguous end-points, each of which can be pin-pointed in their respective geographic zones. If a violation of law occurs, say an obscene phone call, prosecution is possible at either end, but not at points between (assuming intervening jurisdictions). The same logic applies with regard to other common carriers, such as telegraph messages and deliveries of books, videos, and the like, by mail, UPS, or any other private carrier. The only communities arguably affected by the activity in question are those where a tangible, detectable event occurred, not those that were imperceptibly passed through along the way. Broadcast is more scattershot. Transmission occurs from a definite spot, but reception falls upon a more ambiguously defined audience. Nevertheless, reception is finite both in the number of possible signals and in geographic range. And, again, if a violation occurs, if George Carlin broadcasts his seven dirty words routine (*FCC v. Pacifica Foundation*, 438 U.S. 726, 1978),[72] prosecution is possible anywhere in the reception zone, but not geographically beyond it. Theoretically, areas outside the zone of reception are not affected by the transmission.

Transmissions over computer networks defy current understandings of jurisdictional communities based upon physical geography. This is especially critical with regard to "publication" of obscenity, the prosecution of which is based upon a community standard rule (*Miller v. California*, 413 U.S. 15 (1973)).[73] So, a

---

72. For a discussion of this case in the context of cyberspace communications see e.g., Norman Redlich and David R. Lurie, " First Amendment Issues Presented by the 'Information Superhighway," 25 *Seton Hall L. Rev.* 1446, at 1455ff (1995).
73. For further discussion of how computer networks pose problems for our legal definitions of community, see, e.g., Howard Rheingold, *The Virtual Community: Homesteading on the Electronic Frontier* (New York: Addison-Wesley, 1993); William

computer operator in San Francisco can upload image files containing pornographic pictures to a web site that do not violate her local community standards. However, with no outreach effort whatsoever on the part of our California "publisher," or "bookstore owner," those images can be downloaded to any location where Internet access can be obtained, setting up the possibility for a "cybercop" to receive images that are clearly prosecutable in Podunk, Maryland. Can prosecution proceed in the Maryland jurisdiction even if our local Podunk official is the only person equipped in that community to receive them? This is similar to the scenario that led to the 1995 prosecution of Robert and Carleen Thomas, who operated an electronic bulletin board from their home in California and were prosecuted in the Western District of Tennessee. They were found guilty after trial in U.S. District Court, and the convictions were upheld by the 6th Circuit (*U.S. v. Thomas*, 74 F.3d 701 (6th Cir. 1995) (affirming convictions); *reh'g en banc*, denied, 1996 U.S.App.LEXIS 4529 (6th Cir. 1996)).[74] Moreover, the Thomases argued that, given the ability to download images by computer to any location, a system operator would have to meet the standards of the "least tolerant community" and asked the court to consider a new definition of "community." In an effort to buy judicial time, however, the 6th Circuit panel sidestepped that question.[75]

Internet communication, like consumerism, transgresses geographic perimeters and clearly threatens generally accepted conceptions of what constitutes a community.[76] This is an issue that the courts will most assuredly revisit. In a more general sense, electronic communications over a global matrix of networks render international boundaries meaningless and pose significant technological difficulties to any government intent on intervening – whether it is Bejing attempting to shield its people from Western political influence or Washington aiming to insulate its people

S. Byassee, "Jurisdiction of Cyberspace: Applying Real World Precedent to the Virtual Community,"30 *Wake Forest L.Rev.* 197 (1995).

74. The Thomases did, however, use their bulletin board to solicit orders to their mail order business.

75. See *U.S. v. Thomas*, 74 F.3d 701, at *26 (6th Cir. 1995) (affirming convictions); reh'g en banc, denied, 1996 U.S.App.LEXIS 4529 (6th Cir. 1996) (* indicates Lexis pagination).

76. See e.g., Benjamin R. Barber, *Jihad vs. McWorld* (NY: Ballantine Books, 1996).

from the influences of smut peddlers. As the three-judge panel that struck the Communications Decency Act, on First Amendment grounds concluded: "[The Act] will almost certainly fail to accomplish the Government's interest in shielding children from pornography on the Internet. Nearly half of Internet communications originate outside the United States, and some percentage of that figure represents pornography. Pornography from, say, Amsterdam, will be no less appealing to a child on the Internet than pornography from New York City, and residents of Amsterdam have little incentive to comply with the [Act]" *ACLU v. Reno*, 929 F. Supp. 824, 882 (E.D. PA 1996).

We also could see a serious confrontation with established Supreme Court precedent that says that an individual enjoys the right to possess obscene material (with the exception of child pornography) in the privacy of his own home *(Stanley)*, another locational issue. Like the *Miller* community standard rule, this is a long-standing precedent reinforced by subsequent decisions. In *Thomas*, the 6th Circuit appeals panel rejected the *Stanley* "right to possess" argument, stating that "the right to possess obscene materials in the privacy of one's home does not create a correlative right to receive it . . . even if it is for private use only."[77] Although by traditional standards, in order to "possess" material one must first have "received" it (the court's logic appears rather suspect), in a computer mediated reality, the two acts are joined. In the *Thomas* case, files were downloaded (received) and then viewed (possessed). It is not clear how this court (or any other) would address the situation where one, in the privacy of his own home, views obscene (according to his local geographic community) image files available at a remote site without downloading them first. In fact, viewing/possessing can be the equivalent of receiving, since files opened as one surfs the WWW are automatically copied to hard disk as temporary Web navigator cache files.

IV. CONCLUSIONS

As computer-mediated communications systems continue to develop, the courts will face a range of difficult First Amendment

---

77. *U.S. v. Thomas*, at *20, citing *U.S. v. 12 200-Ft. Reels of Super 8mm Film*, 413 U.S. 123, at 128 (1973).

issues – judges are destined to do some hard travelin'. Until now, various forms of communications have appeared separately and in a series. This has allowed the courts to address issues according to technological differences as they have arisen, rather than taking a comprehensive view. Indeed, one can question whether First Amendment doctrine is driven by principle or by technology, or by monied interests able both to marshal principle and exploit technology. In any event, an array of internal contradictions will need to be reconciled with the convergence of communications systems.

What is the core purpose of free speech? Is it to enhance the integrity and autonomy of individuals? To ensure a free market in information and ideas? Or, is it to promote collective deliberation,Madisonian republicanism? Given the speech capabilities over the course of this century, the courts have found room for all three, to carve out different territories and draw lines of distinction. The lines of demarcation collapse, however, in digitized communications, and analogy is rendered highly suspect. At least one important doctrinal effort has paralleled the political economic dynamics observable in the current communications revolution. The Supreme Court has shifted its primary focus in relevant cases from the rights of a *speaker* to those of the *audience*. The public has a right to information, from whatever source, so that it can make "enlightened" decisions. In other words, the First Amendment guarantees us a free market in communication of ideas. This conceptualization fully accepts the commodification of speech. And, because no distinction can be made among potential speech, information, idea, or knowledge sources, all are equalized. There is no tenable difference among individuals, press corporations, business corporations, or any other organization for that matter – we are all protected equally by the First Amendment in the speech market from government interference. It sounds like *laissez faire* economics in new garb.[78] If these are the flowers the Supreme Court is growing, the telecommunications industry will harvest the blossoms;

---

78. For a discussion of this point see e.g., John J. Flynn, "The Jurisprudence of Corporate Personhood: The Misuse of a Legal Concept," in Warren J. Samuels and Arthur S. Miller (eds.), *Corporations and Society* (Westport, CT: Greenwood Press, 1987).

individuals will be given the opportunity to purchase a "First Amendment essence" from the proffered product line. The First Amendment guarantees protection from government action, not the actions of Rupert Murdoch or Bill Gates.

As communication technology has exploded to encompass a wider range of activities, corporations have moved quickly to expand the base of the burgeoning information markets and to secure their positions as information sources and distributors. However, the historical trend of all markets is to consolidate, merge toward oligopolistic control, with fierce measures instituted to ward off competition, and we see the same trend occurring in the information marketplace. Like other items that can be bought and sold, information has been transformed into a commodity that is generated, produced, aggregated, packaged, distributed – there is even an access market. Rather than moving toward a freeform environment, we are likely headed toward one of tighter restrictions on discourse within corporate controlled environments. Like the Internet, the First Amendment has been hailed as a great source of freedom for individuals, but corporations have worked hard to convert it to their own use and to secure it among their constellation of resources. And thus we must take heed of veteran journalist Bill Moyer's (1995) qualified assertion that "the computer will democratize communications if we make sure that there is public access to it and it's not controlled just by a handful of powerful corporations."

Timothy W. Luke
Virginia Polytechnic Institute & State University

The Politics of Digital Inequality:
Access, Capability and Distribution in Cyberspace

Abstract: What is the significance of the World Wide Webs of power and wealth being spun today out along the Internet? How do these informatic networks operate as one of our most vital meaning systems through which we negotiate our shared understandings, conduct war, build our frameworks for peace, and engage in competitive commerce? The nature of the cultures we form, and our resulting network of social relationships, are increasingly shaped in this new virtual community.[1] Since so much of our communication is conducted mostly over digital networks, many of our personal relationships with all of their cultural meanings are being reframed by the forms of "cybersubjectivity" in such networked "infostructures".[2] More importantly, a politics of digital inequality is now surfacing here, and tough questions about very basic conditions of access, capability, and distribution in cyberspace need to be raised. This discussion is only the barest beginning, but it starts thinking through these issues by critically rereading some of the more optimistic rhetorics of transformation now coming from its digital devotees.

I. The Future is Now: Cyberspace as Third Nature

Cyberspace is not a notion about things to come; it is embedded within the material condition of many things already at work today. Any census of Internet users needs to be updated daily or weekly, not monthly or yearly, to keep accurate track of its rates of exponential growth. Many millions of mainframe and personal computers – some 40 million at this time – are linked into this network, directly or through other smaller networks. Exactly how many human users actually utilize the Internet from these multiple points-of-entry is less clear. Numbers can be cited, but they are

1. Douglas Rushkoff (1994) *Cyberia: Life in the Trenches of Hyperspace* (San Francisco: Harper). Howard Rheingold (1993) *The Virtual Community: Homesteading on the Electric Frontier* (Reading, MA: Addison-Wesley).

2. Benedict Anderson (1991) *Imagined Communities* (rev. ed. London: Verso). Manuel De Landa (1991)*War in the Age of Intelligent Machines* (New York: Zone Books). G. Stock (1993) *Metaman: The Merging of Humans and Machines into a Global Superorganism* (New York: Simon & Schuster). C. Emmeche (1994) *The Garden in the Machine: The Emerging Science of Artificial Life* (Princeton: Princeton University Press).

inaccurate even before they are reported. Most of the world's money, much of its communication, transportation, and distribution systems, and many forms of data analysis now move by means of operations in cyberspace. In many ways, this is the age of the smart machine.[3] Cyberspaces might be best understood as the latest manifestation of nature's pluralization. Human beings can reshape their biophysical environmental settings, or a terrestrial "first nature," through purposive-rational action, as illustrated traditionally by the territorialized "second nature" of technological artifacts fabricated as part and parcel of human industrial and agricultural activity.[4] Informationalization goes one more iteration beyond the technical artifice of second nature, creating the ultimate imagined community from the hyperreal domains of digitalized "third nature" in cybernetic telemetrical-ities.[5]

Prevailing notions of power, subjectivity, and community, however, do not fully disclose changes happening in both the industrial technosphere of modern second nature and ecological biosphere of premodern first nature as these elaborate human nature constructs become overlaid, interpenetrated, and recons-tituted with the postmodern "third nature" of an informational cybersphere/telesphere.[6] As Vattimo argues, "the society in which we live is a society of generalized communication. It is a society of the mass media."[7] Power shifts focus, speed overcomes space, orders become disordered, time moves standards, community loses centers, values change denomination as the settings of industrialized human agency are shaken completely. Third nature, at this juncture, assumes informationalized forms on the cyberscape/infoscape/media-scape of telemetricality. It too is an anthropogenic domain, but built on-line out of "bits".[8] If, as Smith contends, "it is in the production of nature that use-value and

3. Shoshana Zuboff (1988) *The Age of the Smart Machine* (NY: Basic Books).
4. Georg Lukács (1971) *History and Class Consciousness* (Cambridge, MA: MIT Press).
5. Anderson (1991) De Landa (1991) *War in the Age of Intelligent Machines* (New York: Zone Books) and Jacques Attali (1991) *Millenium: Winners and Losers in the Coming World Order* (New York: Random House).
6. Jean-Francois Lyotard (1984)*The Postmodern Condition* (Minneapolis: University of Minnesota Press), Frederic Jameson (1991) *Postmodernism, or the Cultural Logic of Late Capitalism* (Durham: Duke University Press). S.G Jones (ed) (1995) *Cybersociety: Computer-Mediated Communication and Community* (London: Sage).
7. G. Vattimo (1992)*The Transparent Society* (Baltimore: The John Hopkins University Press).
8. Robert W. Lucky (1989) *Silicon Dreams: Information, Man and Machine* (New York: St. Martin's Press). Nicholas Negroponte (1995) *Being Digital* (New York: Knopf).

exchange-value, and space and society, are fused together,"[9] then third nature is now recombining society with space by producing new exchange-values in unprecedented ways from the use-values of the electromagnetic spectrum, the industrial era's telecommunication infrastructures, and the digitized restructuring of labor and leisure.[10]

"As a social product," the spatiality of third nature remains, like first and second nature, "simultaneously the medium and outcome, presupposition and embodiment, of social action and relationship."[11] Digitalization shifts the sites of human agency and social structure into registers of informational bits from those of manufactured matter. Most importantly, the setting of agency, the character of power, and the structure of meaning will change in this emergent third nature, especially as cultures and communities must cope with the unstable economy and politics of its cyberspatial domains.

The information superhighways of the World Wide Web represent a vast grid of multimedia/multilingual/multivalent virtual spaces tunneling through a diverse array of monomedia /monolingual/monovalent real-life settings. Like the Cold War system of federal interstate freeways in the United States, the advent of information superhighway traffic often is a blockbuster, breaking apart hitherto more culturally integrated, social homogenous, or politically organized blocks of human settlement, with the information explosions of the digital revolution, into many more diverse and divided informational fragments. For the most part, these exploded fragments also are falling back to earth in ways that worsen the already tremendous material inequalities created during the eras of global industrialization. Anglo-American infotelcos, like the new MCI/BT combine, incessantly beam TV promos at their customers, asserting that the Internet is a utopia, where "there is no race, no gender, no class, no age, only minds in communication," and then begging the basic question: "Is This a Great Time, or What?" The greatness of this time, however, is unclear. Plainly, it is an era characterized by tremendous contradictions between virtual possibilities and real-life actualities. To be informatic about it, many North Americans swap data packets on dial-up connections at 56,000 baud, while phone lines in Madagascar lose most messages at 300 baud – the

9. Neil Smith (1984) *Uneven Development* (Oxford: Blackwell).

10. Timothy W. Luke (1989) *Screens of Power: Ideology, Domination, and Resistance in Informational Society* (Urbana, University of Illinois Press).

11. Ed Soja (1989) *Postmodern Geographies* (London: Verso) p. 129.

slowest possible infotransmission rate.[12] The United States and
United Kingdom publish nearly 40 percent of all scientific articles,
South Africa and Zimbabwe, which are the leading African centers
of scientific research publish 0.439 percent.[13] North America now
annually publishes 461 book titles per million population, and
Africa publishes 29 titles per million population.[14] Kenya has one
phone line for every one hundred people, Canada and the United
States have fifty-four.[15]   Finally, North America has over 5,400
on-line data bases, or 71 percent of the world's total, while Africa
has 8 on-line data bases, or less than 1 percent, a figure that
South America, Eastern Europe, or Asia also do not exceed.[16]
The Internet still is essentially a very Anglophone world in which
IBM, Compaq, Digital, Apple, Hewlett Packard, Microsoft, or
Oracle produce almost all of the hardware and software, and
North American or European telcos support most of the
connectivity arrangements. ASCII implicitly sums up the digital
planet at this time: it is one dominated by American Standard
Codes for Information Interchange.

So MCI is mistaken: the Internet carries many signs of race,
gender, class, age, and nationality in its everyday operations, but
it also might be right in suggesting this is a great time. Oddly
enough, the Net constitutes an utopian space, or a
nowhere/everywhere, which is populated by millions of
"netizens," whose collective sense of their common possibilities
and actualities are corroding many existing principles of
nationality, territoriality and sovereignty, because they are still
pegged to the traditional assumptions of off-line existence. On
one level, the Internet appears to be a vast intranet for the still
quite powerful advanced industrial West, whose influences are
felt as the effects of exocolonizing extranets by the very weak,
arrested, non-industrial Rest, carrying the cyberporn of
Occidentalosis everywhere at microwave or laserlight speed.
There are signs of these tendencies, but, on another level, the
Internet, and all of its many parallel or successor networks, also
constitutes a new supra-national, post-territorial, anti-sovereign,
machinic formation, whose destabilizing effects can be
experienced everywhere and anytime, its on-line virtual practices
pervade off-line real existences.

12. William Wresch (1996) Disconnected: Haves and Have-Nots in the Information
Age (New Brunswick: Rutgers University Press) p. 130.

13. Wresch (1996) p. 84.

14. Wresch (1996) p. 39.

15. United States Bureau of the Census (1993): Wresch (1996), p. 125.

16. Wresch (1996) p. 97.

Given how rapidly cyberspaces are forming all around the world from the (con)fusion of computers with wired and wireless telecommunication networks, we must consider more carefully economic and political questions being raised by cyber-spatialization. Cybertouts and infoprophets among the digiterati, from Alvin Toffler to Nicholas Negroponte, Howard Rheingold to Stewart Brand, Steve Jobs to Bill Gates, have for nearly a generation now promised a brave new world of equality, empowerment, and ease if only everyone would log on. Like so many any other examples of computer "vaporware," however, performance thus far has not matched the promises. By focusing these critical speculations here upon what types of individual and collective subjectivity become possible in these cybernetic domains, we can investigate whether or not some cybersubjects will be more equal than others, which also may challenge our pre-digital assumptions about on-line human agency and social structure.[17]

The following review of recent writings by the digerati or, at least, some fellow travelers, will survey the contemporary debates over telematic networking in this informational new social movement, asking if the virtualization of many economic, political and social activities will, in fact, make it easy to redistribute wealth and opportunities, enhance individual capabilities and skills, or widen popular access and participation? In the end, it concludes, even more perplexed, doubting that virtual surrogates either can adequately substitute for real material inequalities or effectively avoid creating new virtual inequalities as well.

II. Being Digital/Becoming Unequal

Cyberspaces require us to concoct new sensibilities about the time and space – perhaps "postmodern,"[18] maybe "amodern."[19] Their operational architectures on-line set new limits for what are economic, political and social spaces where we act individually and collectively, defining who will be inside/outside, access-granted/access-denied, plug-in ready/plug-in unready, platform-compatible/platform-incompatible, operational/inoperable. Conditions

17. K. Kelly (1994) *Out of Control: The Rise of Neo-Biological Civilization* (Reading, MA: Addison-Wesley). Hans Moravec (1988)*Mind Children* (Cambridge, MA: Harvard University Press). Alvin Toffler (1983)*Previews & Premises* (New York: Morrow).

18. Fredric Jameson (1991)*Postmodernism, or the Cultural Logic of Late Capitalism* (Durham: Duke University Press).

19. Bruno Latour (1993)*We Have Never Been Modern* (Harvester Wheatsheaf).

of network connectivity, then, are a locus for conflict over access, capability and distribution. Cultural authority as well as basic powers of rule-making, rule-applying, or rule interpreting devolve upon network managers, systems operators, and software designers, slipping away from traditional political jurisdictions which cling absurdly to the illusion that the cyberspaces served on their territory adhere precisely to their legalities.[20] These contradictions between a virtual life "on-line" and real life "off-line" must be a central concern for any analysis of how the basic conditions of access, capability and distribution in cyberspace already affect our culture and politics.

a. Living on a Digital Planet

Coming on the cusp of such transformations, we must exercise caution about where what is fixed remains, how what can change shifts, when alterations begin, why old conventions fade, or who causes whom to take a loss or gain. The devotees of the digital age often oversell the positive attributes of cybernetic innovation even as they underplay how so much of what already exists will continue to be just as it is – only it will be improved out of the network. Negroponte is obsessed with telling us that "being digital" implies that we soon shall all live in a world where making, moving, and managing "bits" will replace the embodied modalities of many interactions as they now are conducted through "atoms." Indeed, "the change from atoms to bits is irrevocable and unstoppable."[21] Digitalization means dematerialization. In marking this turning point in human history, he asserts "computing is not about computers any more. It is about living."[22] This claim is completely true, but it needs much more careful discussion than Negroponte and most other digitizers have given us. Living how, living where, living for whom, and by whose leave? These questions rarely are raised by the digerati except in the most ebullient fashion to celebrate microcomputing's coming millenarian moments.

Negroponte dismisses those who worry about "the social divide between the information-rich and the information-poor, the haves and the have-nots, the First and the Third Worlds,"

---

20. Timothy W. Luke (1993) "Discourses of Disintegration, Texts of Transformation: Re-Reading Realism" *Alternatives* 18 pp. 229-258.

21. Nicholas Negroponte (1995) *Being Digital* (New York: Knopf) p. 14.

22. Negroponte (1995) p. 6.

because the "real cultural divide is going to be generational"[23] as "the young" integrate this technology into their lives first. Yet, this glib rehash of 1950s froth about TV and kids totally misses the big questions about access, equality and distribution in the digerati's wired world. Like so many Jacobin revolutionists before him, Negroponte addresses a small, privileged, wealthy elite, whom he addresses abstractly as "you, the reader." While he presumes to speak to/for all of humanity, only about 40 percent of American families own PCs, just 50 percent of American teenagers have PCs at home, and maybe around 40 million people worldwide were surfing the Net.[24] So it is to them, or "you, the reader of Being Digital," that he can say computers are now crawling "into our laps and pockets," so that "early in the next millennium, your right and left cuff links or earrings may communicate with each other by low-orbiting satellites and have more computing power than your present PC.... Mass media will be redefined by systems for transmitting and receiving personalized information and entertainment. Schools will change to become more like museums and playgrounds for children to assemble ideas and socialize with other children all over the world. The digital planet will look and feel like the head of a pin. As we interconnect ourselves, many of the values of a nation-state will give way to those of both larger and smaller electronic communities. We will socialize in digital neighborhoods in which physical space will be irrelevant and time will play a different role."[25] Thus, the digerati commands that "you are expected to read yourself into this book" [Being Digital], just as you must with the digital revolution, so you will begin to "feel and understand what 'being digital' might mean to your life."[26]

What it means for "our lives" now is quite clear: the digital planet is one in which 6 billion people, minus the 40 million or so already on the Internet, will be snared in new worldwide webs of manipulation spun from out of those select digital neighborhoods where physical space is irrelevant and time plays a different role. For those with info-cufflinks or cyber-earrings, personalized information and entertainment will make the digital planet give way to their larger and smaller electronic communities. Nation-states will become more like museums as digital neighborhoods function as playgrounds where web-wise inter-

23. Negroponte (1995) p. 6.
24. Negroponte (1995) p. 5.
25. Negroponte (1995) p. 6-7.
26. Negroponte (1995) p. 8.

connected selves might assemble ideas and socialize all over the world. But those 60 percent of American families and 50 percent of American teenagers without PCs at home, and 5.96 billion other human beings still living off-line will look and feel like pinheads. Being digital means one must become a digital being whose costume jewelry signs you in and out at will of the cyberspatial telemetries projected from low-earth orbit satellites. But for the nearly 70 percent of humanity who still do not have plain old telephone service (POTS) on a personal/family/village level, such rhetoric about cyberchickens coming to everyone's informatic pots is highly alarming.

Being/becoming digital simply is the latest phase of the informational revolution. Like all previous waves of revolution-ization in the key technics of human artifice, whether it is the agricultural revolution of Neolithic times or the industrial revolution nearly three centuries ago, the informational revolution now is arriving with its own social movements of self-interested human groups intent upon transforming all human ecologies, shifting fundamentally the totality of all relationships between human organisms and their environments to serve their revolutionary self-interest as leading-edge actors. The digerati arrogantly see themselves constructing a new world; and, ironically, they are, but not in the ways they believe, as the expanses of third nature proliferate daily the new domains of digitality. New niches of existence are emerging, turning some who were once predators now into prey as others who once endured being prey evolve into predators.[27] Asking who has access on the digital planet, how inequality works in these digital neighborhoods, and what structures determine distribution as we interconnect ourselves are not trivial questions because it boils down to the essence of politics: who, whom? Computers are about living, and because no one should trust the digerati to deliver fantastic technofixes that will obviate any and all of our apprehensions, we should explore the ragged realities of digital inequality.

b. "Computers Everywhere"

Access in an era of informational fast capitalism is a very complicated question. On one level, cybertouts endlessly exalt the advent of "Computers Everywhere," or that installed infrastructure of cybernetic devices numbering nearly three billion

27. Marc Slouka (1995) *War of the Worlds: Cyberspace and the High-Tech Assault on Reality* (New York: Basic).

which control every aspect of our lives at home and work plus another one-hundred million plus business-deployed computer systems in finance, management, banking, design, etc.[28] However, having "access to" these "Computers Everywhere" is actually much more restricted, because it assumes one lives where computer-controlled washers, VCRs, elevators, TVs, stoves, ATMs, automobiles, PCs, or telephones are everyday appliances.[29] This is, in fact, not "an everywhere" that exists anywhere all over the place; it is instead quite confined by social class, income level, personal occupation, or geographic location. VISA's TV commer-cials notwithstanding, there are very few ATMs in Saharan Africa, and despite Sprint's excitement about phone rates one cannot get 10¢ a minute to Kazahkstan.

So getting "access to" the global infostructure's material infra-structures is a real issue, and it is a life chance which is still very unequally distributed. IBM, of course, is cooking up its "solutions for a small planet," and maybe some Kenyan dance bands are composing on PCs, while Italian octogenarians take musicology Ph.Ds at Indiana University over the Net from Tuscany. For the most part, however, actual physical access to a computer and/or the Internet is not a universally shared good. This global village is still quite small, sparsely populated, and very up-scale.

Beyond access to computers everywhere, and once one actually gets to log in to some system, there is the matter of "access in" those cyberspaces that infoprophets dub "the global network," which "is the offspring of Computers Everywhere... the interconnecting tissue of Computers Everywhere. The Global Network is a form of Cyberspace, a place where one can travel electronically, projecting one's being to any place on the planet. The Global Network is the ability to connect any computer to any other computer or connect any person to any other person. The Global Network is instantaneous communication anywhere – by voice, video or data... The Global Network is instant feedback and instant gratification."[30] While the celebrants accentuate how one can travel anyplace in cyberspace to connect to any computer or person with instant feedback and gratification, this statement too mostly is fantasy not fact.

28. Winn Schwartau (1994 *Information Warfare: Chaos on the Information Superhighway* (New York: Thunder's Mouth Press).

29. Bruce Mazlish (1993)*The Fourth Discontinuity: The Co-Evolution of Humans and Machines* (New Haven: Yale University Press).

30. Schwartau (1994) p. 54.

Of course, many relays are embedded in the global infostructure, but along with expertise and equipment up front one also will need funds, clearances, passwords, or connections to make this transit. Many domains are firewalled against unwanted intruders in search of such instant gratification. Most of what is open is not worth browsing, and much of what is worth time and effort to access is tightly closed. Information flows may have meaning as dividing lines between civilizations or nation-states only in as much as they become cultural/economic/political/social borders. Not having access in the Global Network, then, is as important a dividing line as territorial borders or ethnic cultures once were. Beyond the obvious fact that most cyberspaces are Anglophone, consumer-centered, and highly "Americanized," complex encryption also freezes many inequalities into networks to protect informational values, deny access to cyberspaces, preserve financial power, dominate communication grids, or maintain class prerogatives. Still, defining the conditions of getting "access in" the Network is a different kettle of fish than obtaining "access to" the Network, particularly given the abilities of hackers, info-warriors, or phreakers to infiltrate closed cyberspaces. In digital domains, access to and in the Global Networks is what accelerates the economic, political and social inequalities implicit in a culture becoming much more embedded in "Computers Everywhere."

c. "Cosmopolitans" vs. "Locals"

Kanter characterizes this informational divide as the line falling between the "world class," which acts world class in terms of its capabilities and assets and whose members could be considered *"cosmopolitans,"* and the class of *"localists,"* whose constituents are very local in terms of their abilities and resources, which also prompts them to behave as "nativists." Flowing through global markets, "cosmopolitans are rich in three intangible assets, three C's that translate into preeminence and power in a global economy: *concepts* – the best and latest knowledge and ideas; *competence* – the ability to operate at the highest standards of any place anywhere; and *connections* – the best relationships, which provide access to the resources of other people and organizations around the world."[31] Embedded at fixed sites, "the local class are those whose skills are not particularly unique or desirable, whose

31. Rosabeth Moss Kanter (1995)*World Class: Thriving Locally in the Global Economy* (New York: Simon & Schuster).

connections are limited to a small circle in the neighborhood, and whose opportunities are confined to their own communities."[32] To succinctly sum up inequality in a fast capitalist digital economy, Kanter distinguishes between abstract choice and concrete loyalty to differentiate the ethos of these two antagonistic informational classes: "cosmopolitans often value choices over loyalties – even in terms of which relationships deserve their loyalty. Local nativists value loyalties over choices, preferring to preserve distinctions and protect their own group. Cosmopolitans characteristically try to break through barriers and overcome limits; nativists characteristically try to preserve and even erect new barriers, most often through political means."[33]

But what are people loyal to, and how do they choose to organize their lives? Ohmae suggests that cosmopolitans increasingly turn to post-national "region-states" even as the locals cling to bankrupt nation-states. During the industrial era, it was the nation-state that operated as the armature of access to technics and its products on a gross national/domestic scale. The capabilities of the state were embedded within a national system of industrial systems for producing, distributing, and consuming material wealth. Ohmae argues informational flows, technologies and values essentially are eviscerating the nation-state as investment, industry, and individuals now gravitate to those global markets where they can obtain both best-in-the-world products and prices for those products. Increasingly, "the nation-state is increasingly a nostalgic fiction" as well as a "remarkably inefficient engine of wealth distribution."[34] Digitalization becomes the same as equalization for Ohmae inasmuch as it brings forth "a world whose people, no matter how far-flung geographically or disparate culturally, are all linked to much the same sources of global information... the basic fact of linkage to global flows of information is a – perhaps, the – central, distinguishing fact of our moment in history. Whatever the civilization to which a particular group of people belongs, they now get to hear about the way other groups of people live, the kinds of products they buy, the changing focus of their tastes and preferences as consumers, and the styles of life they aspire to lead."[35]

---

32. Kanter (1996) p. 23.

33. Kanter (1996) p. 24.

34. Kenichi Ohmae (1995)*The End of the Nation State: The Rise of Regional Economics* (New York: Free Press) p. 12.

35. Ohmae (1995) p. 15.

Seconding Kanter's observations about these new class divisions arching across a rapidly informationalizing world-system, Ohmae maintains that the nation-state mostly fails as a redistributive device as well as a guardian of sovereignty. Captured by the "resource illusion" (insulating territory from world trade to conserve natural resources) or "national interests" (labelling this land, factory, market as "ours," not "theirs"), the nation-state becomes a protection racket, mostly to protect the biggest, most active racketeers. In the borderlessness of digitalized information, "the traditional national interest – which has become little more than a cloak of subsidy and protection – has no meaningful place. It has turned into a flag of convenience for those who, having been left behind, want not so much a chance to move forward as to hold others back as well."[36] Nationalism, then, is essentially another manifestation of localism/nativism /protectionism poised to prevent cosmopolitans from building fast informationalized capitalism on a global scale. This filtering/braking/retaining function of nation-states is significant on the digital planet only to the degree that national power distorts or enables the efficient circulation of information. As Ohmae asserts, "economic borders have meaning, if at all, not as dividing lines between civilizations or nation-states, but as contours of information flow."[37]

Not to be outdone in the contest to imagine "the road ahead" for those cosmopolitans who love markets in search of global commerce, Microsoft Corporation's Chairman and CEO, William H. Gates, III articulates (along with two associates, Nathan Myhrvold and Peter Rinearson) his vision of "friction-free capitalism" as the essence of global digitalization in his combination 1995 book/CD-ROM, *The Road Ahead*. Indeed, this volume documents the life of one digital being, or Bill Gates, focusing upon how he developed as a cybersubject with a uniquely entwined passion for markets and computers. Because the first time that he "heard the term 'Information Age,' I was tantalized."[38] Gates tells us that he has devoted his life to building this new period of history – a time in which "the new materials men used to make their tools and weapons"[39] will be forged out of digitalized information. Once the transition is made to a world built out of information, "anyone with access and a personal computer

36. Ohmae (1995) p. 64.
37. Ohmae (1995) p. 25.
38. Bill Gates (1995)*The Road Ahead* (New York: Viking) p. 20.
39. Gates (1995) p. 20.

[preferably connected into the Microsoft Network and loaded with Microsoft applications] can instantaneously recall, compare and refashion it"[40] in the reproduction of these vast global flows.

In many ways, the global information superhighways will not lead to a new Third Wave informational society – they already are it: right here, right now. Gates directs his readers to do this little mental maneuver: "When you hear the phrase 'information highway', rather than seeing a road, imagine a marketplace or exchange.... digital information of all kinds, not just as money, will be the new medium of exchange in this market."[41] Most importantly, just as Ohmae argues, the digitalization of everyday life within these global flows "promises to make nations more alike and reduce the importance of national boundaries."[42] As digital computing displaces built environments, fixed work sites, and traditional homeplaces, their dedicated tunneling through the circuitry clouds of big bandwidth switches will provide "a place in our everyday lives because they not only offer convenience and save labor, they can also inspire us to new creative heights."[43]

Readers may well conclude that this magic of the marketplace works: it clearly inspired Gates to new creative heights, transforming him through global flows of PC software into the Multi-Billion Dollar Man – the world's richest person. As Gates sees the Third Wave breaking up all existing social formations, he can hardly wait for "this tomorrow, and I'm doing what I can to help make it happen."[44] What "it" is, of course, is the digital revolution of a cosmopolitan digiterati, working to see their friction-free capitalism being switched into every last little surviving free space of the everyday lifeworld through the Windows 95, thanks to Microsoft, Inc. There are trillions to be made out of accelerating this transition. As Gates addresses Negroponte's collective of on-line "yous," he sees the world's coming digitalized exchanges in exultant terms,

> The global information market will be huge and will combine all the various ways human goods, services and ideas are exchanged. On a practical level, this will give you broader choices about most things, including how you earn and invest, what you buy

40. Gates (1995) p. 21.
41. Gates (1995) p. 6 .
42. Gates (1995) p. 262 .
43. Gates (1995) p. 7.
44. Gates (1995) p. 7.

and how much you pay for it, who your friends are and how you spend your time with them, and where and how securely you and your family live. Your workplace and your idea of what it means to be "educated" will be transformed, perhaps almost beyond recognition. Your identity, of who you are and where you belong, may open up considerably. In short, just about everything will be done differently.[45]

Given this range of borderless possibilities, "at Microsoft," and in keeping with the networked kinematics of informationalization, "we're working hard to figure out how to evolve from where we are today to the point where we can unleash the full potential of the new advances in technology. These are exciting times..."[46] Under this cosmopolitan horizon, Gates enjoins us not to worry about heading out on the information superhighway, because these are exciting times. Once we know where we want to go, we only need to enjoy everything that friction-free capitalism will unleash to help us realize our full superconductive potentials.

Figures that enthuse over "cheap global communications," "the personal computer revolution," or "friction-free capitalism," like Gates, Ohmae, Kanter, Schwartau, or Negroponte, suffer from a classic case of Jacobin elitism as they speak in the name of abstract equality and empowerment amidst concrete conditions of severe inequality and disempowerment to serve their particular interests in the guise of universal change. As the Chairman and CEO of Microsoft Corporation, Bill Gates revolutionizes personal computer use, and freely capitalizes upon the organizational frictions in existing businesses. Yet, in assuming that anyone or everyone can, or will soon, do things just as he does, Gates ironically discloses how we are not all equal in either the virtual or the material world. And, the information superhigh-way will be one more powerful new force for raising barriers of prejudice, inequality, and hierarchy between those who communicate globally as informational superhighwaymen, and those who do not. In this technological new social movement, the world is split between those who foment computer revolutionization and those who are revolutionized, or those world class cosmopolitans who flow friction-free through global commerce and those nativist locals who stay put and get burnt. Because we are not all created equal in the material world, as Jacobin innovators naively assume,

45. Gates (1995) p. 6-7.
46. Gates (1995) p. 19.

we never will be equal in the virtual world. And, instead of solving the material world's sociological problems, the growth of the infobahn will aggravate them, while, at the same time, creating entirely new sociological conflicts and contradictions in cyberspace.

In this vein, Gates openly admits "the power and versatility of digital technology will raise new concerns," and that there are serious questions about "equity issues that will have to be addressed."[47] On the other hand, he also claims "one of the wonderful things about the information highway is that virtual equity is far easier to achieve than real-world equity."[48] And, in this state of wonder, Gates makes a remarkable foundational claim: "We are all created equal in the virtual world, and we can use this equality to help address some of the sociological problems that society has yet to solve in the physical world. The network will not eliminate barriers of prejudice or inequality, but it will be a powerful force in that direction."[49] Assuming that everyone has, or easily can access, their own high-end work station, big bandwidth net connection, unlimited network time, and sophisticated software resources, the digerati see a world of virtual equality, cyberliberty, and netcentric fraternity coalescing in clouds of electrons clinging to each and every dataport. Unfortunately, their ideologies slide in and out of familiar Jacobin ellipses in which too much materialistic wherewithal is assumed to be present, constant, and limitless, because it is, by and large, for them. The possibility that others might not be so blessed is either an utterly implausible notion or even a sign of their unworthiness.

Taking that track marked by Microsoft as "the road ahead," however, is leaving most people in the dust. While Gates and others enthuse endlessly over the emancipatory possibilities of a netcentric world, it is clear that not everyone gets to head out on the highway looking for adventure. And those that do also will not move at the same speed, attain the same range of access, operate with the same level of complexity, or sample the same spectrum of information. Gates is right about the infobahn; it is not a highway, it is a point of sale, trading pit, or commercial site at which an info-mart positions cosmopolitan symbolic analysts such that they always will be more equal than most others.

---

47. Gates (1995) p. 251.
48. Gates (1995) p. 258.
49. Gates (1995) p. 258-259.

III. The Politics of Digital Inequality

The cyberspaces of third nature are not universally accessible to anyone anytime anywhere. They instead are extremely concentrated at certain venues, enveloping and enriching particular sites in only a few domains not unlike the other industrial-technological systems which transformed the second nature of developed regions during the Industrial Revolution. Clearly, one can access them remotely, and interoperate amidst some connections from many places with the right equipment and adequate resources, but these prerequisites are exceptional in most real life situations. Moreover, making the world digital in access or equal in capability is destined simply to generate digitalized inequalities, uncapabilities, and inaccessibilities.

The large-scale of these globalized production circuits also is undercutting the relative value of physical property, real estate, or material wealth. Because so many discrete components are integrated into any one commodity chain, and because so many competitive alternatives are available on the material side of the equation, it is information about the totality of the industrial-technological process – who does what, when, how, and why – that constitutes the greatest power and value-adding significance in today's global economy. Having marketable skills, owning a supply of vital resources, or controlling an efficient factory are not a sufficient condition for success today without informed access to markets, the capability of extracting resources for a specific application, or putting the factory to use on a globally distributed production line. Control of the means of informational organization is what constitutes decisive power today, and many are wielding this power in ways that are causing unemployment and underemployment on a large scale. What does this mean for overall levels of social equality?

At this juncture in the 1990s, it is quite obvious that many firms "have learned how to use information technologies to reduce the number of white-collar and middle management jobs. That is what downsizing is all about."[50] And, as part and parcel of the downsizing process, many hitherto secure, well-paid employees are being turned into "contingent workers," or "involuntary part-timers, temporary workers, limited-term contract workers, and previously laid-off 'self-employed' consultants who work for wages far below what they had previously been receiving" as

---

50. Lester Thurow (1996)*The Future of Capitalism.* (New York: William Morrow and Company) p. 183.

they also receive "less fringes, fewer paid holidays, and must accept great economic risks and uncertainty... for part-timers the probability of having pensions or health benefits is less than a third of those of full-time workers, their skill-adjusted wages are much lower, and most of the jobs open to them are dead-end jobs."[51]

Having access in the Net does allow one to operate as a telepresence who can work in virtual firms, shop in virtual stores, interact in virtual neighborhoods. Given one's physical location, this engagement recasts his or her actions as those of a virtual laborer, a virtual citizen, or a virtual neighbor. Hence, the level and scope of access in cyberspace, in turn, is turning into a measure of status, class, power, and wealth since, just like real space, not all offices, stores, territories, or neighborhoods are open to just anyone whenever they wish. Tapscott argues the digital economy is "a molecular economy" as old social, economic, or cultural formations are disaggregated into dynamic molecules and clusters of activity – "mass" becomes "molecular" in every aspect of living.[52] Molecularization, however, also comes with increasing atomization. Many molecularized bits will not find new niches in their disaggregation, and such conditions of inaccessibility are now a key strain in digitalizing economies.

The computerization of society, then, is not a trivial change that will leave things just as they are now only done better with computers. Instead molecularizing change is transforming social institutions and cultural practices as thoroughly as motorization did over a century ago. Just as the automobile reordered the built environment, reconstituted industrial economies, reshaped social mores, and rearranged social classes, one sees digitalization doing the same today. Already the industrial infrastructure has shifted as more Americans make semiconductors than build construction equipment, more work in data processing than in petroleum refining, and more make computers than fabricate automobiles.[53] Old mass production industries are shedding workers, and with their mass of working men and women going by the wayside, the economy is becoming more and more stratified. The "successful fifth," or top 20 percent of households that Reich[54]

---

51. Thurow (1996) p. 29 .

52. Don Tapscott (1996)*The Digital Economy: Promise and Peril in the Age of Networked Intelligence* (New York: McGraw Hill) p. 51.

53. Tapscott (1996) p. 9 .

54. Robert Reich (1991)*The Work of Nations: Preparing Ourselves for 21st Century Capitalism* (New York: Knopf).

mainly fills with symbolic analysts and Tapscott finds are worth $180,000 or more, now control 80 percent of all wealth.[55] And, these rates of concentration are accelerating.

The celebrants of such virtual offices and factories mostly are to be found among the cosmopolitan cadres of world class corporate management. Thurow's observations on this point, as related by Tapscott,[56] speak directly to the empty promises of equality in Gates' friction-free marketplace. Thurow asks his audience in a recent speech to U.S. business leaders, "Who do you think has more high school graduates – the United States or China?" He relies: "If you guess China, you're right – by a couple of hundred million. Now why hire a graduate in the U.S. for $30,000 per year when I can get an equivalently educated person in China for $100 per month?" Many U.S. businesses have already answered with a resounding, "We don't."

Digitalization greatly enhances the opportunities of capital to water down the wage, speed up the line, or runaway with the shop, because the virtual workplace can seek, and will find, a mix of the highest skill levels with the lowest wage costs out on the Net.

As a result, Tapscott notes: "Millions of so-called virtual aliens are clicking away on key boards in Shanghai, New Delhi, and Hong Kong – fully networked and employed as members of the U.S. economy. Except that they don't pay U.S. taxes or live in the United States."[57] The U.S. loses jobs that should/could/would pay $30,000 per year, but these off-shore virtual shops do not gain their dollar equivalents. This is not a uniquely American problem. Asea Brown Boveri, for example, pays German workers $30.33 an hour, and Polish workers $2.58 an hour. Since Polish workers also work 400 hours more a year than German ones, it is no surprise that ABB has added 21,150 positions in former CMEA countries as it has cut 40,000 jobs in North America and Western Europe.[58] Of course, not all of these changes are related to informationalization, but digital means of organizing production are greatly accelerating those changes that they do not cause.

During the 1980s, as Thurow notes, all of the gains in male employee earnings went to the top 20 percent of the work force, and 64 percent went to the top 1 percent. If total incomes are factored into the mix, 90 percent of all income gains went to the

55. Tapscott (1996) p. 33.

56. Tapscott (1996) p. 6.

57. Tapscott (1996) p. 6.

58. Thurow (1996) p. 168.

top 1 percent. So, not too surprisingly, the pay of the average CEO in the Fortune 500 increased from 35 to 157 times that of an average worker.[59] As the U.S. Bureau of the Census records, real wages of full-time male workers from 1973 to 1992 fell 23, 21, 15 and 10 percent respectively for the bottom, second, third, and fourth quintiles of labor – only the top quintile gained, and its increase was 10 percent.[60] Even real GDP per capita rose 33 percent from 1973 to 1994, wages for all non-supervisory (male and female) workers fell 14 percent, leaving the level of real wages where they were in the late 1950s.[61]

Rifkin suggests that it is Reich's symbolic analysts or Kanter's cosmopolitans who are benefiting from this radical upward redistribution of income. These knowledge workers are "a diverse group united by their use of state-of-the-art information technology to identify, process, and solve problems. They are the creators, manipulators, and purveyors of the stream of information that makes up the postindustrial, postservice global economy."[62] At the same time, nearly one in six, or 37 million Americans, are living in poverty, according to 1992 figures with 42 percent of them living at the inner core of major cities.[63] In many ways, digitalization provides an extremely efficient means of virtualizing "the revolt of the elites"[64] inasmuch as an emergent bit-based *Gemeinschaft* leads to severe restructuring in the atom-based built environments and social institutions of America's once industrial *Gesellschaft*. The infamous "secure community" in exurbias out beyond suburbia with its own private schools, high walls, rent-a-cops, and restrictive covenants will promote more of this hollowing out of public spaces by allowing its residents to interact with one another mostly on the infobahn. These info-islands, in turn, will have highly inegalitarian socioeconomic profiles. One study already has shown 27 percent of homes whose owners completed high school have PCs, while 63 percent of university

59. Thurow (1996) p. 21.

60. U.S. Bureau of the Census (1972) *Current Population Reports, Consumer Income* (Washington, D.C.: Government Printing Office, p. 137). U.S. Bureau of the Census (1992) *Current Population Reports, Consumer Income* (Washington, D.C.: Government Printing Office) p. 198.

61. Council of Economic Advisers (1995) *Economic Report of the President 1995* (Washington, D.C.: Government Printing Office) pp. 276, 311, 326.

62. Jeremy Rifkin (1995) *The End of Work: The Decline of the Global Labor Force and the Dawn of the Post-Market Era* (New York: G. P. Putnam's & Sons) p. 174.

63. Rifkin (1995) pp. 177, 180.

64. Christopher Lasch (1994) "The Revolt of the Elites: Have They Cancelled Their Allegiance to America?" *Harper's* 289 November pp. 46-48.

educated households have them. And, 21 percent of households with incomes under $30,000 have computers, but 66 percent of those with an income over $70,000 have them.[65] At the apex of society, those who are the most likely world class "cosmopolitans," making over $70,000 a year with a $180,000 plus net worth and having nearly 7 of 10 homes equipped with computers, are dematerializing the once secure positions at the base of society still held by those who tend to be "localists," who make do on $30,000 or less a year, have barely 2 in 10 households with computers, and dance around daily with karoshi to evade the next corporate downsizing being driven by the digitalization of their work.

Learning to love the rationality of such markets is, of course, the global mantra of neoliberal digital ideologists, like Gates, Kanter or Ohmae. Nonetheless, the accelerating informational-ization they describe already is provoking acute struggles over access and distribution in the developed world and elsewhere. While many devotees of informational fast capitalism see it creating a friction-free market, Rifkin casts this new era in world history as "one in which fewer and fewer workers will be needed to provide the goods and services of the global population," but this transnational perestroika of productive capital is taking "a drastic toll on the lives of millions of workers."[66] The acceleration of global exchange, on the one hand, will lead to "growing numbers of permanently displaced workers who have little hope and even fewer prospects for meaningful employment;"[67] while, on the other hand, those who hang onto their jobs must endure greater frictions, a tighter time-squeeze, and systematically imposed overwork as downsizing, retrenchment, and kanban engineering turn workers into overworked superconductors of capital. When long hard work delivers a satisfying standard of living, many ordinary people tolerate its rigors. In the post-1973 era, however, digital-ization has brought lower living standards, less security, and emptiness as the reserve army of the proletariat grows by leaps and bounds in its competition with virtual aliens, cyber-illegals, and digital scabs for its daily bread.

Hence, the telematic class struggle turns into a specialized type of info-warfare between owners and workers, producers and consumers, the informed and uninformed, those with access confirmed and access denied, the few who are net-capable and

65. Tapscott (1996) p. 34.
66. Rifkin (1995) p. xvi-xvii.
67. Rifkin (1995) p. vii.

those many who are net-incapable. Of course, this dematerialization of wealth and power is not total. Any peek at local narcocapitalist markets or deindustrialized neighborhoods will reveal those who control the cash and/or coercion still count, even though the digiterati want to virtualize money as "e-cash" (because cash is dirty, mobile, unruly) and register all firearms in nation-wide databanks (because unregistered guns or gun-users are the main criminal element threatening their world class lifestyles). But, on a global scale in major markets, corporations are becoming hollowed out as they reduce their core holdings to technological know-how, product marketing intelligence, or financial information.

For most people, this tendency is a profound threat. Information is precious usually because so few can know or use it. As land, real property, or social entitlements decline in value, so too does the material well-being of most people. Not surprisingly, as Reich observes, informationalized societies fragment into "the successful fifth" of symbolic analysts, who are informationally competent, and "the failed four-fifths" of metal-bending, paper-pushing, sod-busting, or service-performing laborers who are rapidly becoming informationally-obsolete or superfluous. Nation-states, in turn, are fragmenting, as the fictive "yous" in the world class that Negroponte or Gates see "becoming digital" are being interconnected globally in strings of information passing through the hands of the symbolic analysts from the successful fifth, and the anonymous multitudes of those "remaining atomic" are trapped behind in miserable deadzones contained by every increasingly irrelevant nation-state. As Bill Gates assures us, "education is the best preparation for being able to adapt," and "as the economy shifts, people and societies who are appropriately educated will tend to do best."[68] Yet, being able to adapt also is often the best preparation to provide appropriate education, and few regions, peoples, or cities amidst the failed four-fifths have the best preparation to see economic shifts, to educate themselves as appropriate, or to do their best in a changing world. If they did, then we would not have inequality in the material world. And, it is unclear how the virtual world will alleviate these severe inequities.

The "cyber-nation" is perhaps a new domain coming under numerical control from within existing nation-states; hence, the control of numbers, the source of codes, grantor of access, or the point of connections will be the fulcrum of cybernational authority

68. Gates (1995) p. 254 .

in this new social formation. As numerical control mediates humans' control over their collective and individual digital being, one can anticipate that the ideological bias, class prerogatives, or group interests of the controlling class in each cyber-nation also will be much more difficult to discern as well as resist.

Indeed, digital beings also must recognize how totally their on-line lives are now subject to on-line injury, debilitation or death. An informational subjectivity can be "killed," or "crippled," or "injured" by destroying, modifying or stealing all or part of their informational modes of existence. Security is a major worry out on the Net, because info-war is, and can be, waged by all against all. Individuals, corporations, and states all face the threat of info-attack, and info-defenses need to be part of any digital being's operational routines. "Access to" hardened heavily encrypted sites, like cyber-nations, and then "access in" them once anyone gets there again will mark inequalities in digital domains. Little people, or local nativists, will be readily attacked and quickly damaged, because so much of their cybernetic subjectivity will be easily accessible, modifiable, destructible, nonredunant. Another mark of world class cosmopolitan status may well be having better, more flexible security as a virtual (and material) being.

As long as digital information has value, and to the extent that anyone can tap this value anytime from anywhere, intruders or abusers will surf through these anarchic network spaces in search of financial information, telephone numbers, psycho-demographic data, industrial secrets, or infrastructure commands that might be leveraged to extract wealth or power. Not only will nation-states attempt to turn these into strategic assets, but firms and experts also will aspire to capture them for tactical advantages. Before this onslaught, individuals will find their privacy, wealth, and behaviors subject to tremendous surveillance, if not outright domination.

IV. Conclusions

Caught in the shockwaves coursing off fast capitalism's time-space compression, some postmodernist dirges mimic Marx, regretting how "everything solid melts into air"[69] as digitalization transforms material being into digital being. Yet, one need not go overboard with their cyber-angst, believing "the result is an inability to map our contemporary terrain, to envision space and representational

---

69. Marshall Berman (1982) *All That is Solid Melts into Air* (New York: Verso).

forms, and thus to weave things together, to conclude, to be able to act."[70] The digerati are mapping, and then colonizing these terrains very effectively. So buying some vertigo effect with informationalization will only promote defeat. Foucault's sophisticated characterization of disciplinary forces as the mediation of action at a distance acquires greater quiddity in cyberspace.[71] Behind the screen, but looped into the spreading skein of internet/intranet connections, cyberspace operates entirely around the disciplinary principles of action at a distance.[72] So too then are many motions those of distant actors enacting their remote agency through disciplinary grids of coded communication.

On a more basic level, however, Deleuze might be more correct about the phenomenology of power in these emergent cyber-nations. Foucault's mechanistic construction of positive power dynamics,[73] exercising their disciplinary effects in fairly rigid enclosures of discursive prerogative, institutional inertia or panoptic surveillance, in fact, could lose its resonance in the network of networks now infiltrating each facet of everyday life. While Foucault envisioned control being mediated through the distribution of bodies/functions/organizations in space, Deleuze reimagines the codes of connectivity and platforms of performativity digitally switching domination on-and-off on demand when and where guidance is needed to sustain the operationality of entirely wired/sireless social formations.[74] Rather than solid embodiments of centered authority, one laces into a decentered New World Order equivalent of the Cold War era's command/control/communication-intelligence, or C3i, on-line to keep these virtual regimes, as central server hosts, in-line so that their interoperating human users, as distributed clients, do not/cannot/will not either go off-line or get out-of-line in any local or wide area network.

The normativity of disciplinary expectations may well be displaced by the performative rules of modulating/demodulating an inescapable gridwork of instructional code to every client from

70. Christine Boyer (1996) *Cybercities: Visual Perception in the Age of Electronic Communication* (New York: Princeton Architectural Press) p. 19.

71. Michel Foucault (1991) *The Foucault Effect: Studies in Governmentality* (Chicago: University of Chicago Press).

72. Michel Foucault (1979)*Discipline and Punish: The Birth of the Prison* (New York: Vintage).

73. Michel Foucault (1980)*The History of Sexuality, vol. 1, An Introduction* (New York: Vintage).

74. Giles Deleuze (1992) "Postscript on Societies of Control" *October* 59 pp. 3-7.

their most appropriately scaled central servers, which mediate authority as access/no access instructions on their lines of flight in kanban combinations of command/control/communication-intelligence. Manipulative systems of domination, then, can acquire a distributed network architecture as it migrates away from the mainframes of centralized panopticism and closed systems of single-source discursive direction. Object-oriented programming will embed the instructions in the bits coursing through the space of flows; so those who would rule through these flows in various spaces must program all objects and subjects to accept these orientations.[75]

If Deleuze is correct, then our direct awareness of political domination will become even more attenuated in cyberspace. The loss of feudalism's negative/destructive agent of power in the booming and buzzing confusions of bourgeois society with its positive/ productive agencies of power already has been disorienting enough for anyone struggling to decipher the present regime. The inequalities implicit in Deleuze's reappraisals of digitized authority, however, are even more profound, as the visible lines of flight, denoting who dominates whom, are deleted in the encryption of various complexly-layered computer domains. Microsoft Corporation and its Chairman /CEO, Bill Gates, pretend that "the road ahead" leads into an immediate future in which transparent, polycentric, nonhierarchical, multiplex, open archi-tectured forms of life on line will define new democratic, egalitarian, humane communities.

Yet, at the same time, the infostructures sustaining these digital beings' new modes of being digital require that large slices of these cyber-commons be enclosed in opaque, monocentric, hierarchical, uniplex, closed architectured ways, if only to maintain/innovate/administer the networks' net-workable connections. Translating more of our ways of life or means of livelihood into digitized formats must create greater and greater digital inequality as it grants the digital format and/or digital formatters formidable powers, which few now imagine must be either checked and balanced or divided and separated.

This paper originally was presented at the annual meeting of the American Political Science Association, August 29-September 1, 1996.

---

75. Timothy W. Luke (1996) "Liberal Society and Cyborg Subjectivity: The Politics of Environments, Bodies, and Nature" *Alternatives* 21 pp. 1-30.

144

Anna Sampaio and Janni Aragon
UC Riverside

'To Boldly Go (Where No Man Has Gone Before)': Women and Politics in Cyberspace

Abstract: In this article we examine competing perspectives on new technologies paying particular attention to the interpretations of language offered by poststructuralists as well as variant strands of feminism. In borrowing from these theories, we attempt to spell out some of the implications of new technologies to the lives of women, especially the manner in which they construct new language systems, new subject positions, and ultimately new political practices. Throughout the article, we maintain that cyberspace communication challenges traditional concepts of language, and by extension traditional constructions of historical agents as masculine and rational actors. In its place, these new technologies provide a context for more fluid formations of language which themselves are largely void of many of the cultural indicators (such as age, race, sex, or physical appearance) which have constricted women's expression. Ultimately, while we are optimistic about the opportunities which cyberspace creates for women users and feminist politics in general, we also recognize a number of limitations to these opportunities. In particular, we conclude this article with a discussion of how questions of authenticity and ownership of information, which are necessary attendants of cyberspace anonymity, have mitigated against communication between and by women.

Introduction

Among social and political theorists as well as contemporary cultural critics there is little consensus on how to approach the proliferation of new technologies that have impacted many Americans both professionally and personally. There are multiple interpretations of the significance of electronic mail and web pages emerging from the humanities to the sciences. And yet, the multiplication of perspectives surrounding these issues does not mean that each interpretation has received equal attention or been held with the same regard. On the contrary, there is a body of literature (one informed by Daniel Bell's work) which has contributed to a general theory of these developments, one which argues that these new technologies are merely extensions of more traditional print and speech media, and thereby subject to the same political social norms as the former.[1] However, despite the dominance of this perspective (particularly among the organic and human sciences), there exists an alternate interpretation, one that is grounded in the poststructuralist tradition of language which views electronic mail and web pages as new forms of social interaction capable of restructuring human subjectivities, and which ultimately require a different epistemological position to analyze them.

In the following essay, we argue that these new technologies have introduced an epistemological challenge to traditional conceptions of language and social construction. Furthermore, we argue that this new language not only disrupts the production of more traditional subjectivities, but also allows for the production of alternate subject positions, and by extension alternate political practices. Paying particular attention to the role these new technologies play with regard to the experiences of women generally and feminist activists in particular, we also examine the benefits and limitations of cyberspace communication. Ultimately, we conclude that while these developments offer possibilities for a more constructive politics and the development of a more democratic public space, they also contain their own constraints and hierarchies that require new political strategies of resistance.

The Cartesian Self v. the Poststructural Subject

One of the most enduring claims which pervades much of the literature on new technologies is derived largely from an extension of Cartesian subjectivity grounded in traditional Western philosophy. This view sees individuals as agents in history who are capable of standing outside the world of objects and are allowed to control the world and its object through instrumental reason. Grounding their theories within this view of rational and autonomous human agency theorists are able to maintain that developments in electronic communications and cybernetic technology have in no way upset the Cartesian subject. In fact, in the view of these theorists, the new developments have merely

1. See Daniel Bell (1973)*The Coming of Postindustrial Society* (New York, Basic Books) and"The Social Framework of the Information Society" in Tom Forester (ed) *The Microelectronics Revolution* (Oxford, Blackwell). In addition, see Anthony Giddens (1987) *Social Theory and Modern Sociology* (Stanford, Stanford University Press); as well as, Jürgen Habermas (1970) *Toward a Rational Society* translated by Jeremy Shapiro (Boston, Beacon); and Robert Markley (1996)"History, Theory and Virtual Reality" in Robert Markley (ed)*Virtual Realities and Their Discontents* (Baltimore, John Hopkins University Press).

extended this subject position by promoting the institutional mechanisms of writing that are associated with the autonomous rational subject.[2]

Marshall McLuhan's writings on media and communication were influenced by this understanding of subjectivity. In particular, in the bulk of his early writings McLuhan distinguished between print and oral communications and maintained that "alphabetization," and its extensions into written communications, were destroying the tribal world of dialogue and face-to-face contact evidenced in early civilizations. Thus, he claimed that the privileging of the eye in the technology of writing and printing brought about a cultural and cognitive shift typified by Western logic and the emergence of the rational agent.[3] While McLuhan proceeded to applaud efforts at dismantling the age of print (and consequently proved somewhat incapable of adequately theorizing the value and meaning of television to modern societies), he was nonetheless instrumental in relating the formation of new technologies to the creation and promotion of the rational and autonomous subject.[4]

Thus, in the view of authors such as McLuhan, new technologies can most appropriately be understood as tools for maximizing efficiency among acting human subjects. That is, they frame these changes as largely extensions of print media (or in some instances, as with "chat rooms," as extensions of speech media) which simplify and streamline familiar routines. As such it is argued that these new communication experiences should fall under the traditional laws and cultural norms that govern written and oral practices. One example of this logic was the formulation of federal laws aimed at regulating electronic databases during the mid 1970s. Specifically, the Privacy Act of 1974 and the Freedom of Information Act regulated databases kept by the Federal government and restricted the kind of

2. More recent writings, such as Susan Bordo (1987) *The Flight into Objectivity: Essays on Cartesianism and Culture* (Albany, State University of New York Press); and Sandra Harding (1991) *Whose Science? Whose Knowledge? Thinking from Women's Lives* (New York, Cornell University Press) have effectively argued that the traditional autonomous rational subject is also masculine.

3. "If a technology is introduced either from within or from without a culture, and if it gives new stress or ascendancy to one or another of our senses, the ratio among all of our senses is altered...Tribal, non-literate man, living under the intense stress on auditory organization of all experience, is as it were, entranced." Marshall McLuhan (1962) *The Gutenberg Galaxy: The Making of Typographic Man* (Toronto, University of Toronto Press) p. 24.

4. See Marshall Mcluhan and Harley Parker (1968) *Through the Vanishing Point: Space in Poetry and Painting* (New York, Harper and Row).

information that could be stored in them. In addition, these laws limited the use of the information to "the purpose for which it was gathered" and prohibited the selling of mailing lists in certain circumstances. It also allowed some individuals to review records that had been kept on them. But while these laws failed, in part, because they did not cover the actions of states, municipalities, or private agencies nor did they set up an agency to enforce these laws, they were also incapable of halting the spread of information because they misread how new technologies had transformed both access to and reproduction of materials. [5]

To the extent that these authors admit that new technologies have altered human communication in any basic manner, their comments are most often concentrated on the changes to patterns of time and space. In other words, language, and by extension electronic communications, are nothing more than the transparent representation of an author's writing or speech. Within this view, new technologies simply increase the representational power of language by reducing the constraints of time and space, in particular by reducing the temporal and spatial distancing of meaning.

However, those who focus on new technologies as strictly an extension of print media or as a means to simplify and streamline familiar routines do not go far enough in questioning dominant theoretical perspectives surrounding these developments. In particular, this view fails to interrogate the social and cultural construction of the new forms of communication and the subsequent impact they have on users. As Mark Poster noted in a discussion of these new technologies:

> For the issue of communication *efficiency* which is at stake in the above discussion, does not raise the basic question of the *configuration* of information exchange or what I call the wrapping of language... what is at stake are new language formations that alter significantly the network of social relations and the subjects they constitute.[6]

Alternative perspectives on these developments have been offered by the emerging class of poststructural intellectuals in the United States who view electronic communication as a language or

5. Michael A. Abib (1984) *Computers and Cybernetic Society* (New York, Academic).
6. Mark Poster (1990) *The Mode of Information: Poststructuralism and Social Context* (Chicago, University of Chicago Press) p.8.

discursive system which not only effects (and is effected by) social conditions but which constructs entirely new subjects.[7] Following the tradition of structuralism,[8] these theorists generally argue that language is fundamental to social reality in as much as subjects are constructed and given meaning through the structure of communication. In a similar vein, feminist critics such as Sandra Harding and Rosemary Hennessy have borrowed from post-structuralism to argue that gendered subjectivity is also constructed by language and can provide useful tools for challenging the effects of unequal gender relations.[9] Thus, an adequate account of these new technologies should be grounded in discursive analysis and must be capable of "decoding" the linguistic dimension of these new structures of social relationships. In addition, poststructuralists maintain that the dominant perspective is inadequate because it assumes the presence of an autonomous rational male subject; when in fact subjectivities are being continuously multiplied, dispersed, and even deconstructed in cyberspace. In short, poststructuralists attempt to rewrite the history of technology from the perspective of symbolic exchange as opposed to the agency of autonomous rational actors.

Two key elements in this poststructural view of commun-ications are the way discourse and language are implicated in new forms of domination and the manner in which temporal and spatial changes have occurred within our postindustrial context.[10] In particular, with regard to our understanding of

7. See Jean Baudrillard (1983) *Simulations* translated by Paul Foss et al, (Beithchman, New York, Semiotext(e)); David J. Bolter (1990)*Writing Space: The Computer in the History of Literacy* (Hillsdale, New Jersey, Lawrence Erlbaum); Jacques Derrida *Of Grammatology* translated by Gayatri Chakravorty Spivak, (Baltimore, Johns Hopkins University Press); George Landow *Hypertext: The Convergence of Contemporary Critical Theory and Technology* (Baltimore, Johns Hopkins University Press); Richard Lanham (1993) *The Electronic Word: Democracy, Technology, and the Arts* (Chicago, University of Chicago Press); and Jean-François Lyotard (1984) *The Postmodern Condition: A Report on Knowledge* Minneapolis (University of Minnesota Press)

8. It should also be noted that there is a growing body of literature in the area of cultural studies which examines the construction and impact of new technologies. However, where the focus in those accounts rests largely on the cultural significance of cyberspace, our attention in this essay is drawn primarily to the use of language captured in the analysis of post-structuralism and more specifically how that language relates to women's subjectivity.

9. Sandra Harding (1991) Whose Science? Whose Knowledge? Thinking from Women's Lives (New York: Cornell University Press) and Rosemary Hennessy (1993) Materialist Feminism and the Politics of Discourse (New York: Routledge).

10. Giles Deleuze (1977) *Dialogues* (Paris, Flammarion); Giles Deleuze (1993) *The Deleuze Reader* Constantin V. Bouncas (ed) (New York, Columbia University Press); and Michel Foucault (1977) *Language, Counter-Memory, Practice: Selected*

women's experience in politics and feminist theory in the US, this notion of discourse helps to specify a new form of domination and resistance, one that is grounded in the complex intersubjectivity that has permitted particular cultural and intellectual trends to become dominant and fix women and other marginalized subjects in sedentary and essentialized positions. These new forms of domination and resistance expressed by poststructuralists take multiple forms with some of the more benign manifestations occurring in early feminist theory which often assumed the formation of a concrete and easily identifiable category of "women" as an already constituted coherent group with identical interests and desires. This form of feminist theorizing is evident in the research by Nancy Chodorow, Carol Gilligan, and Shulamith Firestone which simultaneously promotes academic inquiry into the experiences of women while construct-ing barriers around the very meaning and expression of "womanhood." Nancy Fraser and Linda Nicholson explain:

> [The early Women's Studies] assume methods and concepts which are uninflected by temporality or historicity and which therefore function de facto as permanent neutral matrices for inquiry. Such theories...are insufficiently attentive to historical, and cultural diversity and falsely universalize features of the theorists' own era, society, culture, class, sexual orientation, and ethnic or racial group.

A more extreme example of the discursive domination eluded to in poststructural theory is evident in women's encounters with pornography. In addition to offending some women's sensibilities or creating hostile environments, post-structuralists point out that pornography is also problematic because it constructs a fairly specific and limited image of women and their sexuality that is then imposed on women by virtue of its widespread dissemination and reproduction in popular culture. In both cases, this understanding of discourse and domination allows for a more complex analysis of the multiple layers of discrimination and prejudice faced by women as well as the

Essays and Interviews Donald F. Bouchard (ed) (New York, Cornell University Press); Edward Soja (1989) Postmodern Geographies: The Reassertion of Space in Critical Social Theory (London and New York, Verso); and Edward Soja (1993) "Postmodern Geographies and the Critique of Historicism," in Postmodern Contentions: Epochs, Politics, Space John Paul Jones III et al (eds) (New York and London, The Guilford Press).

complex nexus of potential strategies and practices available to resist these forces. A prominent example of potential strategies for women which addresses these aspects of discourse and makes use of new technologies can be found on the homepage by the Guerrilla Girls who promote a feminist agenda through artistic and cultural productions and who don gorilla masks in their escapades, proclaiming to potential adversaries: "We could be anyone, we are everywhere."[11]

In the analysis of temporal and spatial dimensions, post-structuralists have also tended to argue that everyday conceptions of time and space have ignored the nuances and complexities of these systems. Specifically, much of social theory today relates to "space" as simply a static, material object or boundary while time is interpreted simply as "progress" or a natural forward motion. What these everyday meanings of space and time omit, and what David Harvey and Edward Soja point out, is that underneath these seemingly common sense perceptions of space and time lie ambiguity, contradiction, and tension. Furthermore, they argue that space and time horizons materially affect the kinds of decisions we make, the type of cultural logic we ascribe to and even the values and standards imbued in that cultural logic. In short, space and time are shaped by (and shape) our political, economic, and cultural processes. As well, the organization of space and time in social life provides a framework of experience that helps establish standards of truth which give meaning to our individual and collective subjectivities. For these reasons, Harvey and Soja argue that space and time need to be theorized in a more sophisticated manner than has been done through everyday practice. Thus, by borrowing from the poststructural view of time/space as well as the understanding of language and its relation to forms of domination, we will detail the manner in which new technologies allow for alternative language systems to emerge and for these languages to construct alternate subjectivities, as well as the implications these new subjects bring for a different type of feminist politics.

Learning to Speak the Language

Within structural linguistics Ferdinand de Saussere suggested that all human activity and subjectivity is structured by the organization of signifiers within language. Saussere argued that each referent is represented by a sign and signifier in language

11. Guerilla Girls at http://www.voyagerco.com/gg/gg.html

and while there is no inherent or necessary connection between referents and signifiers there are cultural norms that maintain a stable relationship between the two. In short, structural linguists and semioticians as well as their poststructural pursuants maintain that in addition to its capacity for communicating information, language has another very different role in structuring the subject who speaks as well as the one that is spoken to. However, Roland Barthes anticipated the arguments from French post-structuralists when he argued that a rupturing of the relationship between signs, signifiers and referents would not only impact the flow of common languages, but more importantly would obstruct the meaning of social reality.

Similar arguments have been posited by authors such as Jean Baudrillard and Mark Poster with regards to our present context. In particular, Jean Baudrillard coined the term "simulacra" to describe the state of image and representation which our postmodern moment has created. He argues that there are no longer any "true" or essential identities, instead by virtue of our state of hyper-commodification we are left with a series of detached and distanced, alienated, and isolated images which are merely "copies of a copy," holding no claims to essential truth.[12]

Baudrillard's notion of representations and the politics which follow from it, are grounded in his four successive phases of the image or four "modes of obtaining practical knowledge about the real life world." The first phase is captured by reference to the metaphor of a mirror. In this period the world is seen as a set of rational logics mixed with irrational noise and distortion. The belief among scholars and academics in this period was that by virtue of empirical study and critical engagement with the "truths" about the world which empiricism mirrors, humans are able to make practical sense of the world and eventually make it a more satisfying experience.

The second stage, captured by Baudrillard's use of a mask metaphor, maintains that practical (understood as "good") knowledge about the real world must be dug out because it has been masked or hidden by false/counterfeit appearances. This requires that those interested in arriving at some truth about the world dig for insight beneath the empirical world of directly measurable reflections.

Baudrillard's discussion of the third and fourth phases in the history of image and representation are especially important because they speak to one of the principle features within

12. Soja (1993) p. 120.

postmodern aesthetics and politics; namely, the attempts to discredit the "cult of originality." It is in the third phase that he begins to develop the concept of simulacra, or that level of critical epistemology which signals a shift from belief in the mere masking of appearances to the substitution of signs or representations of the real for the real itself. Therefore, for Baudrillard this third phase, which emerged during the 20th century, marks a moment when image begins to mask a growing absence in reality, when the sign or messenger not only becomes more important than the signified/message but ultimately gives meaning to it. In addition, Baudrillard argues that while all of these shifts/phases in the history of image/representation are indicative of changes in reality (or at least our perceptions of reality) and thus require new analytical frameworks to understand them, they also signal the invalidation of empiricism and positivistic methods for uncovering "truths" about the world.

Ultimately, Baudrillard's analysis leads to the fourth and final stage where all images become their own pure simulacra with no relations to any reality. This nihilistic stage presumes that there is no truth to be found in any formal (or informal) analysis, and thus we are left with a condition where academics and scholars engage in deconstruction simply for deconstruction's sake with little or no interest in the creation of alternative narratives.

Using a similar framework, Mark Poster argues that decoding the new electronic communications requires a theory that is able to account for the linguistic dimension of these media as well as the "fetishitic importance within contemporary culture given to 'information'."[13] As such, Poster offers his 'mode of information' theory borrowing from both Baudrillard and Marx, and rewriting history from the perspective of symbolic exchange as opposed to ownership of the means of production or the development of the sign.

In Poster's account, there are three distinctive stages in human history. The first stage is marked by the inception of face-to-face communications – orally mediated exchange characterized by symbolic forms of correspondence. In this stage, the construction of subjectivity is embedded in the experience of one-on-one communications and the emphasis on enunciation of sounds. The second phase of Poster's analysis is the stage of written exchanges mediated by print, and characterized by the

13. Poster (1990) p. 5. *The Mode of Information: Poststructuralism and Social Context* (Chicago: University of Chicago Press).

representation of signs. In this stage, the construction of subjectivity shifts to the formation of an autonomous active and rational subject forged through the individual logic of reading and writing. Finally, in Poster's analysis, the third stage is captured in our present moment of electronically mediated exchange characterized by informational simulations. In this stage, the subject/self is "decentered, dispersed, and multiplied in continuous instability."[14]

Ultimately, in their analyses both authors point to a condition which is prevalent in the age of these new technologies. In Baudrillard's terms it is the "free floating mix of signifiers" and in Poster's analysis it is the displacement of the representational character of language and specifically the removal of the referent from its language system. In the language of these new technologies it means that traditional social/cultural markers such as sex, age, race, as well as temporal and spatial boundaries which fix the language of everyday life and which are inscribed in both print media and speech are absent, resulting in a condition of virtual anonymity.[15] As a result, the dialogue concerning women and their role as a sex-class shifts into an era of heightened reliance on cyberspace.

An example of this type of loss within electronic communications is the shift from analog recordings of sound, recordings which attempt to imitate both the sound and sense of the recording moment, to digital recordings in which sound is reduced into a digitized language of zeros and ones. This same type of reduction also occurs in electronic mail and database collection; that is, where information in speech and writing was once wrapped in a cultural context which provided clear signifiers to forms of identity, by reducing communication to a complex code of zeros and ones and reproducing information from that code we inevitably reconfigure the cultural context and its signifiers. This is not to say that all of the previous indicators of identity have been removed in cyberspace; in fact, an early analog recording of Prince such as the 1981 *Controversy* album produced on vinyl carries with it many of the same cultural indicators as his 1996 *Emancipation* work which is a digitally mastered compilat-

---

16. Poster (1990) p. 6.

15. His point has been underscored by the availability of anonymous e-mail accounts in countries such as Finland. Until recently, internet users around the world were able to use a source in Finland to obtain, in a manner of speaking, fake identities. They could then use the fake ID in sending electronic mail or posting messages on the Internet without fear of revealing their identities. See "Privacy a Hot Issue on the Internet," *Los Angeles Times* 8 September 1996.

ion produced on compact disc. However, we maintain that the configuration of language and the relations it produces are substantially altered through this new "mode of information" as is the case with the types of encounters between people on cyberspace chat rooms as opposed to face-to-face meetings in coffee houses, bars or libraries. Moreover, the types of indicators which are threatened or even removed in the new technologies are more often those which constrain women and racial minorities, especially those markers which identify one's sex, race, age, or geographical background as well as qualities of aesthetic appearance which have largely been relegated to the domain of women. Thus, where analog recordings and more traditional speech and writing practices rely on the reproduction of connotative meanings embedded in cultural contexts, digital recordings and electronic communications lose much of this material by imposing a binary reduction of information into a language of zeros and ones.

In addition to these changes, digital encodings and electronic manipulation of language obstruct the temporal and spatial limits of communication. Specifically, they disrupt the organizing power of distance among more traditional communications media by allowing the user to record/listen and send/receive information at their own pace as well as when they want and where they want. In other words, because of these new technologies "reproduction of information is exact, transmission is instantaneous, storage is permanent and retrieval is effortless,"[16] resulting in a challenge to the figurative structuring powers of time and space.

The effect of this loss of key cultural signifiers or the disruption of the relationship between referent and sign/signifier is that new informational technologies threaten the prominence of the autonomous rational masculinized subject as well as the existence of traditional hierarchies inscribed within print and spoken language systems. To be clear, this disruption of a masculinized subject is not merely the effect of more women going on line. While recent statistics on internet users compiled by Nielsen and Commercenet, an Internet industry consortium, reported that the number of women users increased from 33% in August 1995 to 40% in April 1996, the focus on increased participation (or even increased outlets for women in cyberspace) does not address more fundamental questions about the configuration of racial and/or gendered categories that we have

16. Poster (1990) p. 72.

outlined in this article.[17] In addition, because the new language systems also interrupt the space/time coordinates that help fix the language of everyday life they also open up the possibility for challenges to the control of information.

Thus, communication is in the process of becoming more open to new interpretations based on the space of creation, that is cyberspace. In this space users often choose not to follow rules of grammar and punctuation, thus modifying the language of communication. Likewise, the new codes developed also welcome the use of symbols in lieu of words. The colon no longer denotes merely a punctuation mark, but rather it signifies eyes on a face, happy or sad. Cyber-communication also augments logocentric notions of communication contesting the boundaries of written speech. In this context, the attention given to presentation, by way of deliberate (and even unconscious) misspellings and mispronunciations, allows the messenger to become as important as the formal message itself. Put simply, this new language challenges linguistic forms of privileging that exist outside of cyberspace. Hence, the words and symbols transform themselves into "action, a resistance" in a distinctive, empowering way.[18] Therefore, hooks is correct in warning that language is a site of struggle, yet within the realm of cyberspace language changes to cover all cybercommunication from electronic mail, listservs and web sites.[19]

In addition to these effects, women's "narrative" is given a renewed sense of legitimacy by virtue of computer communications. Specifically, Madan Sarap alludes to the ways in which women's narratives or stories have not been perceived as scholarship according to mainstream society, and yet the "text" of computer conversations often involves streams of consciousness, inductive reasoning, and the use of lived experience as evidence, thereby validating a type of communication that has generally been defined as "feminine."[20] Therefore cyberspace contains a different structural and cultural ethos for women's participation.

Needless to say, while this challenge to traditional forms of social control opens the door for more democratic cultural and

17. "The Net May Snare Us All" *Los Angeles Times* 8 September 1996.

18. bell hooks (1990) *Yearning: Race, Gender, and Cultural Politics* (Boston, South End Press) p. 147.

19. bell hooks (1990) p. 145.

20. Madan Sarap (1993) *Post-Structuralism and Postmodernism* (Athens, University of Georgia Press).

political trends, the conditions provided by these new language systems are in no way utterly free from constraints of power, ownership and control. In the following section we will build on the discussion of new language systems to describe the challenge that has been issued to the traditional subject position and the alternate identities that are constructed in its place. In particular, we will focus on the depersonalization of the text, the dispersal and multiplication of subject positions and the reconstruction of semi-anonymous subjects.

Deconstructing Identity (and Reconstructing Subjects)

While research regarding the structure of language in new technologies is worthy of study in itself, it is also significant because it points to more dramatic changes that have occurred in the construction and meaning of our own subject positions. Recent studies detail the types of physical changes caused to our bodies through consistent contact with computer terminals. These changes range from muscle and bone damage in the form of carpal tunnel syndrome and blurred visions, to the actual restructuring of DNA through low levels of radiation.[21] However, and more importantly, what the new communications systems contribute and ultimately call into question is the very shape of our subjectivity: its position in the world, its perspective on that world and its location in the world.

In particular, one of the most instrumental qualities of the new technologies for women and feminist activists comes in the challenge to the traditional Western subjects which are understood primarily as autonomous, rational, and masculine, and the ensuing possibilities that are opened up for women constructing new feminist identities. Specifically, the traditional autonomous male ego is interrogated and eventually displaced in the language of these new communications by virtue of its separation from an essential self/referent, the removal of traditional markers of cultural context and identity, and the dislocation of subject positions and hierarchies which had been fixed in part by the figurative boundaries of space and time.

Beginning with the condition of the autonomous male ego who comes to dominate his world through rationality, we see that in the space of the internet these subjects have been depersonalized, decentered, multiplied, and reconstructed.

21. Paul Brodeur "Annals of Radiation: The Hazards of Electromagnetic Fields, III-Video Display Terminals" *New Yorker* June 26, 1989, p. 39.

Autonomy is removed through the depersonalization of the text. That is, by virtue of the loss of traditional cultural markers that gave meaning to one's own personality, the subjects of electronic communications become collections of words and images.

While internet users themselves cannot be divorced from their real life contexts and the sensibilities derived from these contexts informs the identities they take on in cyberspace, the only information we have to interpret those identities is derived from the language and form of their e-mail messages or Web pages. Although this language is produced from a very specific context, information about this context is not readily available to the online community and this itself produces a condition in which no inherent link can be made to the language of the user in virtual reality and an essential self in real life. In addition, unlike print media which requires a meditative state of isolation and the use of one's own cognitive resources thereby re-enforcing the bounds of individuality, logging on to the internet necessarily connects individuals to a nexus of other users.

In a similar manner, the subjects of electronic communications are effectively emasculated by the removal of gender cues from the text. As Mark Poster commented, "for the first time individuals engage in telecommunications with other individuals without considerations that derive from... their voice, their *sex*, or many of the markings of their personal history."[22] As such, the space of electronic communications becomes neither distinctively masculine, nor feminine, but anonymous; thereby allowing for the construction of imaginary selves. The specificity of gender is transformed via electronic communication especially if a woman chooses not to name her sex in "chat rooms" specific to education, politics or popular culture. In the space of the internet, writing subjects are free to construct their identities in the manner of their choosing, leading to a variety of outcomes such as women logging on as men, or individuals assuming the identity of some larger public figure (i.e. actors or elected officials). In essence then, electronic communications dematerializes the "text" and specifically de-genders communication within its "text" by removing traditional gender cues.

However, the loss of autonomy and masculinity does not suggest that we are left with simply a free-floating collective of signifiers without referents. In fact, we argue that conversation in these new technologies is still bound by rules of reason and

22. Poster (1989) p. 117, emphasis added. The Mode of Information: Poststructuralism and Social Context (Chicago: University of Chicago Press).

rationality. However, unlike more traditional forms of print and speech media, the assumption of a universal or grounded rationality is unfounded within these communications. That is, especially within the World Wide Web, cultural trends and competing logics are allowed to flourish without the imposition of a universally accepted norm of rationality. This practice results in the proliferation of subcultures and alternate groups through newsgroups or World Wide Web sites that have their own internal logic which may (and often does) contradict or conflict with the proposed logic of other sites, such as the types of feminism practiced on the home pages of The Eagle Forum, NOW and the Guerrilla Girls.[23]

For example, in "Feminist Assault on Reasonableness" a news-letter presented in *The Phyllis Schlafly Report*, Schlafly attacks the increase of feminists within the legal field. Specifically, she explains that feminist lawyers are trying, "to establish a license for women to kill their allegedly abusive spouses," and she continues to discredit violence against women. In contrast, NOW covers the same issues in such a manner that women's rights are under attack and require protection. NOW's mission statement declares that the courts and government should ensure women's equal rights. An even more opposing opinion is represented by the Guerrilla Girls – a self proclaimed conscience of the art world, composed of a contingent of women artists. The group dons guerrilla masks in order to "focus on the issues and not particular personalities." Their use of posters and other projects powerfully criticizes sexism in a grass-roots style. Thus, while each of these sites or groups actively support women in their own specific manners (either by protecting traditional values of womanhood or by protecting women from those traditional values), together they represent opposing views of women's "place" in society.

Finally, as was mentioned earlier, within the space of the new technologies traditional subjects are also dislodged from their locations both temporally and spatially. Essentially, distance no longer becomes an obstacle as subjects are able to exchange information in a manner that is instantaneous. Thanks to teleconferencing, we no longer need to be in the same place at the same time in order to exchange messages in group situations. Individuals who participate in discussion groups or "chat rooms" are able to access all types of information when and where they

23. The Eagle Forum at http://www.basenet.net/~eagle.eagle.html
NOW at http://www.now.org/
Guerrilla Girls at http://www.voyagerco.com/gg/gg.html

choose. The result of this disjunction of familiar time/space configurations is that information – and by extension the language which constructs and represents subjects in these new technologies – is easily multiplied, reproduced, and dispersed leaving us to believe that no authentic "self" can occur within cyberspace. In addition, the flexibility of time/space in electronic communications not only challenges the autonomy of traditional subjects but also facilitates collective authorship, thereby allowing women to make linkages to other useful sites and promulgate information to users.

Nevertheless, to suggest that new technologies have killed all forms of subjectivity in addition to the autonomous masculine ego is an exaggeration. New subjectivities do emerge on the internet, subjects which are semi-anonymous and imaginary. Current research has also demonstrated that certain social divisions are replicated online and actually reinscribe users in repressive social orders. However, our intent is not to examine the replication of social stratification in cyberspace as much as it is to examine the language and usage of the new technologies and the extent to which the possibility for constructing alternative subjects appears.

Looking specifically at the case of women, we see that the condition of anonymity provides the opportunity to explore various forms of identity that would be difficult to express in other contexts. Whereas markers such as gender and race had once served to inscribe and fix women within fairly sedentary hierarchies, in the new information systems other qualities such as handle names and typing speed are more salient qualities in identifying users. Thus, the idealized notions of women's identity are displaced and positively receptive to multiple definitions. Chela Sandoval, in "Cyborg Feminism and the Methodology of the Oppressed," refers to a new knowledge "the differential mode of oppositional consciousness, a cyberconsciousness."[24] "Cyberconsciousness" is similar to the Mestiza consciousness, Womanism, Third World Feminism, Standpoint Feminism, Queer Theory and other names used to designate oppositional feminist theories in so much as it presents a form of activism that is conscious of the material, cultural and social boundaries that affect women but which also interrogates the very categories of maleness and femaleness.

---

24. Chela Sandoval "Cyborg Feminism and the Methodology of the Oppressed" in *The Cyborg Handbook* Chris Hables Gray (ed) (New York, Routledge).

For women, this means a new "space" for communication, representation, and, of course, self-determination. Women as subjects, not objects, have the opportunity to make information, disseminate it and then interpret it; thereby, increasing their active participation in a more democratic arena of communication. The often marginalized subject, woman, can utilize cyberspace as a site of creation and resistance. Specifically, women can decenter their typically proscribed subjectivity in their own manner in cyberspace. Control of these subjects in cyberspace proves a ubiquitous notion considering that sites can change daily or even within minutes, especially considering that until recently regulation was not a threat to cybercommunication.

Linguistic feminism, as explained by Kathy E. Ferguson, supports challenging "the dimensions of the speaking subject by calling upon the energies, semiotics and deconstruction, a deliberately unfocused invocation of multiple sides of meaning in identities, bodies and pleasures."[25] Thus, for the cyberuser the reading and writing subject contests identities within the fiberoptics of cybercommunication by maintaining new subject-ivities with the death of the traditional subject. Linguistic feminism practiced in cybercommunication facilitates the reconstruction of identities, which in turn promotes cyberspace as an outlet of release and communication, in some cases where such freedom never existed.

Ultimately, we feel that the key contribution which the new technologies and their attendant language structures contribute to women's activism and mentoring is the paths for resisting essentialized understandings of women's identity. By allowing women (and all users) an anonymous space in which to construct their identities, alter their identities, and simultaneously multiply their identities, the internet challenges the discursive power of traditional masculinized subjects as well as the dominating tendencies of some feminists whose discursive practices inscribe women within essentialized norms of "womanhood" or "activism."[26]

In addition, while the internet affords women opportunities to contest forms of discourse through language, it has also been effective at undermining the gatekeeping role of traditional print media and opening up new opportunities for the publication and dissemination of women's work. Feminist organizations

25. Kathy E. Ferguson (1993) *The Man Question: Visions of Subjectivity in Feminist Theory* (Berkeley, University of California Press) p. 121.
28. Fraser and Nicholson (1989).

which have made use of these new media in disseminating information include Ms. Net (the online version of Ms. Magazine), the Center for American Women and Politics (CAWP), and Geekgirl ("the worlds first cyberfeminist zine").[27]

However, the opportunities afforded by the anonymity of cyberspace are not without costs. While these new spaces challenge essentialisms and provide avenues for dissemination of information not previously available, they also bring into question all claims to truth, authenticity, authorship and ownership. In short, it becomes impossible for women to claim a "place of their own"[28] in cyberspace because no claims to a true woman's space can be validated. We will discuss the implications of these limitations as well as others in our final section; however, first we feel it is necessary to detail how the new subject positions of the internet help reconfigure effective and useful political strategies for women.

Playing with Politics

The new language systems and the altered sense of subjectivity which the new electronic communications bring also suggest a different type of politics in cyberspace. Possibly one of the most obvious manifestations of these politics are revealed in the manner which traditional legal systems deal with cyberspace. We mentioned earlier how the federal government attempted to regulate databases and the information gathered within them but failed in part because of misconceptions on the part of Congressional legislators. The same misapplication of law has occurred in cases of copyright infringement and privacy. Both types of law attempt to protect the private ownership of some material commodities either by securing some form of written

27. Ms. Net at http://www.womweb.com/msnet.htm
Center for American Women and Politics (CAWP) at
http://www.rci.rutgers.edu/~cawp/
Geekgirl at http://www.geekgirl.com.au
We would like to thank our anonymous reviewer at *New Political Science* for suggesting the latter addition to our article.

28. Microsoft has attempted to capitalize on the increased number of women logging on to the internet, and the desires of some to create authentic spaces for women's expression by printing an ad in a recent issue of *Vanity Fair* magazine which stated: "The Microsoft Network thinks Virginia Wolf was right: WOMEN need a room of their own." (*Vanity Fair* April 1997). The promotion is intended to entice female subscribers to an online chat room dedicated to women; however, as we stated before the ability of women to create such viable spaces on the internet are mitigated by the anonymity of cyberusers and the nature of cyberspace language which obscures authentication.

communications, as in the case of copyrights, or by protecting a private space from intrusions. Yet, when we speak of the information and the space which users inhabit in the new technologies we see the obvious complications that such laws bring. Copyright laws are made obsolete by the ease and speed with which information on the internet can be accessed, downloaded, and copied. In addition, ownership of private space means little in cyberspace as was evidenced in November 1988, when it was reported that ARPAnet, a web of military, corporate, and university computers, was infected by a computer virus. Despite the fact that ARPAnet was temporally shut down and that the FBI was called into investigate the incident, no known crime was committed.[29] As most internet users now know, this does not mean that the internet is virtually free from all dominating tendencies (especially forms of state control), but it does suggest that the more traditional cultural, legal, and political practices drawn from print and speech media do not readily apply to the new technologies. However, despite the implications of these legal politics, we ultimately feel that more impressive changes in the field of politics come from the new social situations that are formed in cyberspace. Clearly, cyberspace is a new realm for resistance, cultural criticism and dialogue. The democratic nature of cyberspace helps instill the politics of increased participation, since no one voice is "louder" than another in communication between users.[30] The ontology of cyberspace becomes one located at the center and margins of political communication, fixed only to the extent that one uses the technology. Therefore, in cyberspace candidates can attempt to "Get out the Vote," complain about lack of funding, or as we saw in 1996, Web users can stage a global blackout in defense of cyberspeech. Cybercommunication also promises feminist activists an opportunity to intensify their movement with more efficient ways of disseminating information quickly and globally. Information about protests, meetings, books,

29. By now most of us are at least vaguely familiar with the most recent attempts to control internet activities through passage of the 1996 Communications Decency Act. However, shortly after the passage of the bill a federal appeals court in Pennsylvania declared the law unconstitutional and in June 1997, the Supreme Court upheld the Pennsylvania court's ruling. In their opinion, the court stated that "the desire to protect children [from pornography on the internet] does not justify an unnecessarily broad suppression of speech addressed to adults." See Jube Shive Jr., David G. Savage, and Elizabeth Shogren "Law Curbing Indecency on Internet Overturned" *Los Angeles Times* 27 June 1997.

30. For further discussion, see Michelle Kendrick (1996) "Cyberspace and the Technological Real" in Robert Markley (ed) *Virtual Realities and Their Discontents* (Baltimore, Johns Hopkins University Press).

and groups are readily available at the user's fingertips. Users can forward important messages or addresses to all of their colleagues, friends and family members, multiplying the reach of the information.

Presumably, the influence of these new technologies on women's lives in the political and personal context is immeasurable. For the techno savvy, and not so savvy, this has meant surfing the web, looking for sites of interest and communicating with others. For some women, though, cyberspace has become a treasured tool of communication and source of information. We can participate in conversations or merely read them with people from any city across the country or in other countries. Women can sign up on various listservs in order to obtain information regarding political issues, such as current party platform stances, abortion rights, family care or job announcements in specific disciplines. Women who use the web can also transform their page or bookmarks into their own cyberdatabases of information. Many sites serve as information clearinghouses by and for women, such as Femina, Virtual Sisterhood, CLNET'S Chicana Studies, and,TAP: Ada Project.[31] Others, like Geekgirl,[32] serve as a cultural and educational sites for women or grrls covering virtually every imaginable topic.

Donna Haraway, in her celebrated article "A Manifesto for Cyborgs," explained that cyborg writing demonstrates survival power for the writer.[33] In the same way, the user in cyberspace utilizes cybercommunication, as a political device to communicate and educate, therefore reconstructing social realities. Historically, the conception of the cyborg or other cybernetic technological contraptions appear "at moments of radical social and cultural change."[34] We are at the cusp of an era where one medium, cyberspace, holds transformative ramifications for popular

31. Femina at http://femina.cybergrrl.com/
Virtual Sisterhood at http://www.igc.apc.org/vsister/vsister.html
CLNET'S Chicana Studies at
http://latino.sscnet.ucla.edu/women/womenHP.html
TAP: Ada Project at http://www.cs.yale.edu/homes/tap/tap.html

32. Geekgirl at http://www.next.com.au/spyfood/geekgirl/

33. Donna Haraway (1990) "A Manifesto for Cyborgs: Science, Technology, and Socialist Feminism in the 1980s" in *Feminism/Postmodernism* p. 217. The word "cyborg" was coined by Manfred E. Clynes in "Cyborgs and Space" co-authored by Nathan S. Kline in 1970, in a solicited article by *Astronautics;* however they refused to publish the article. A revised version of the article was recently published as, "Cyborg II; Sentic Space Travel" in Chris Hables Gray (ed) (1995) *The Cyborg Handbook* (New York, Routledge).

34. Jennifer González (1995) "Envisioning Cyborg Bodies; Notes from Current Research" in *The Cyborg Handbook* (New York, Routledge).

culture, science, oppositional politics and implicitly every imaginable topic opening the doors to a new era of politics. Daily we travel across new cyberterritory that influences the paradigm of knowledge and communication. This new mode of commun-ication repoliticizes what constitutes communication and representation for women in politics.

Limitations

Despite the encouraging prospects presented to women through developments in cyberspace communications, there are a number of substantial limitations which render its benefits somewhat suspect. One problem with computer research concerns contem-porary cyberspace sources. One can readily find texts that are written primarily by ancient (i.e. Plato, Aristotle), early modern (i.e. Hegel, Kant), and modern philosophers (i.e. Marx, Gramsci),[35] however, it is much more difficult to obtain texts from such contemporary feminist authors such as Carole Pateman and Nancy Hirschmann.[36] At the same time, there are some electronic journals such as *Ctheory*, [37] that provide access to recent articles.

As we mentioned earlier, cyberspace also changes the publishing field for all users, regardless of academic standing, by allowing all participants the potential to publish articles, poems, recipes and the like. However, this notion thoroughly alters our understandings of authorship, because authorship is problem-atized in cyberspace. We contend that one of the primary limitations to the new technologies is the curtailment of authorization and the command of information that is associated with it. In essence, by deconstructing the presence of authority as necessarily autonomous, rational, and masculine, the language systems of these communications disrupt the potential for users to claim authority over a concept. What this means to feminists participating on the internet or feminist activists interested in mentoring women in political science, is that the legitimacy of information we submit or exchange in newsgroups, "listservs,"

35. A useful site for accessing texts by these authors and others is available through ALEX, a catalogue of electronic texts on the internet at http://apsa.trenton.edu.70/11/PolThe

36. By pointing out the difficulties involved in acquiring information from feminist authors we do not mean to suggest that there is no research available in this field on the web. In fact, we were able to find "texts" written by Mary Wollstonecraft and Charlotte Perkins Gilman as well as excerpts of articles from bell hooks, Andrea Dworkin, and Catharine MacKinnon.

37. *CTheory* at http://www.ctheory.com/

or web sites is threatened. As an example of this, various women's newsgroups such as Systers, Women in Telecommunications, and Women on the Well have documented the presence of "imposters" on the lists, such as men claiming to be women, who listen in on discussions and use the forum as a chance to vent their anti-women/anti-feminist critiques by "flaming" at the women in the group.[38]

The challenges presented to women's empowerment by virtue of the loss of authority, authenticity, and ownership are further complicated by the fragmentation of identities in cyberspace. The destablization and multiplication of subjects in electronic communications leads to a condition where it becomes difficult to privilege one form of identity over any other. For women and people of color, this condition can compromise the experiences of oppression in a larger context by permitting every manifestation of identity, from the subculture of novelty cars to the collective histories of resisting sexism, to carry equal weight.

Ultimately, we feel that all the benefits and obstacles presented to women's activism in the new technologies are somewhat muted by the overarching limitations of cyberspace imposed by its own spatial boundaries. Both the possibilities for constructing more democratic public communications and the challenges to it are confined to the space of the new information system and don't readily speak to the lives we live outside of cyberspace. Thus, one of the challenges which we offer to readers of this paper is to consider how the gains and benefits of the new information systems can be applied in our daily practices and struggles.

Conclusion

Borrowing from poststructuralism and looking specifically at the condition of women in politics, we have attempted to spell out some of the theoretical implications of new information technologies, particularly the manner in which they construct new language systems, new subject positions, and ultimately new political practices. However, in detailing the role played by these systems in the lives of women, we do not mean to suggest that electronic communications have created a fully anonymous democratic space, or forms of "distortion free communication," where all users can engage in complete identity reconstruction

38. Natalie Engler "A Woman's Place in Cyberspace" *Fast Company* Premiere Issue.

free from hierarchies or dominating tendencies. In fact, we have tried to point out that while these new language systems and technologies may have little direct political impact at this time, they do open the doors to a more substantial critique of language and domination and reconfigure strategies of resistance.

And yet, despite our attempts to analyze some of the theoretical explanations for these new technologies and how they speak to women in particular, we also realize that a more thorough examination must consider both internal and external dimensions of domination. That is, outside of the language that is constructed and communicated through these new technologies there also lie issues of access and ownership. Thus, we present the arguments in this paper as a beginning for more extensive research into the productions of new technologies generally, and the effects they have on the lives of women in particular.

Douglas Kellner
University of California Los Angeles

Intellectuals, the New Public Spheres, and Techno-Politics

Abstract: This article makes a distinction between those intellectuals who are functional to the State, and those who adopt a critical-oppositional stance. I examine the concept of oppositional intellectual, and argue that while technology has long been of marginal importance to intellectual activity, media literacy and the capacity to utilize new technologies has now -at the end of the twentieth century- become of central importance. I review political struggles conducted over and through such technologies as community radio, public access television and the Internet. My central theme is that the new technologies of communication can be used equally well by right and left, and that progressive intellectuals must develop skills in the new technologies if they are to participate effectively in the politics of the twenty-first century.

The category of the intellectual, like everything else these days, is highly contested and up for grabs. Zygmunt Bauman contrasts *intellectuals as legislators,* who wish to legislate universal values (usually in the service of state institutions), with *intellectuals as interpreters,* who merely interpret texts, public events, and other artifacts, deploying their specialized knowledge to explain or interpret things for publics.[1] He claims that there has been a shift from modern intellectuals as legislators of universal values, who legitimated the new modern social order, to postmodern intellectuals as interpreters of social meanings, and thus theorizes a de-politicalization of the role of intellectuals in social life.

In contrast, I want to make a distinction between *functional intellectuals,* who serve to reproduce and legitimate the values of existing societies, and *critical-oppositional intellectuals* who oppose the existing order.

Functional intellectuals were traditionally the classical ideologues, whereas today they tend to be functionaries of parties or interest groups, or mere technicians who devise more efficient means to obtain certain ends, or who apply their skills to increase

---

1. Zygmunt Bauman (1987) *Legislators and Interpreters: Or Modernity. Postmodernitv, and Intellectuals* (Oxford: Polity Press) and (1992) *Intimations of Postmodernity* (New York and London: Routledge).

technical knowledge in various specialized domains (medicine, physics, history, etc.), without questioning the ends, goals, or values that they are serving, or the social utility or disutility of their activities. Functional intellectuals are thus servants of existing societies; they are specialists in legitimation and technical knowledge.

Critical intellectuals were traditionally those who utilized their skills of speaking and writing to denounce injustices and abuses of power, and to fight for truth, justice, progress, and other universal values. Sometimes oppositional intellectuals voice their criticisms in the name of existing values which they claim are being violated (i.e. truth, rights, rule by law, justice, etc.); and sometimes they voice criticisms in the name of values or ideas which are said to express higher potentialities of the existing order (ie. participatory democracy, socialism, genuine equality for women and blacks, ecological restoration, etc.). In the words of Jean-Paul Sartre, "the duty of the intellectual is to denounce injustice wherever it occurs."[2] For Sartre, the domain of the critical intellectual is to write and speak within the public sphere, denouncing oppression and fighting for human freedom and emancipation. On this model, a critical intellectual's task is to bear witness, to analyze, to expose, and to criticize a wide range of social evils. The sphere and arena of the critical/oppositional intellectual is the word, and his or her function is to describe and denounce injustice wherever it may occur.

In the following reflections, I want to discuss some challenges from postmodern theory to the classical conceptions of the critical-oppositional intellectual and examine some of the ways that the new technologies and new public spheres offer possibilities for democratic discussion and intervention. Consequently, I will also discuss some changes in the concept of the public sphere and how new technologies and new spheres of public debate and conflict suggest some new possibilities for redefining intellectuals in the present era.

---

2. It has not been generally noted that the problematic of defining the nature and function of the intellectual was a major theme of Sartre's philosophy, or that he reformulated his concept of the committed intellectual in the 1970s, during his last decade of political and intellectual activity. For some examples of his discourse on intellectuals, see Sartre 1962, 1970, 1974, and 1975 and the discussions in Kellner "The Latest Sartre," Telos 22 (Winter 1974-5) pp. 188-201 and Kellner (1995b) "Intellectuals and New Technologies" in Media, Culture & Society 17 pp. 427-448.

The Public Sphere and the Intellectual

Democracy involves a separation of powers and popular participation in governmental affairs. During the era of the Enlightenment and 18th century democratic revolutions, public spheres emerged where individuals could discuss and debate issues of common concern.[3] The public sphere was also a site where criticism of the state and existing society could circulate. The institutions and spaces of the 18th century democratic public sphere included newspapers, journals, and a press independent from state ownership and control, coffee houses where individuals read newspapers and engaged in political discussion, literary salons where ideas and criticism were produced, and public assemblies which were the sites of public oratory and debate.

Bourgeois societies split, of course, across class lines and different class factions produced different political parties, organizations, public spaces, and ideologies with each class attracting specialists in words and writing known as intellectuals. Oppressed groups developed their own insurgent intellectuals, ranging from representatives of working class organizations, to women like Mary Wollstonecraft fighting for women's rights, to leaders of oppressed groups of color, ethnicity, sexual preference, and so on. Insurgent intellectuals attacked oppression and promoted action that would address the causes of subjugation, linking thought to action, theory to practice. Thus, during the 19th century, the working class developed its own oppositional public spheres in union halls, party cells and meeting places, saloons, and institutions of working class culture. With the rise of Social Democracy and other working class movements in Europe and the United States, an alternative press, radical cultural organizations, and the spaces of the strike, sit-in, and political insurrection emerged as sites of an oppositional public sphere.

At the same time, intellectuals in modern societies were conflicted beings with contradictory social functions. The classical critical intellectual – represented by figures like the French Enlightenment ideologues, Thomas Paine, Mary Wollstonecraft, and later figures like Heine, Marx, Hugo, Dreyfus, Du Bois, Sartre, and Marcuse – was to speak out against injustice and oppression and to fight for justice, equality, and the other values of the Enlightenment. (Indeed, the Enlightenment itself represents one of the most successful products of the critical individual, a

3. Jurgen Habermas (1989) *The Public Sphere* (Cambridge, Mass.: The MIT Press).

discourse and movement which assigns intellectuals key social functions). And yet conservative intellectuals attacked the Enlightenment, and its prodigy the French Revolution, and produced discourses that legitimated every conceivable form of oppression from class to race, gender, and ethnic domination.

Against the Enlightenment and Sartre, Michel Foucault complained that Sartre's vision of the intellectual represented an ideal of the traditional intellectual, one who fought for universal values but assumed the task of speaking for humanity. Against such an exalted, and in his view exaggerated conception, Foucault argued for a conception of the *specific intellectual* who intervened on the side of the oppressed in specific issues, not claiming to speak for the oppressed, but intervening as an intellectual in specific issues and debates.

Foucault's conception of the specific intellectual has been echoed by a turn in postmodern politics toward new social movements and the hope that they can replace the state and parties as the fulcrum for contemporary politics. For writers like Laclau & Mouffe,[4] power is diffuse and local and not merely to be found in macroinstitutions like the workplace, the state, or patriarchy. In their view, a macro-politics that goes after big institutions like the state or capital has been replaced by a micropolitics, with specific intellectuals intervening in spheres like the university, the prison, the hospital, or for the rights of specific oppressed groups like sexual or ethnic minorities. Global and national politics and theories are rejected in favor of more local micropolitics, and the discourse and function of intellectuals is seen as more specific, provisional, and modest than in modern theory and politics, subordinate to local struggles rather than more ambitious projects of emancipation and social transformation.

In my view, such a binary distinction between macro and micro theory and politics is problematic, as are any absolutist commitments to either modern or postmodern theory *tout court..*[5] It is clear from the events of 1989 surrounding the collapse of communism that the popular offensives against oppressive

4. Ernesto Laclau and Chantal Mouffe (1985) *Hegemony and Socialist Strategy* (London: Verse Books).

5. On the variety of, often conflicting, postmodern politics, see the surveys in Steven Best and Douglas Kellner (1991) *Postmodern Theory: Critical Interrogations* (London and New York: Macmillan and Guilford); Steven Best and Douglas Kellner(1997) *The Postmodern Turn.* (New York: Guilford Press) and *The Postmodern Adventure* (New York: Guilford Press). Also Hans Bertens (1995) *The Idea of the Postmodern* (London and New York: Routledge).

communist power combined micro and macropolitics; moving from local and specific struggles rooted in union halls, universities, churches, and small groups to mass demonstrations forcing democratic reforms, and even to classical mass insurrection aiming at the overthrow of the existing order, as in Romania. In these struggles, intellectuals played a variety of roles and deployed a diversity of discourses, ranging from the local and specific to the national and general.

Thus, whereas I would argue that postmodern theory contains important criticism of some of the illusions and ideologies of the traditional modern intellectual, it goes too far in rejecting the classical role of the critical intellectual. Moreover, I shall suggest that aspects of the modern conception of the critical and oppositional intellectual remain useful. I would, in fact, reject the particular/universal dichotomy in favor of developing a normative concept of the critical public intellectual. The public intellectual – on this conception – intervenes in the public sphere, fights against lies, oppression, and injustice and fights for rights, freedom, and democracy á la Sartre's committed intellectual. But a democratic public intellectual on my conception does not speak for others, does not abrogate or monopolize the function of speaking the truth, but simply participates in discussion and debate, defending specific ideas, values, or norms or principle that may be particular or universal. However, if they are universal, they are like human rights – they are contextual, provisional, normative and general, and not valid for all time. Indeed, rights are products of social struggles and are thus social constructs and not innate or natural entities (as the classical natural rights theorists maintained). Nevertheless, rights can be generalized, extended, and can take universal forms – as with, for instance, the UN charter of Human Rights which holds that certain rights are valid for all individuals, at least in this world, at this point in time.

Consequently, one does not need all of the baggage of the universal intellectual to maintain a conception of a public or democratic intellectual in the present era. Intellectuals may well seek to occupy a higher ground than particularistic interests, a common ground seeking public interests and goods. Intellectuals should not abrogate the right to speak for all, but they should be aware that they are speaking from a determinate position with its own biases and limitations. Moreover, intellectuals should learn to get out of their particular frame of reference for more general ones, as well as to be able to take the position of the other, to empathize with more marginal and oppressed groups, to learn from them, and to support their struggles. To perpetually criticize oneself, to develop the capacity for self-reflection and critique as well as self-expression is thus part of the duty of the democratic intellectual.

New Technologies. New Public Spheres, and New Intellectuals

In the following discussion, I will argue that although the public intellectual should assume new functions and activities today, the critical capacities and vision of the classical critical intellectual are still relevant. Thus I suggest building on models of the past, rather than simply throwing them over, as in some types of postmodern theory. First and foremost, I want to suggest that rethinking the intellectual and the public sphere today requires rethinking the relationship between intellectuals and technology.

In a certain sense, there was no important connection between the classical intellectual and technology. To be sure, intellectuals (especially scientific scholars like Leonardo de Vinci, Galileo, or Darwin) deployed technologies, and entire groups like the British Royal Society were concerned with technologies and were indeed often inventors themselves. Some intellectuals used printing presses and were themselves printers, and many, though not all, of the major intellectuals of the 20th century probably used a typewriter – though I personally know of no major studies of the relationship between the typewriter and intellectuals. Yet a classical intellectual did not have to intrinsically deploy any specific technology and there was thus no intimate connection between intellectuals and technology.

However, I want to argue that in the contemporary high-tech societies there is emerging a significant expansion and redefinition of the public sphere, and that these developments, connected primarily with media and computer technologies, require a reformulation and expansion of the concept of critical or committed intellectual, as well as a redefinition of the public intellectual. Earlier in the century, John Dewey envisaged developing a newspaper that would convey "thought news," bringing all the latest ideas in science, technology, and the intellectual world to a general public, which would also promote democracy.[6] In addition, Bertolt Brecht and Waiter Benjamin saw

6. See the discussion of this project in Daniel Czitron (1982) *Media and the American*

the revolutionary potential of new technologies like film and radio and urged radical intellectuals to seize these new forces of production, to "refunction" them, and to turn them into instruments to democratize and revolutionize society. Sartre too worked on radio and television series and insisted that "committed writers must get into these relay station arts of the movies and radio."[7]

Previously, radio, television, and the other electronic media of communication tended to be closed to critical and oppositional voices both in systems controlled by the state and in private corporations. However, technologies like public access television and community radio are open to intervention and use by critical intellectuals. For some years now, I have been urging progressives to make use of new broadcast media and have been involved in a public access television program in Austin, Texas. Since 1979 we have produced over 600 programs and won the George Stoney Award for public affairs television.[8] My argument was that radio, television, and other electronic modes of communication were creating new public spheres of debate, discussion, and information and that intellectuals who wanted to engage the public, to be where the people were at, and who thus wanted to intervene in the public affairs of their society, should make use of these new media technologies and institutions, and develop new communication politics and new media projects.

One can argue that the hegemony of Reagan and the Right in the United States in 1980s was related to the Right's effective mobilization of conservative intellectuals and their use of television, radio, fax and computer communication, direct mailings, telephones, and other sophisticated political uses of new technologies, as well as more traditional print media. Furthermore, one could argue that Clinton's victory over Bush in 1992, and the surprising success of the Perot campaign, were both related to effective uses of communication technologies. The right-wing Republican success in the 1994 Congressional elections

Mind: From Morse to McLuhan (Chapel Hill: University of North Carolina Press) p. 104.

7. Jean-Paul Sartre (1974) The Writings of Jean-Paul Sartre   Michel Contat and Michel Rybalka (eds) (Evanston, Northwestern University Press) p. 177. For discussion of his Les temps moderne radio series, see pp. 177-180.

8. Douglas Kellner (1979) "TV, Ideology, and Emancipatory Popular Culture," Socialist Review 45 (May-June, 1979) pp. 13-53; (1985) "Public Access Television: Alternative Views" Radical Science Journal 16, Making Waves, pp. 79-92: (1990) Television and the Crisis of Democracy (Boulder, Col: Westview); and (1992) The Persian Gulf TV War (Boulder, Col: Westview).

can also be related to their use of talk radio, computer bulletin boards, and other technologies. It is generally acknowledged that the Clinton administration deployed more effective communications politics in the 1996 election than the Dole campaign. Thus, effective communication politics are now essential to political success in national and local conflicts and often which side has the most effective politics of communication wins the struggle in question.

Consequently, I would argue that effective use of technology is essential in contemporary politics. First broadcast media like radio and television, and now computers, have produced new public spheres and spaces for information, debate, and participation that contain both the potential to invigorate democracy and to increase the dissemination of critical and progressive ideas – as well as new possibilities for manipulation, social control, and the promotion of conservative positions. But participation in these new public spheres computer bulletin boards and discussion groups, talk radio and television, and the emerging sphere of what I call cyberspace democracy require critical intellectuals to gain new technical skills and to master new technologies.

I am therefore suggesting that there is thus a more intimate relationship between intellectuals and technology than in previous social configurations. To be an intellectual today involves use of the most advanced forces of production to develop and circulate ideas, to do research and involve oneself in political debate and discussion, and to intervene in the new public spheres produced by broadcasting and computing technologies. New public intellectuals should attempt to develop strategies that will use these technologies to attack domination and to promote empowerment, education, democracy, and political struggle – or whatever goals are normatively posited as desirable to attain. There is thus an intrinsic connection in this argument between the fate of intellectuals and the forces of production.

Toward a Radical Democratic Techno-Politics

A revitalization of democracy in capitalist societies will therefore require a democratic media politics. Such a politics could involve a two-fold strategy. First, there must be an attempt to democratize existing media to make them more responsive to the "public interest, convenience, and necessity." In the United States, the media watchdog group FAIR (Fairness and Accuracy in Media) has developed this alternative, criticizing mainstream media for failing to assume their democratic and journalistic responsibilities and calling for an expansion of voices and ideas within the media system. Second, oppositional media must be developed; alternatives to the mainstream, built up outside of the established media system. In my view, both strategies are necessary for the development of a democratic media politics, and it is a mistake to pursue one and neglect of the other.

Developing a radical democratic media politics thus involves continued relentless criticism of the existing media system, attempts to democratize and reform it, and the production of alternative progressive media. Democratizing our media system will require expansion of the alternative press, a revitalization of public television, an increased role for public access television, the eventual development of a public satellite system, expanded community and low-power radio, democratized computer networks, and oppositional cultural politics within every sphere of culture, ranging from music to visual to print culture.[9]

Community and Low-Power Radio

Community radio has long provided an alternative set of voices to the highly commercialized mainstream radio. Citizen-band (CB) and short-wave radio allows individuals to directly communicate with each other. Many countries have also experimented with low-power community radio, which enables groups to bring individuals out of their homes to public places to engage in discussion or communal activity. Low-power radio enables individuals to directly communicate with their neighbors through call-in telephone connections, or through discussions in nearby studios, and thus provides democratic and participatory institutions.

Low-power radio, however, is subject to quick suppression by the state, as happened in Japan which had an extensive low-power radio culture in play that was shut-down almost overnight when the state outlawed low-power broadcasting. In Brazil, by contrast, low-power radio in flourishing. In the US, there have

9. My examples in the following analysis come from my of experience in the United States, though they are to some extent generalizable, concerning the possibilities for oppositional deployment of new technologies across a broad spectrum of media practices. For my previous studies of radical media politics see Kellner (1990) and (1995b).

been some low-power radio experiments, but the government too has cracked down on these local attempts to democratize radio (most recently, shutting down black liberation radio in Illinois).

Community radio has also been curtailed by saturation of FM and AM frequencies and in most places there is simply not room for legal community radio stations. For example, during the early 1990s in Austin, Texas, a vicious battle took place between the University of Texas and a local community-based co-op radio group for the remaining FM frequency band.[10] Hence, it has been difficult to develop new radio outlets for public communication within the limited spectrum allotment, although fiber-optic community cable system and the Internet may make possible a dramatic expansion of community and alternative road which could even make possible Brecht's vision of a radio system in which every individual is a sender.

Public Access Television

Public access television has been an established venue for alternative democratic communication in the US for some decades now. The rapid expansion of public access television in the 1970s provided new possibilities for progressive individuals and groups to produce video programming that cuts against the conservative cast which dominates mainstream television. Progressive access programming is now being cablecast regularly in such places as New York, Los Angeles, Boston, Chicago, Atlanta, Madison, Urbana, New Orleans, Austin, and perhaps as many as 2,000 other towns or regions of the country. Public access television, in most cases, provides free equipment and airtime to individuals and groups who want to make their own programming. Usually, one must take a course to actually use studio and editing equipment and a few systems lease the equipment and airtime, but, for the most part, where there are public access channels, the cable systems make them available for public use and they are usually managed by an independent body, answerable to the community, and often financed by the cable system.

10. To its disgrace, the University of Texas refused to share the spectrum with the community group, despite a court order to do and community pressure to come to a rational solution, until state judge ruled that they must share the spectrum with th community group and blocked appeal. In a corporate-controlled society, in which universities too function like big corporations there are always obstacles to democratic communication which is terrain of struggle between those who want to control and restrict communication and those who wish to democratize it.

When cable television began, the Federal Communications Commission mandated in 1972 that new cable systems (and after 1977, all cable systems) in the 100 largest television markets would be required to provide channels for public access. This mandate suggested that cable systems should make available three public access channels to be used for state and local government, education, and community public access use. "Public access" was construed to mean that the cable company should make available equipment and air time so that literally anybody could make noncommercial use of the access channel, and say and do anything that they wished on a first-come, first-served basis, subject only to obscenity and libel laws and prohibitions against advertising and pitches for money. However, creating an access system also required, in many cases, setting up a local organization to manage the access channels, though in other systems the cable company itself managed the access center.

In the beginning, few, if any, cable systems made as many as three channels available, although some systems began offering one or two access channels in the early to mid1970s. The availability of access channels depended, for the most part, on the political clout of local governments and committed, and often unpaid, local groups, who had to convince cable companies (almost all of them privately owned) to make available an access channel. Here in Austin, for instance, a small group of video activists formed Austin Community Television in 1973 and began broadcasting with their own equipment through the cable system that year. Eventually, we received foundation and CETA government grants to support our activities, buy equipment, and pay regular employees salaries. A new cable contract signed in the early 1980s called for the cable company to provide $500,000 a year for access and after a difficult political struggle we were able to get at least $300,000-$400,000 a year to support Austin Community Television activities.

A 1979 Supreme Court decision, however, struck down the 1972 FCC ruling on the grounds that the FCC did not have the authority to mandate access, an authority which supposedly belongs to the US Congress. Nonetheless, cable was expanding so rapidly and becoming such a high-growth competitive industry that city governments considering cable systems were besieged by companies making lucrative offers (20 to 80 channel cable systems) and governments were able to negotiate access channels and financial support for a public access system. Consequently, public access grew significantly during the early 1980s.

Where there are operative public access systems, individuals have promising, though not sufficiently explored, possibilities to produce and broadcast their own television programs. In Austin, Texas, there have been weekly anti-nuclear programs, black and chicano series, gay programs, countercultural and anarchist programs, an atheist program, feminist and women's programs, labor programming, and a weekly progressive news magazine, *Alternative Views*, (with which I am involved) has produced over 470 hour-long programs from 1978 to the present on a wide variety of topics. We mix news reports from alternative sources with discussion, documentaries, and video-footage from alternative sources. *Paper Tiger Television* in New York combines critique of corporate media by media critics with imaginative sets, visuals, editing, and so on. A labor-oriented program in Pittsburgh, *The Mill Hunk News*, used to combine news reports of labor issues with documentary interviews with workers, music-videos, and other creative visuals; while *Labor Beat* in Chicago uses documentary footage, music, drama, and collages of images, as well as interview and talking head formats, to present alternative information.

There have been some experiments with national progressive satellite networks, although they have suffered from inadequate funding and the failure of often conservative-owned cable systems to carry progressive programming. While public access television is still in a relatively early stage of development, it contains the promise of providing a different type of alternative television. Despite obstacles to its use, public access still provides the one institution in the commercial and state broadcasting systems that is at least potentially open to progressive intervention. It is self-defeating simply to dismiss broadcast media as tools of manipulation and to think that print media are the only tools of communication and political education open to progressives. Surveys have shown that people take more seriously individuals, groups, and politics that appear on TV; thus the use of television could help progressive movements and struggles gain legitimacy and force. The Right has been making effective use of new technologies and media of communication, and for progressives to remain aloof is a luxury that we can no longer afford.

Of course, many will claim that democratic politics involves face-to-face conversation, discussion, and producing consensus. But for intelligent debate and consensus to be reached, individuals must be informed, and radio, television, and computers are

not proposing that media politics supplant all political activity and organizing, but I am arguing that a media politics should be developed to help activist groups and individuals obtain and disseminate information. In Austin, for example, the *Council for Public Media* has been working to inform activist groups how they can obtain information through new computer technologies and how they can use the press, broadcast media and other methods of communication to get their messages out.[11]

Indeed, if progressive groups and movements are to produce a genuine alternative to the Right, they must increase their mass base and circulate their struggles to more segments of the population. After all, most people get their news and information from television, and the broadcast media arguably play a decisive role in defining political realities, shaping public opinion, and determining what is or what is not to be taken seriously. If progressives want to play a role in local and national political life, they must come to terms with the realities of electronic communication and computer technologies in order to develop strategies to make use of new technologies and possibilities for intervention.

The Democratization of Computers and Information

Other possibilities for expanding a system of democratic techno-polities reside in new computer and information technologies. It appears that there will be a merger of entertainment and information centers in the homes of the future with all print media information and all visual media entertainment and information resources available for home computer/entertainment center access. But the threat (and likelihood if alternative concepts are not developed and disseminated) is that information and entertainment material will be thoroughly commodified, available only to those who can afford to pay. Consequently, it is necessary to begin devising public alternatives. To avoid corporate and government monopolization and control of information, new public information networks and centers are necessary. For

---

11. Our group published a bi-monthly media monitor assessing coveirage of important issues in local and national media. In addition, we had a telecommunications group dedicated to the use of computers for social change; an alternative media group, involved in community radio and public access television; and media theory and activism groups concerned with theorizing the role of the media, the development of oppositional media and movements, and strategies and tactics for using the media in social change. I am indebted to members of this group for ideas expressed in this study.

computers, like broadcasting, can be used for or against democracy.

Computers are a potentially democratic technology. While broadcast communication tends to be one-way and uni-directional, computer communication is often two-way, or even omni-directional.[12] Whereas TV viewing is often passive and receptive, computer involvement can be interactive and participatory. Individuals can use computers note only for word-processing but to communicate with others directly via modems which use the telephone to link individuals with each other. Modems can tap into community bulletin boards, web sites, or computer conferencing programs, and make possible a new type of public communication. For instance, many computer bulletin boards and web sites have a political debate conference where individuals can type in their opinions and other individuals can read them and if they wish respond. This constitutes a new form of public dialogue and interaction.

Computer data bases and web sites also provide essential sources of information and new technologies that tremendously facilitate information-searching and research. Mainstream data bases include *Lexis/Nexis* and *Dialogue* which contain a tremendous array of newspapers, magazines, journals, transcripts of TV programs, news conferences, congressional hearings, and newsletters. Alternative data bases include *Peacenet* which has over 600 conferences on topics of ecology, war and peace, feminism. I was able to research my book on the media and the Gulf war, for instance, because I was able to access information on various topics from a variety of sources simply by typing in key words which enabled me to discern the conflicting media versions of the Gulf war and to put in question the version being promoted by the Bush administration and Pentagon. Eventually, many of the lies and disinformation promoted by the US government in the war were thoroughly exposed by a variety of sources, accessible to computer data base searches.

But the politics of information in the future must also to see that alternative information is accessible in mainstream computer

12. But does not need to be. Call-in and talk radio and television, as well as electronic town meetings, can involve two-way communication and participatory democratic discussions. Theorists like Baudrillard who argue against television and the media on the grounds that they promote only one-way, top-down communication essentialize the media and freeze the current forms of the media into fixed configurations, covering over the fact that media can be reconstructed, refunctioned, and constantly changed.

data bases, as well as alternative ones.[13] In particular the development of the World Wide Web offers exciting possibilities. Independent and alternative groups and individuals are now creating their own web sites, making information available to people all over the world. Moreover, the Internet may be a vehicle for new forms of alternative radio, television, film, art, and every form of culture as well as information and print material. New multimedia technologies are already visible on web sites and Internet radio and television is now struggling beyond its infancy. This would greatly proliferate the range and diversity of voices and texts and would also no doubt give a new dimension to the concept of information/cultural overload. Indeed, it should be clear by now, that progressives must gain a whole new set of literacies to use and deploy the new technologies. However, in conclusion, I want to limit my focus to new technologies and techno-politics of the present day.

Techno-Politics and Political Struggle

Since the new technologies are dramatically transforming every sphere of life, the key challenge today is how to theorize this great transformation and how to devise strategies to make productive use of the new technologies. Obviously, a radical critique of dehumanizing, exploitative, and oppressive uses of the new technologies in the workplace, schooling, public sphere, and everyday life, is more necessary than ever; but so are strategies that use the new technologies to rebuild our cities, schools, economy, and society. I want to focus, therefore, in the remainder of this section on how new technologies can be used for *increasing* democratization and empowering individuals.

Given the extent to which capital and its logic of commodification have colonized ever more areas of everyday life in recent years, it is somewhat astonishing that cyberspace is by and large decommodified for large numbers of people – at least in the overdeveloped countries like the United States. In the

---

13. *Dialogue, Lexis/Nexis,* and the other mainstream computer data bases with which I am familiar exclude such publications as *Mother Jones. The Utne Reader, The Progressive. Z Magazine,* and other progressive periodicals - though they are always incorporating more sources. Alternative publications like *The Utne Reader* and *Z Magazine,* however, have produced a variety of lively electronic salons and interactive sites. Moreover, in recent years, emailing lists, bulletin boards and web sites run by radical economic, sociological, and political groups download articles from mainstream and alternative media into their computer networks, allowing people to access material, often free of charge.

US, government and educational institutions, and some businesses, provide free Internet access and in some cases free computers, or at least workplace access. With flat-rate monthly access charges (which I know do not exist in much of the world), one can thus have access to a cornucopia of information and entertainment on the Internet for free. The Web is thus one of the few decommodified spaces in the ultracommodified world of techno-capitalism.

Obviously, much of the world does not even have telephone service, much less computers, and there are admittedly vast inequalities in terms of who has access to computers and who participates in the technological revolution and cyberdemocracy today. Critics of new technologies and cyberspace repeat incessantly that it is young, white, middle or upper class males who are the dominant players in the cyberspaces of the present. However, while this is true, statistics and surveys indicate that many more women, people of color, seniors, and other minority categories are becoming increasingly active. Moreover, it appears that computers are becoming part of the standard household consumer package and will perhaps be as common as television sets by the beginning of the next century, and certainly more important for work, social life, and education than the TV set.

Thus, cyberdemocracy and the Internet should be seen as a site of struggle, as a contested terrain, and progressives should look to its possibilities for resistance and circulation of struggle. Dominant corporate and state powers, as well as conservative and rightist groups, have been making serious use of new technologies to advance their agendas and if progressives want to become players in the political battles of the future they must devise ways to use new technologies to advance the progressive agenda and the interests of the oppressed and forces of resistance and struggle.

Fortunately, there are by now copious examples of how the Internet and cyberdemocracy have been used in progressive political struggles to inspire a progressive media politics. A large number of insurgent intellectuals are already making use of these new technologies and public spheres in their political projects. From the beginning, the peasants and guerilla armies struggling in Chiapas, Mexico used computer data bases, guerrilla radio, and other forms of media to circulate news of their struggles and ideas. Every bulletin from the Zapatista Army of National Liberation was immediately circulated through the world via computer networks.[14] In January 1995, when the Mexican government moved against the Zapatistas, computer networks were used to inform and mobilize opposition to the Mexican government's repressive action. There were many demonstrations in support of the rebels throughout the world; prominent journalists, human rights observers, and delegations travelled to Chiapas in solidarity and to report on the uprising, and the Mexican and US governments were bombarded with messages arguing for negotiations. The Mexican government accordingly backed off their repression of the insurgents and as of this writing in August 1997, they have continued to negotiate with them.

Audiotapes were used to promote the revolution in Iran and have also been used to promote alternative information by political movements throughout the world.[15] The Tianaman Square democracy movement in China and various groups struggling against the remnants of Stalinism in the former communist bloc and Soviet Union used computer bulletin boards and networks, as well as a variety of forms of communications, to circulate news of their struggles. Opponents involved in anti-NAFTA struggles made extensive use of the new communication technology.[16] Such multinational networking and circulation of information failed to stop NAFTA, but created useful alliances for the struggles of the future.

Thus, using new technologies to link information and practice, to circulate struggles, is neither extraneous to political battles nor merely utopian. Even if material gains are not won, often the information circulated or alliances formed can be of use. For example, in a celebrated case, two British activists were sued by the fastfood chain McDonald's after they distributed leaflets denouncing the corporation's low wages, advertising practices, involvement in deforestation, harvesting of animals, and promotion of junk food and an unhealthy diet. The activists counterattacked, organized a McLibel campaign, assembled a McSpotlight website with a wealth of information criticizing the corporation, and assembled experts to testify and confirm their

14. See Harry Cleaver (1994) "The Chiapas Uprising" *Studies in Political Economy* 44: pp. 141-157; the documents collected in Zapatistas (1994); and the various websites, mailing lists, and documents archived on the World Wide Web.

15. John Downing (1984) *Radical Media* Boston: South End Press.

16. Joseph Brenner (1994) "Internationalist Labor Communication by Computer Network: The United States, Mexico and Nafta," unpublished paper. Howard Fredericks (1994) "North American NGO Networking Against NAFTA: The Use of Computer Connunications inCross-Border Coalition Building," XVII Internatioal Congress of the Latin American Studies Association.

criticisms. The five-year civil trial ended in July 1997 when the British courts found in favor of McDonald's but awarded the corporation a derisory amount in damages. The long proceedings and the trial's outcome created unprecedented bad publicity for McDonald's and news of the case was circulated throughout the world via Internet websites, mailing lists, and discussion groups. The McLibel group[17] claims that their website was accessed over twelve million times while *The Guardian* newspaper reports that the web site "claimed to be the most comprehensive source of information on a multinational corporation ever assembled and was indeed one of the more successful anticorporate campaigns."[18]

Many labor organizations are also beginning to make use of the new technologies. Mike Cooley has written of how computer systems can reskill rather than deskill workers, and Shosana Zuboff has discussed the ways in which high-tech can be used to "informate" workplaces rather than automate them – expanding workers knowledge and control over operations rather than reducing and eliminating it. The Clean Clothes Campaign, a movement started by Dutch women in 1990 in support of Filipino garment workers has supported strikes throughout the world, exposing exploitative working conditions.[19] Most labor organizations – such as the North-South Dignity of Labor group – note that computer networks are useful for coordinating and distributing information, but cannot replace print media that is more accessible to union members, face-to-face meetings, and traditional forms of political struggle. Thus, the trick is to articulate communication politics with actual political movements and struggles, so that cyber-struggle is an arm of political battle rather than its replacement or substitute. The trouble with some cyber-revolutionaries is that they focus exclusively on issues internal to the internet, and do not interact with actually existing political struggles. By contrast, the most efficacious Internet struggles have intersected with real struggles ranging from campaigns to free political prisoners, to boycotts of corporate projects, to actual political struggles, as noted above.

17. MacLibel Group at http://www.envirolink.or4/mcspotlight/home.html
18.*The Guardian* February 22nd, 1996.
19. Clean Clothes Campaign
at http://www cl eanc lo thes . org/l /index . html
In 1997, activists involved in Korean workers strikes and Merseyside dock strike
in England used websites to gain international solidarity at Labournet, see
http://www.gn.apc.org/lbournet/docks/

Hence, to capital's globalization from above, cyberactivists have been attempting to carry out globalization from below, developing networks of solidarity and circulating struggle throughout the globe. To the capitalist international of transnational corporate globalization, a Fifth International of computer-mediated activism is emerging that is qualitatively different from the party-based socialist and communist Internationals. Such networking links labor, feminist, ecological, peace, and other progressive groups, providing the basis for a new politics of alliance and solidarity to overcome the limitations of postmodern identity politics.[20]

Moreover, a series of struggles around gender and race are also mediated by new communications technologies. After the 1991 Clarence Thomas Hearings in the United States on his fitness to be Supreme Court Justice, Thomas's assault on claims of sexual harassment by Anita Hill and others, and the failure of the almost all male US Senate to disqualify the obviously unqualified Thomas, prompted women to use computer and other technologies to attack male privilege in the political system in the United States and to rally women to support women candidates. The result in 1992 was the election of more women candidates than in any previous election and a general rejection (at least in that election) of conservative rule.

As a result many feminist groups have now established web sites, mailing lists, and other forms of cybercommunication. Likewise, African-American insurgent intellectuals have made use of broadcast and computer technologies. John Fiske[21] has described some African-American radio projects as the "techostruggles" of the present age. African-American "knowledge warriors" are using radio, computer networks, and other media to circulate their ideas and counter-knowledge on a variety of issues, contesting the mainstream and offering alternative views and politics. Likewise, activists in communities of color, like Oakland, Harlem, and Los Angeles are setting up community computer and media centers to teach the skills necessary to survive the mediazation of culture.

Obviously, right wing and reactionary groups are also using the Internet to promote their political agendas. In a short time, one can easily access an exotic witch's brew of ultraright websites maintained by a myriad neo-Nazi groups including the Ku Klux

20. On the latter, see Best and Kellner (1991), (1997) and forthcoming.

21. John Fiske (1994) *Media Matters* (Minneapolis, Minn.: University of Minnesota Press).

Klan, the Aryan Nations and various Patriot militia groups. Internet discussion lists also promote these views and the ultra right is extremely active on many computer forums, as well as their radio programs and stations, public access television programs, fax campaigns, video and even rock music production. These groups are hardly harmless, having promoted terrorism of various sorts ranging from church burnings to the bombings of public buildings. Adopting quasi-leninist discourse and tactics for ultraright causes, they have been successful in recruiting working class members devastated by the developments of global capitalism.

The Internet is thus a contested terrain, used by Left, Right, and Center to promote their own agendas and interests. The political battles of the future may well be fought in the streets, factories, parliaments, and other sites of past struggle, but all political struggle is already mediated by media, computer, and information technologies and will increasingly be so in the future. Those interested in the politics and culture of the future should therefore be clear on the important role of the new public spheres and must intervene accordingly.

CONTRIBUTORS

Janni Aragon is a third-year graduate student in Political Science at the University of California, Riverside. She is currently working on a dissertation entitled, "Desperately Seeking the Self: Feminist Interpretations of the Enlightenment."

Cynthia L. Cates is an Assistant Professor at Towson University where she teaches judicial process and court policymaking. Formerly, she was a senior analyst with the U.S. Advisory Commission on Intergovernmental Relations, specializing in the impact of federal court decisions on state and local governments. She has published articles in *Publius, State Constitutional Commentaries and Notes, Journal of Politics and Law*, among others journals. A book with Professor McIntosh on Judicial Entrepreneurship is scheduled for Fall 1997 publication, and they are currently working on an historical analysis of corporation activity in First Amendment cases before the U.S. Supreme Court.

Timothy Luke is Professor of Political Science at Virginia Polytechnic Institute and State University in Blacksburg VA. He is a member of the Editorial Board of *New Political Science* and is author of *Screens of Power: Ideology, Domination, and Resistance in Informational Society.* Urbana, University of Illinois Press, 1989.

Douglas Kellner is now Professor of the Philosophy of Education at the University of California Los Angeles.

Wayne V. McIntosh is an Associate Professor at the University of Maryland, College Park, specializing in law and politics. He has published one book, *The Appeal of Civil Law*, and a number of articles in political science and multidisciplinary journals, including the *American Political Science Review, Law and Society Review*, and *Journal of Politics and Law*. A book with Professor Cates on Judicial Entrepreneurship is scheduled for Fall 1997 publication, and they are currently working on an historical study of corporate influences in First Amendment controversies.

David Resnick is Associate Professor of Political Science and Director of the Center for the Study of Democratic Citizenship at the University of Cincinnati. He has published numerous articles on the history of political theory. Recently he has been doing research and writing on Cyberspace and, along with Michael Margolis, is the author of a forthcoming book with Sage Publications on politics and the Internet.

Juliet Roper is a lecturer in the Dept. of Management Communication at the University of Waikato, Hamilton, New Zealand. Her on-going research is in the area of public relations and political communication, particularly the discourse of election campaigns and media.

Anna Sampaio is a candidate in Political Science at the University of California, Riverside who is currently teaching in Ethnic Studies at California State University, Hayward. She is also in the process of completing a doctoral dissertation examining discursive politics surrounding the creation of subjectivity within Chicano/a and Latino/a studies and its encounters with movements toward postmodernism and positivistic empiricism.

John Streck is a graduate student in the Department of Communication Studies (Media Studies) at the University of Iowa.

Chris Toulouse (http://www.urbsoc.org) is assistant professor of Sociology at Hofstra University. Among others, he is webmaster for the Community Web, the web site of the Community & Urban Section of the ASA , and the Labour Party International.

Milton Keynes UK
Ingram Content Group UK Ltd.
UKHW020030071024
449327UK00032B/3010

9 780415 921671